D1001878

WITHDRAWN

SCSU

JAN 2 3 1997

H.C. BULEY LIBRARY

Terrorism, Drugs and Crime in Europe after 1992

Other books by the same author

Across the River (as Richard Jocelyn), London, Constable, 1957.
The Long, Long War, New York, Praeger, and London, Cassel, 1966.
Protest and the Urban Guerrilla, London, Cassell, and New York, Abelard Schumann, 1973.
Riot and Revolution in Singapore and Malaya, 1948–63, London, Faber & Faber, 1973.
Living with Terrorism, London, Faber & Faber, and New York, Arlington House, 1975.
Guerrillas and Terrorists, London, Faber & Faber, 1977, and Athens, Ohio, Ohio University Press, 1980.
Kidnap and Ransom, London and Boston, Mass., Faber & Faber, 1978.
Britain in Agony, London, Faber & Faber, 1978, and Harmondsworth, Penguin, 1980.
The Media and Political Violence, London, Macmillan, and New Jersey, Humanities Press, 1981.
Industrial Conflict and Democracy, London, Macmillan, 1984.
Conflict and Violence in Singapore and Malaysia 1948–83, Boulder, Col., Westview Press, 1984, and Singapore, Graham Brash, 1985.
The Future of Political Violence, London, Macmillan, and New York, St Martin's Press, 1986.
Kidnap, Hijack and Extortion, London, Macmillan, and New York, St Martin's Press, 1987.
Terrorism and Guerrilla Warfare: Forecasts and Remedies, London, Routledge, 1990.

Terrorism, Drugs and Crime in Europe after 1992

Richard Clutterbuck

First published 1990
by Routledge
11 New Fetter Lane, London EC4P 4EE

Simultaneously published in the USA and Canada
by Routledge
a division of Routledge, Chapman and Hall, Inc.
29 West 35th Street, New York, NY 10001

HV
9960
.E86
C58
1996

© 1990 Richard Clutterbuck

Phototypeset in 10pt Times by
Mews Photosetting, Beckenham, Kent
Printed and bound in Great Britain by
Biddles Ltd, Guildford and King's Lynn

All rights reserved. No part of this book may be
reprinted or reproduced or utilized in any form or
by any electronic, mechanical, or other means, now
known or hereafter invented, including photocopying
and recording, or in any information storage or
retrieval system, without permission in writing from
the publishers.

British Library Cataloguing in Publication Data

Clutterbuck, Richard
    Terrorism, drugs and crime in Europe after 1992.
    1. European Community countries. Terrorism. Prevention
    I. Title
    363.32094   B 10665390
                         53.96
    ISBN 0-415-05443-5
          0-415-05843-0 (Pb)

Library of Congress Cataloging in Publication Data

Clutterbuck, Richard L.
    Terrorism, drugs, and crime in Europe after 1992 / Richard
Clutterbuck.
        p. cm.
    Includes bibliographical references (p.
    ISBN 0-415-05443-5   0-415-05843-0 (Pb)
        1. Criminal justice. Administration of – European Economic
Community countries. 2. Terrorism – European Economic Community
countries. 3. Drug traffic – European Economic Community countries.
4. Crime – European Economic Community countries. 5. Europe 1992.
I. Title.
HV9960.E86C58   1990
364.94–dc20   90-8279
                                                            CIP

For Rachel
who encouraged me to write it

Contents

Preface		xi
Abbreviations		xiii
Prologue		xvii

Part I Introduction

1	**The challenge of 1992**	3
	Terrorism, drugs and computer crime	3
	Towards a united European Community	4
	The world in the 1990s	6
	The nature of the terrorist threat	7
	International crime and the drug trade	8
	What has worked and what has not?	10
	European co-operation	11
	Technological development	11
	European judicial systems	12
	The right to kill and the right to live	13

Part II Threat and response 1969–89

2	**Foreign terrorists in Europe**	17
	Yassir Arafat and the PLO	17
	The PFLP, PFLP–GC and JRA	19
	The Abu Nidal Group	21
	Other Arab terrorists operating in Europe	22
	Latin American and Chinese drug traders	24
	Foreign terrorists in Europe in the future	24

Contents

3　**Italy**　26
　Right- and left-wing terrorism　26
　The anatomy of the Italian state　28
　The origins of the Red Brigades (BR)　30
　Organization of a professional terrorist movement　32
　The kidnap and murder of Aldo Moro (1978)　34
　Emergency legislation　37
　The return of General Dalla Chiesa　39
　The Penitence and Dissociation Laws　42

4　**West Germany**　46
　The rise of the Red Army Faction (RAF)　46
　The Schleyer kidnap – peak and decline　48
　The Revolutionary Cells (RZ) and Autonomous Groups　51
　Neo-Nazi terrorists　53
　Foreign terrorists in Germany　53
　Government, police and intelligence　55
　The Berufsverbot　56
　Anti-terrorist laws and civil liberties　57

5　**France, Benelux, Denmark and Ireland**　61
　Foreign terrorists in France　61
　Action Directe (AD)　62
　Separatists and others in France　62
　Anti-terrorist legislation　64
　Belgium　67
　The Netherlands　68
　Luxembourg, Denmark and the Irish Republic　69

6　**Northern Ireland**　70
　The origins of the IRA　70
　The IRA campaign, 1969–89　72
　IRA organization and tactics　74
　Emergency legislation in Northern Ireland　78
　The Anglo-Irish Agreement　82

7　**Great Britain**　85
　Indigenous terrorism in Great Britain　85
　The IRA in England　86
　Foreign terrorists in Britain　89
　Anti-terrorist legislation　92

8　**Spain, Portugal and Greece**　95
　The origins of ETA　95

The ETA offensive 97
The challenge from the right 99
The government's response 101
Prospects for the future in Spain 103
Portugal 105
Greece 106

9 **International crime and drug trafficking** 108
The international Mafia and the drug barons 108
The cocaine trail 111
Computer crime and extortion 114
Laundering illegal money 116

10 **European co-operation against terrorism** 119
Interpol 119
The United Nations 120
The Tokyo, Hague and Montreal Conventions 120
TREVI and bilateral co-operation 121
The Council of Europe 122
The Economic Summit 124
Shengen and the European internal market 125

Part III Technological development

11 **Computerized intelligence systems** 129
Technical and human intelligence 129
The computer and the brain 131
Logical inferences 132
Expert systems 133
Neural computer systems 135

12 **Identification and detection of impersonation** 136
Identity cards, passports and visas 136
Anti-impersonation 137
Detecting hijackers 139

13 **Searching for guns, explosives and drugs** 142
The challenge 142
Aids to the searcher 143
Vapour detection 144
Neutron bombardment 145
Other research 146
Multiple methods 146
Airport and airline security 146

Contents

Part IV Public safety and civil rights

14 **Detection, arrest and civil liberties** 153
   Finding the needle in the haystack 153
   Racketeering, laundering, bribery and intimidation 156
   Arrest and detention 157
   Interrogation 158
   European judicial co-operation 160
   Banning political parties and terrorist broadcasts 161
   Reserve powers and legislation in draft 162

15 **Trial and sentence in face of intimidation** 165
   Trial without jury 165
   Video and CCTV to protect juries and witnesses 166
   Evidence 168
   Capital punishment 169
   Life-meaning-life sentences 171
   Rehabilitation 172

Part V What is to be done?

16 **Future development of the threat** 177
   The rise and decline of terrorist movements 177
   Terrorist weapons 180
   Computer games and white-collar crime 182
   Drugs and international crime 184

17 **Fighting the war in a united Europe** 186
   What has worked best so far 186
   Free movement of goods, capital and services 188
   Free movement of persons 189
   Identification and anti-impersonation 190
   Air travel security 190
   A world war on drug trafficking 191
   International crime and money laundering 193
   The rule of law 195
   Political and professional co-operation 196
   Widening co-operation to the East 198

   Notes and bibliography 202
   Index 218

Preface

When the internal borders of the European Community are opened soon after the end of 1992, the benefits to EC countries will be enormous. The present delays of truck traffic at border checks are estimated as costing as much as 5 per cent of the EC's Gross Domestic Product, but the acceleration of economic activity unleashed by free flow of people, goods, capital and services will generate a great deal more than that. The history of the USA illustrates this. Though their states are internally self-governing, they constitute a sovereign territory of 3.5 million square miles, with a vast range of raw materials from arctic, temperate and tropical regions, with the products of industry moving freely by an unfettered land, sea and air transport system to a market comprising over 210 million of the world's most affluent people. This formula has provided a very high standard of living and the ability to exert enormous influence on the world by virtue of their national wealth.

Whether the United European Community, to which all members are committed, takes the form of a federation, or something less, its 320 million people could match the prosperity and political influence of the USA, provided that they become a genuinely single market and exercise a united foreign policy, both political and economic. Corporations could still compete as freely as Ford and General Motors, and states (for example for factory or exhibition sites) as freely as Indiana and Illinois. If they could have had this same vision at the Congress of Vienna in 1814, and if the gradual process of unification which began with the European Coal and Steel Community in 1952 had been achieved in the nineteenth century, that is by 1892 instead of 1992, Europe would not have exhausted its wealth and peoples in 1914–18 and 1939–45, and would almost certainly be richer and more powerful than either of the other two great federations, the USA and the USSR. Now, with those two giants at last on speaking terms, and on the verge of joining forces to maintain international order (as envisaged in the original UN Charter in 1945), the opportunities for a united Europe have never been better.

These is now far less risk of major wars, but we have instead three other threats which could, over the years, do almost as much damage to the community: drug trafficking, computer crime and terrorism. Unless we take drastic steps to check them, all three could grow alarmingly when the movement of terrorists, criminals and the tools of their trade is no longer inhibited by routine border checks.

This book is about how we can prevent that happening. Those three forms of crime are linked: the multinational narcotics rings use and sponsor terrorism and both they and terrorists abuse computers for extortion and laundering of money.

Part I assesses the problems. Part II examines the experiences of EC member countries in the past twenty years as a guide to the future, and particularly their emergency anti-terrorist laws. Part III looks at the technological aids now available or coming on stream. Part IV balances security measures against civil liberties. And Part V comes to conclusions about what to do. Different readers will have different interests, so each part is designed to stand on its own, with repetition avoided as far as possible by cross-references and a full table of contents.

Security against the small but vicious minorities of criminals, drug traffickers and terrorists inevitably involves some restrictions. Most people welcome the search of passengers and baggage before boarding aircraft, and prefer breathalysers to drunken drivers. Powers of search on the streets, however, can be abused, and the prevention or detection of such abuse is as important as the powers themselves. In a Europe with freedom of movement from the Mediterranean to the Baltic, striking the right balance between public safety and civil liberties will be a challenge. If this book helps to stimulate informed debate on this subject, it will have achieved its object.

I owe a lot to my first five readers: my secretarial neighbours Iris Sanders and Claire Turner; Sue Joshua the commissioning editor, Ruth Jeavons the desk editor and Christine Firth the copy editor. A writer always knows what he means, but if it is not crystal clear to any of these first readers it will not be clear to others. All five told me when this was so and their professionalism and enthusiasm have been a tonic to me.

Richard Clutterbuck
Exeter

Abbreviations

For most foreign acronyms and in other cases where it is judged to be more helpful to the reader, an English description (in parentheses) is given instead of spelling out the words.

AD	Action Directe (France)
AG	Autonomous Groups (Germany)
AI	Artificial Intelligence
ALF	Animal Liberation Front *or* Arab Liberation Front
ARB	(Breton Revolutionary Army) France)
ASALA	(Armenian Liberation Army)
ASU	Active Service Unit
BBC	British Broadcasting Corporation
BBE	(Dutch Marines Anti-Terrorist Commando)
BEFA	(Central Police Surveillance System) (Germany)
BfV	(Federal Office for Protection of the Constitution) (Germany)
BKA	(Federal Criminal Office) (Germany)
BND	(Federal Intelligence Service) (Germany)
BR	(Red Brigades) (Italy)
CCC	(Combatant Communist Cells) (Belgium)
CCTV	Closed Circuit Television
CDU	(Christian Democratic Union) (Germany)
CESIS	(Intelligence Executive Committee) (Italy)
CIA	Central Intelligence Agency (USA)
COT	Computerized Organic Tracer
CSPPA	(Committee for Solidarity with Arab and Middle Eastern Prisoners) (France)
DC	(Christian Democratic Party) (Italy)
DEA	(Drug Enforcement Administration (USA)
DFLP	Democratic Front for the Liberation of Palestine
DNA	(Genetic molecule in body fluids)
DP	Detection Probability

DST	(Surveillance Service) (France)
EC	European Community
ECST	European Convention for the Suppression of Terrorism
El Al	Israeli Airlines
ETA	(Freedom for the Basque Homeland) (Spain)
ETA-M	(ETA – Military Wing) (Spain)
ETA-PM	(ETA – Politico-Military Wing) (Spain)
FAA	Federal Aviation Authority (USA)
FACES	Facial Analysis Comparison and Elimination System
FAR	False Alarm Rate
FBI	Federal Bureau of Investigation (USA)
FDP	(Free Democratic Party) (Germany)
FLNC	(Corsican National Liberation Front) (France)
F-PC	Fatah – Provisional Command (Palestinian)
FP 25	(An ultra-left terrorist movement) (Portugal)
FRAP	(Revolutionary Front for Proletarian Action) (Belgium)
F-RC	Fatah – Revolutionary Council (Abu Nidal Group) (Palestinian)
GAL	(Anti-Terrorist Liberation Group) (Spain)
GEO	(Special Operations Group) (Spain)
GRAPO	An extreme Marxist group) (Spain)
GSG9	(Anti-Terrorist Commando) (Germany)
HB	(People's Unity – political party supporting ETA) (Spain)
HED	Hydrogenous Explosive Detection
HOLMES	Home Office Large and Major Enquiry System
IATA	International Air Transport Association
ID card	Identity card
INLA	Irish National Liberation Army
Interpol	International Criminal Police Organization
IRA	Irish Republican Army
JRA	Japanese Red Army
KGB	(Soviet Intelligence Bureau)
KLM	(Royal Dutch Airlines)
KPD	(Communist Party of Germany)
LIPS	Logical inferences per second
MEP	Member of the European Parliament
MIK	(Military Industrial Complex) (Germany)
MI5	(British domestic intelligence service – *colloquial*)
MI6	(British foreign intelligence service – *colloquial*)
MNF	Multinational Peacekeeping Force (Lebanon)
MSI	(Neo-fascist political party) (Italy)

NATO	North Atlantic Treaty Organization
NDP	(National Democratic Party) (Germany)
OAS	(Secret Army Organization) (France)
OPEC	Organization of Petroleum Exporting Countries
Pan Am	Pan-American Airlines
PASOK	(Socialist Party) (Greece)
PCI	(Communist Party of Italy)
PCP	Palestine Communist Party
PFLP	Popular Front for the Liberation of Palestine
PFLP-GC	Popular Front for the Liberation of Palestine – General Command
PIN	Personal Identification Number
PKK	(Parliamentary Control Commission) (Germany)
PL	(Front Line) (Italy)
PLF	Palestine Liberation Front
PLO	Palestine Liberation Organization
PNF	Palestine National Fund
PNV	(Basque Nationalist Party) (Spain)
PPSF	Palestine Popular Struggle Front
PR	Proportional Representation *or* Public Relations
RAF	Red Army Faction (Germany)
Risc	Reduced instruction set computers
RUC	Royal Ulster Constabulary
RZ	Revolutionary Cells *or* Red Zora (Germany)
SAS	Special Air Service Regiment *or* Scandinavian Air Services
SDLP	Social Democratic and Labour Party (Northern Ireland)
SEA	Single European Act
SEP	Surrendered Enemy Personnel
SISDE	(Political Intelligence Service) (Italy)
SISMI	(Military Intelligence Service) (Italy)
SO	Scheduled Offence
SPD	(Social Democratic Party of Germany)
TNA	Thermal Neutron Activation
TREVI	(EC Ministerial Anti-Terrorist Committee)
TWA	Transworld Airlines
UDR	Ulster Defence Regiment
UN	United Nations
UVF	Ulster Volunteer Force
VIP	Very Important Person

Prologue

Five years on . . .

A selection of press and radio news reports, May 1995

Swanley, 1 May   Yesterday I saw the government's new security check in action. I was sitting opposite two smartly dressed young men of what they call 'Middle Eastern appearance' (Why don't they say Arabs?) half-way through the Channel Tunnel on the Paris–London express. A policewoman was working her way down the coach like a ticket collector.

'Could I see your passports or identity cards, please?' asked the policewoman.

Spot checks on this route were announced by the Home Secretary last week following the recent wave of bombings in London claimed by the North African Liberation Front.

One of the two men – he looked the older of the two – produced a French ID card, the other a Libyan passport with what appeared to be a French visa card. Like my own ID card, each of these had a black strip along the edge with the electronic data. The policewoman put the ID card in the slot in the minicomputer fixed to her belt. A small diode, like a ball-point pen, hung from the computer. The passenger was clearly accustomed to this and extended his hand. The policewoman passed the diode across the vein pattern on the back of the hand, as if she were logging up the bar codes at a supermarket check-out.

'Thank you, sir.'

She did the same with the visa card and the younger man's hand. This time, however, something on the computer's tiny visual display unit perplexed her. She did the test again. She pocketed the card.

'I'm afraid I shall have to ask you to come up to the front coach so that we can check it again as soon as we arrive at the Swanley terminal, sir.'

'Why? What have I done?'

'I cannot make your vein-check reading match your visa, sir. We have a data link from Swanley to the French national police computer. It should take only a few minutes – so long as they give a positive clearance.'

The man began to object but thought better of it. When we stopped at Swanley I looked along the train towards the special coach at the front, where a police team got on board with a black box with a cable extension to the police and immigration check-point on the platform. Soon afterwards, I saw our smart Middle Easterner leaving the train handcuffed to a policeman – presumably on his way to help them with their enquiries. So it *does* work . . . even with a French visa.

Gatwick, 4 May The new check-in channels at Gatwick opened yesterday, replacing the temporary set-up we have all been living with for the past year. At the check-in desk they took both my bags, hand and hold, and added them to a small dump of baggage at the entrance to a conveyor belt. I watched for a minute or two and noticed that the bags were going on to the belt at about six a minute. As I moved on through the passport and immigration checks I watched the conveyor belt which ran parallel to the passenger corridor. I saw four operators, about five yards apart along the line, gazing at screens and dials and the like as the bags went by. I realized that the belt was not, in fact, continuous, but a series of belts, so that each operator could stop each bag for as many seconds as was needed. Then the operator reactivated the belt and the bag moved on and tipped automatically on to the next belt. Sometimes, however, the operator pressed a buzzer and a handler was ready to lift the bag across to a parallel 'reject' belt. At the end of the corridor we emerged into the baggage search hall. There was a large bench and the bags were waiting behind it. I asked one of the guys behind the bench what the four checks were. He said 'X-ray, vapour and two neutron checks – TNA and HED.' I didn't ask him what these were but I noticed that both my bags were in the 'rejected' area. I identified them and they were opened for a hand search on the bench. The searcher made a thorough job of it. He told me that the 'TNA' (whatever that is) had picked up a rather ripe piece of cheese in my suitcase and the 'HED' had reacted to a carton of fruit juice in my brief-case! He said that they find they have to check about one bag in twenty. When he had finished, he stamped both the baggage labels and my boarding card with some kind of electronic code

– 'to make sure you all three get on the same aircraft'. He told me that the actual flow through this procedure is as fast as before, because the same number of bags go on to the conveyor belt at the same rate – and come off at the same rate. But there are a lot more pairs of eyes and pairs of hands on the way. So now you know why you pay that £5 'airport surcharge' on your air ticket!

London, 15 May I say 'London' but I'm not allowed to say where, except that it was between five and ten miles from the Old Bailey. I've been on a jury only once before, and it was certainly nothing like this. The jury summons said that I was required to attend for interview and selection but that I would receive details of when the case was to be tried later – at least four weeks later. My interviewer was an official of the 'jury ombudsman service' and he asked all the usual kinds of questions, I suppose to unearth my prejudices. When the call came, the twelve of us found ourselves in a small top-floor conference room in the council offices of a London borough – no, I *can't* say which. The judge had apparently decided that there was a risk of the jury's being nobbled or threatened, and ordered a 'video jury' trial. It's all done by closed circuit TV. In front of us were five screens, one each showing the judge, prosecuting counsel, defence counsel, witness and accused. They were all full face, and seemed a lot closer than they do in the court. It was just like watching television. The accused had a bit of blarney about him, but his lawyer was a bastard. Some of the witnesses were a bit shifty: they looked anywhere but at the camera. They tell me that in some trials the witnesses are on video too, seen only by the jury. It was easy enough to tell who was lying. Actually we let the guy off, in spite of his rotten lawyer. But none of them knew who we were, any more than Neil Kinnock knows who he is talking to on TV. There was no camera in the jury room.

New York, 20 May The CIA/KGB link-up has so transformed the terrorist scene since 1993 that it is no surprise that the UN Security Council today passed unanimously a resolution approving the establishment of a joint NATO/Warsaw Pact headquarters to act on behalf of the UN in directing the war on cocaine. The new command post will be located in Kingston, Jamaica, and will organize naval and air patrols in the Caribbean, with soldiers supplementing local forces in policing isolated airstrips and harbours. There will also be training teams for special forces. All the Caribbean Island governments, together with Mexico, Colombia, Peru, Brazil and most of the other Latin American states, have agreed to provide facilities. I understand that there will later be a similar 'Heroin Task Force HQ' in Karachi. NATO and the Warsaw Pact comprise twenty-two nations, and all of these have agreed in principle to provide contingents, even if, in some cases, only token ones. Following the massive troop withdrawals on both sides, there was talk of disbanding the two headquarters. It was the NATO and Warsaw Pact Commanders, Generals John K. Adams and Andrei Suvarov, who jointly proposed adapting these two tried and tested international military command headquarters to the world-wide war on drugs, with the additional role of co-ordinating anti-terrorist operations when the occasion demands.

Part I

Introduction

Chapter one

The challenge of 1992

Terrorism, drugs and computer crime

In June 1985 a TWA aircraft was hijacked to Beirut and one American was killed before the other passengers were released. As a direct result of this (and of its massive and emotive television coverage) 6 million Americans cancelled their vacation plans in Europe and the Mediterranean in 1986. There could be few better illustrations of Sun Tzu's ancient Chinese proverb: 'Kill one, frighten ten thousand'.

During 1987 and 1988 there were repeated rumours of huge concessions (diplomatic and financial) by the US, French and German governments to secure the release of individual hostages from Lebanon.

In 1984 the US, French, Italian and British governments withdrew their Multinational Peacekeeping Force (MNF) from Lebanon as a direct result of two suicide bombs which killed 241 US Marines and 60 French soldiers in their bases.

Whether Western governments and people should or should not be swayed by terrorism, they are. There is no logic about this. The annual killing rate per million of the population in Northern Ireland is by far the highest in Europe, yet it is only half the annual death-rate in Northern Irish road accidents,[1] and far less than half the criminal homicide rate per million in Los Angeles or Washington, DC. Compared with world wars or even regional wars, or with famines, floods and earthquakes, the terrorist killing rate is minute.

The explanation is that we identify with the individual victims of terrorism because we see their faces (and the faces of those who love them) nightly on television. Whether they want to or not, democratic governments cannot afford to ignore the intensity of public emotion which is aroused. When even one or two of its citizens' lives are held in the balance in a major terrorist incident, a government has to give it overriding priority. When other countries are involved, either as sponsors of terrorism or as half-hearted allies, public passions may prejudice working relationships with those countries when national interests would be better served by those relationships' being restored.

In 1984 the President of the General Assembly of Interpol said that the most pressing problems in international crime were the narcotics trade, white-collar crime and terrorism.[2] The narcotics trade certainly causes more deaths than terrorism world-wide (from drug overdoses and murders), though as yet most of these are outside Europe, where the main damage is to society and to the economy. Computer crime is growing at an alarming rate and it could generate even more illegal money than the drug trade. In fact they are closely linked; all three may be greatly affected by the implementation of the Single European Act after 1992, but because of its perverse influence on public perceptions and on political decisions, terrorism is the main concern of this book.

Towards a united European Community

After 1992, the intention of the Single European Act (SEA) is that it will be as easy to cross the frontier between France and Italy as between Kansas and Missouri, or to consign a truckload of goods from Athens to London, without check-points, as easily as from New York to San Francisco.

Yet Europe has problems which the USA does not have. At most borders in the European Community (EC), there are changes in languages, changes in the law and, in some cases, radically different judicial systems. In the USA the great majority of teenagers and adults, of all races, were educated with English as the medium of instruction, and are there because they or their ancestors wanted to be citizens of the USA rather than of their mother countries. There are many immigrants in the EC who still look first to their motherlands and their mother tongues.

Foreign terrorist groups already find it much easier to find cover and operate in the EC than they would do in the USA. The challenge to be faced is that they will find it easier still after 1992 in the EC, unless member countries can harmonize their measures for prevention and response, and co-operate in applying them.

The EC is already making strides towards political as well as economic union. The Council of Ministers has now reduced the areas in which unanimity is required, and can in other matters pass legislation binding on all its members, unless twenty-three out of seventy-six votes[3] are against it which, with the weighted voting system, means that it can be vetoed only if three of the largest countries (France, Germany, Italy or the UK), or two of those countries plus any one of the smaller countries except Luxembourg, or five of the smaller ones, all vote together against it. By these means, nearly 300 legislative proposals needed for the 1992 internal market have been passed. The trend is towards increasing the powers of the Council of Ministers over those of the twelve national governments.

Similarly the powers of the European Parliament, which has been directly elected since 1979, are gradually extending at the expense of those of national parliaments. Progress here has been and will probably continue to be slower than with the Council of Ministers, chiefly because the Members of the European Parliament (MEPs) are not regarded by the voters as their representatives in the same way as the members of their national parliaments or their ministers; also because the European Parliament's debates are in public, and there is less chance of useful behind-the-scenes discussion amongst 518 MEPs than amongst 12 ministers. So it is more difficult for them to reach compromises than for the Council of Ministers, whether at the summit or at departmental level, meeting together in private. It is hopeless to conduct delicate negotiations entirely in front of the television cameras.

Apart from ease of movement, there are other likely developments which may increase rather than reduce conflict. There will be a greater flow of cheap labour into countries whose governments and trade unions permit them to undercut the wage levels of nationals; this may lead to a greater response to neo-Nazi politicians which could explode into violence. Environmental pressure groups have already become violent in Germany (mainly against property rather than people) and this trend may spread. As the East–West accord develops, both Eastern and Western Communist parties may be regarded by the ideological and intellectual left as traitors for accommodating capitalism, and this could increase the bitterness and the frustration, much as the strength of the Communist Party of Italy (PCI) and its co-operation with the parliamentary process embittered the Red Brigades (BR) in Italy in the 1970s. The escalation from violent demonstrations to bombing of installations to killing people is sadly a familiar by-product of frustration.

The policy of the European internal market will be to make up for removing internal frontiers by strengthening its external frontiers. Seaports and airports are both internal and external. Airports should present no insurmountable problem, since most international airports already have separate access for international and domestic flights. Major international seaports, like Southampton, accustomed to ferries from the Isle of Wight, France and world-wide, are equally geared for it. Smaller ports will be harder to secure, small fishing and yachting harbours harder still. Countries with deserted sandy beaches could be made more secure only with expensive surveillance equipment and personnel. Land frontiers – mountainous, wooded or rural – present few obstacles to small groups of terrorists or criminals. The EC would therfore be unwise to rely too much on a secure external frontier. Once in Greece, the intruder could be in London or Madrid without further check – unless subjected to irregular spot checks anywhere on the way.[4]

The world in the 1990s

The microelectronics revolution is the fastest industrial revolution of all time, and may prove to be the most profound. The rate of change it is bringing to European societies may be at its fastest in the early 1990s, in the fields of robotics and information technology. The percentage of the population of industrial countries employed in manual work (agriculture, mining, manufacture, etc.) had already fallen from 42 per cent in 1972 to 29 per cent in 1982 and will be between 10 and 20 per cent by the end of the century. The majority employed in service industries will therefore rise to over 75 per cent in the early years of the European single market. This majority does not create wealth, but merely opens the way for its creation, processes and distributes it and provides leisure and other facilities for the producers. To pay for these service industries, the actual producers of wealth will have to produce a great deal more – much more than was produced by more people in longer working hours in the past. They should be able to do this comfortably with the higher productivity resulting from robotics and information technology. In fact, if we are to avoid the constant burden of 10 per cent or more unemployed, we shall probably have to reduce the working week to about thirty hours, four shifts, or four days; this will mean still more leisure, more leisure industries, so still more surplus wealth needed to pay for them.

So far from closing the gaps between rich and poor, internationally and domestically, these changes are likely to widen them. The economic growth rate of industrial countries will be faster than that of the Third World countries. Though their economies too will grow, so will their populations, and they will fall further and further behind. The information explosion will ensure that their peoples know that there are places where the grass is greener, and that there are ways of getting to them. The pressure for immigration, therefore, will grow, and, if legal immigration is restricted, there will be more and more attempts to find other ways: witness the tip of the iceberg in the form of the Vietnamese boat people and other 'economic migrants.

Within industrial societies there will be widening gaps between the skilled and the unskilled, especially in the service industries, where there will be a new kind of rich and poor. The 'information rich' will be those who master and keep pace with the new information technology; who may be able to work a relatively stress-free day at home with their intelligent computers, teleconference screens, fax and other aids; and who will have fulfilling well-paid jobs. The 'information poor' will be those who are unable or unwilling to keep up with using the technology, and will fall into duller and duller routine jobs, if they have jobs at all.[5]

Most homes will have a choice of up to fifty television channels, including some via satellite. Authoritarian governments are likely to control these channels and use them to mould their people's minds. Democratic governments will generally give them free rein, which will enable anyone who has the money, from inside or outside (including politically-minded TV barons, the PLO and Colonel Gadafi), to disseminate whatever propaganda they wish in the form of news and current affairs or entertainment. This flood of information will make it easier for those who wish to destabilize democratic societies. This may tempt some democratic governments to become more authoritarian to counter it. It is uncertain how the European internal market would handle the situation if some national governments went this way and others did not.

The rapid growth of plastic money and of the instant electronic transfer of money abroad through the international banking system will affect the choice of targets for both criminal and terrorist operations and will facilitate the laundering of illegal money from either of these sources. These and associated problems, and possible solutions to them, are discussed in Chapter 9, 14, 16 and 17.

The nature of the terrorist threat

Indigenous European terrorist movements range from those with a hard core of 10 or 20 to movements like the IRA (Irish Republican Army) and ETA (the Basque terrorists) with a hard core of 50 to 100 and a fringe of active supporters of 200 to 300, needing a budget of about £5 million a year. All of the ideological movements, such as the Red Brigades (BR), the Red Army Faction (RAF) and Action Directe (AD), at their peak were in the 50–100 category, though most were cut back in the 1980s to small gangs of 10 or 20.

The richest of all is the conglomeration of Palestinian movements under the umbrella of the Palestine Liberation Organization (PLO), which has assets estimated at $5 billion and an annual income of about $1.25 billion.[6]

The bitterness and frustration amongst the Arabs over their inability to get rid of Israel, despite their huge superiority in numbers and wealth, is so intense that, even if there were a political settlement, there would be some Arab rejectionist groups who would continue to use violence both in the Middle East and Europe to overturn it. The same applies in Northern Ireland, where rejectionist groups would include both Republicans and Unionists. Neither the Palestinian nor the Northern Irish problem will go away.

Unlike the Northern Irish Catholics, the Basques are in a majority in their region of Spain and enjoy a high degree of autonomy. The conflict there is therefore more likely to fade away as the terrorists realize that they are losing popular support by their violence.

Other nationalist movements (such as the Corsicans in France) may also be defused, but experience sadly shows that new ones are almost certain to arise, or old ones re-emerge. Some of those outside the EC may also try to fight their battles on West European streets, as the Armenians, Croats, Arabs and Iranians have already done, and as, possibly, Slovenes, Slovaks, Ukranians and other Soviet national communities may do in the future. Like the Palestinians, the more they fail at home the more they will seek to make an impact on the international stage.

The ideological left and right suffered major set-backs in Western Europe in the 1980s and, with the possible exception of the Revolutionary Cells (RZ) in Germany, seem likely to continue to decline. Nevertheless, experience has shown that two or three ruthless and dedicated people, with the propaganda skills to attract support from idealistic or disgruntled sections of the population, can build a new and highly lethal terrorist movement quite quickly. Chapter 3 gives an account of the growth of one such movement from just such beginnings – the Red Brigades in Italy. In less than ten years, a handful of ideologically motivated people were able to create a movement which made the Italian political and judicial systems dance to its tune for three years before they were shocked into taking firm measures to break it – measures which were viewed by some as ethically dubious.

The rise and (where appropriate) the fall of the most important terrorist movements operating in Europe is described in Chapters 2 to 8, as a guide to how similar movements – of whatever political, racial or religious colour – may arise and be organized in the future.

International crime and the drug trade

In the long term the growth of the narcotics trade could prove to be the greatest of all the threats to human civilization. The damage it does to its growing number of addicts is in many cases incurable. Its estimated annual turnover of $500 billion (£300 billion) is far greater than the budgets of all the terrorist movements in the world put together. The profits not only give enormous economic and political power to the drug barons, but also finance a horrifying amount of crime all over the world.

The Sicilian Mafia is selected for a brief case study in Chapter 9. It has permeated the top levels, in varying degrees, of politics, the police, the intelligence services, industry and the judiciary all over Italy; in some areas it has dominated them.

The cocaine trail is also examined, from Latin America to the streets of the USA and Europe. Bolivia and Peru produce the majority of the world's coca crop. Most of the refining to make cocaine is done in Colombia where the drug barons use their enormous wealth and their murder squads to dominate some areas of Colombian society as much as the Mafia do in Italy.

World-wide, the distribution and marketing of drugs is run by organizations precisely modelled on commercial multinational organizations. As an indication of the enormous profits made down the line, the raw material (coca) needed to make one kilogram of pure cocaine costs about £14 in Colombia). By the time it has been smuggled into Europe, the wholesaler pays £35,000 for it – a gain of 250 to 1. Its street value, split into doses, is about £70,000 – a further gain of nearly 2 to 1 or a total gain of 500 times the production cost. With so much money to spend, these multinationals and their dealers have no difficulty in hiring willing smugglers, using speedboats or light aircraft, or simply concealing cocaine in the heels of their shoes, or in capsules which they swallow in Colombia or in a Caribbean island and excrete intact after arrival in the USA. The barons can also pay whatever bribes may be needed by corrupt officials to turn a blind eye. And the distributors or the addicts themselves can convert cocaine into the higher-priced and more addictive 'crack' simply by heating it with an easily obtainable chemical in a microwave oven.[7]

The USA and European countries can and must help the Latin American and Caribbean governments to fight their war against cocaine trafficking; also the Asian and Middle Eastern governments fighting the heroin traffic, in which the multinational distribution is largely run by Triad Secret Societies based in Hong Kong. Specific proposals for a 'world war on drugs' are in Chapter 17. The ultimate cure, however, must lie at the demand end – on American and European streets. The tempting solution of killing the profits by legalizing drugs, and the alternatives of suppression, are discussed in Chapter 9. Whichever methods are used, drastic action will be needed because the number of addicts is increasing and the traders will build up their wealth and resources as each year goes by.

Like drug addiction, computer crime is growing at an alarming rate and the courts are so lenient that fear of getting caught provides little deterrent. The victims of computer fraud are mainly large corporations (especially banks) or government departments. The computer manufacturers have been slow in building in reliable prevention against fraud and hacking, presumably because the competition to produce faster and more 'user friendly' machines at lower cost leaves security with a low priority; also because the big corporate users share their priorities and may prefer to avoid the adverse publicity of revealing that there are fraudsters inside their business by prosecuting them. Nevertheless, the ease of manipulating computers undetected provides opportunities for laundering money, which in turn aids the more dangerous crimes of kidnapping, extortion, terrorism and drug trafficking.

Other means of money laundering also need to be countered: the setting up of shell companies to absorb money on account of imaginary services, and the rapid electronic transfer of money between international banks all over the world in countries whose governments ask no questions.

These problems and possible solutions are discussed in Chapter 9, in particular the question of how far banks and corporations can be compelled by law to open their accounts to police inspection if ordered by the courts, and how such orders might be enforced internationally. Will money laundering become easier when Europe's internal borders are opened for the free flow of persons, goods, capital and services? If so, what further measures will be needed to prevent it?

What has worked and what has not?

Almost all EC counties (excepting Belgium) introduced emergency legislation and special police powers to deal with their terrorist problems in the 1970s and 1980s. These are examined to assess their effectiveness in Chapters 3 to 8, and are re-examined in the light of the changes which will arise in the European single market after 1992 in the later chapters of the book.

The Italian experience (Chapter 3) is considered in more depth than the others because it taught the most lessons. In 1974–5 a dynamic and able Carabinieri General, Carlo Alberto Dalla Chiesa, was appointed to tackle the growing threat of terrorism and was given wide powers. When he was on the verge of nipping it in the bud, the government posted him away and disbanded his highly successful anti-terrorist organization, largely because the predominant Christian Democratic Party needed to placate left-wing parties in Parliament in order to remain in power. For the same reason the Italian government emasculated their intelligence organization in 1976. They paid heavily for this in 1978–80 by suffering a spate of kidnaps and murders of politicians, judges, prison officers and executives. This prompted them to reappoint General Dalla Chiesa and reactivate his team, with the powers he needed, and, largely due to his skill in exploiting the opportunities offered by the *pentiti* (repentant terrorists), he led the way in breaking both left- and right-wing terrorism before they moved him to Palermo to tackle the Mafia – who murdered him within six months.

The German and French governments also provided some very useful experience in the fields of intelligence, emergency legislation, the maintenance of the judicial process in the face of organized disruption and intimidation, and the use of specially selected and trained anti-terrorist commandos. These are described in Chapters 4 and 5. Similar measures were tried in the face of larger-scale violence in the United Kingdom, especially in Northern Ireland. Again, some worked well and others did not. The *'pentiti'* achieved astonishing results in Italy. Their equivalents, the 'supergrasses', yielded dramatic initial successes in Northern Ireland, but the resulting convictions were quashed by the Appeal Courts, unwilling to accept convictions on uncorroborated evidence from one witness with a strong incentive to give it. It could be that the Italian courts were encouraged to be more robust by the large number of murders of judges. While the success of *pentitismo* has reduced terrorist murders in Italy to a trickle, over 400 people have been killed in Northern Ireland since the 'supergrass' convictions were quashed. The ethics of these contrasting decisions are examined in context in Chapters 3 and 6. What has worked and what has not will be reassessed in Chapter 17.

European co-operation

There have been many attempts at West European (and world) co-operation against terrorism. What have been the limitations of Interpol? Of the United Nations? Of the Tokyo, Hague and Montreal Conventions against hijacking (all ratified by more than 100 states)? And of the 1977 Council of Europe Convention for the Suppression of Terrorism? Have the policies evolved at the summit meetings between the seven most economically powerful capitalist countries (Britain, Canada, France, Germany, Italy, Japan and the USA) been more effective? Collectively these governments have enormous power, but are they likely to be restrained by national self-interest from using it?

EC ministers and officials meet regularly to co-ordinate anti-terrorist policies under the TREVI organization (see pp. 121–122). This has undoubtedly resulted in better bilateral co-operation between their professionals (police, etc.). But again, will all EC governments have the political will to apply this capability to the full in the face of sacrificing their economic and political self-interests?

What will be the effect of removal of internal borders on all these agreements? And will co-operation be extended to involve the USSR and Eastern Europe? These questions are considered in Chapters 10 and 17.

Technological development

National police computers, linked between some EC countries, have already revolutionized criminal and anti-terrorist intelligence; the fact that terrorism and crime have continued to grow is a disturbing indication of how much faster they will grow unless the technology to counter them keeps ahead in the race. Computer development is constantly enlarging the volume of personal data which can be stored and increasing the speed with which it can be processed. Coupled with the continuing miniaturization of computers and their falling price, this may make it possible for an immigration official, or a police officer doing a spot check with a portable computer in Edinburgh, to call up relevant data from the police computer in Germany – provided that the person being questioned has a machine-readable identity card, passport or visa.

This raises serious questions of civil liberties, and, if these systems are to be introduced at all, an effective safeguard will be needed to prevent their abuse. Will this be possible? And how best can we balance the prospect of George Orwell's *1984* nightmare with protection from more and more sophisticated terrorism and crime? Does every citizen have a civil right to conceal his or her identity? Or to impersonate someone else? All of these questions are considered in Chapters 11, 12 and 14.

Less controversial is the development of means to detect bombs. Detection of metal alone is now totally inadequate: bomb fuses need contain little or no metal. Moreover, firing circuits can be concealed in a normal and serviceable calculating machine or cassette recorder, as was done by the terrorists who blew up a Pan-American Flight 103 over Lockerbie in December 1988, killing 270 people. There are many means now of detecting explosives: dogs, vapour sniffers and various forms of neutron bombardment. Other means are under development, such as the measurement of dielectric properties and infra-red thermal imagery. No single one will guarantee 100 per cent detection, but successive checks by each in turn may get very close to it. These techniques, and the economic and organizational implications of using them, are discussed in Chapter 13.

European judicial systems

Throughout the 1970s and 1980s the greatest problem facing all West European judiciaries dealing with terrorism and organized crime was intimidation: of witnesses, of juries, and sometimes of judges; and, with an indirect effect on justice, of politicians, officials, police and journalists; also of members of the public who sometimes found it safer to turn a blind eye. The various methods used to combat this are discussed for each of these countries in Chapters 2 to 10.

Possible police methods for countering racketeering, extortion and the laundering of 'dirty money' will be discussed in Chapter 9. Judicial means (such as placing the onus of proving a legitimate source of money and property on the accused person) are further pursued in Chapter 14, which also discusses judicial control to prevent abuse of emergency powers granted to the police.

In Germany, Italy and the United Kingdom, lawyers have sometimes abused their privileges in order to disrupt court proceedings or to pervert the course of justice, and changes in procedure have been necessary to overcome this. Also the videotaping of police interrogation may justify a revision, not of the 'right to silence' (which must remain), but of the right of the judge and jury to take refusal to answer questions into account in assessing guilt. This is discussed in Chapter 14.

Intimidation or corruption of juries has led a number of countries to introduce trial without jury for terrorist offences, and this might well need to be extended to trials of members of organized and violent criminal gangs. Other possible means of overcoming intimidation, for example by greater use of video cameras, are examined in Chapter 15. So are possible changes to combat the particular menaces of the drug trade.

The opening of internal frontiers will strengthen the case for a European Judicial Area, in which EC citizens can be tried in courts in any country with witnesses from any other country. But problems of harmonizing the judicial systems may be hard to resolve. It will also be important to facilitate extradition of accused persons between EC countries. These and other questions are discussed in Chapters 14 and 15.

The right to kill and the right to live

Throughout this book, both in case studies of the past and in consideration of measures to face the challenges of the future, the balance has been weighed between the need to protect the lives, possessions and well-being of the community without unwarranted erosion of their civil liberties. Most violence in EC countries is carried out by small minorities motivated either by criminal greed or by determination to force their political views on the majority who do not want them. The right of a minority to kill must never be allowed to override the right of the majority to live.

Part II

Threat and response 1969–89

Chapter two

Foreign terrorist groups in Europe

Except in the United Kingdom and Spain, foreign groups now constitute a greater terrorist threat in West European countries than do their own indigenous movements. With so many immigrants from so many different races, able to move relatively freely within the EC, foreign terrorists can easily merge into the background, before and after their operations, in nondescript hotels and lodging houses accustomed to travelling immigrants. They can, if necessary, lie low for many months on end during the reconnaissance phases. Though they come mainly to fight their own battles on European streets, they do also sometimes attack European targets (persons or property) to apply coercion on European governments. In this chapter the foreign movements most likely to operate in Europe will be discussed briefly as a prelude to examining their specific tactics and techniques in the subsequent chapters devoted to individual European countries.

Yassir Arafat and the PLO

Palestinian terrorists of various complexions have killed many more people on the streets of Europe (including other Arabs) than any other foreign terrorists. Most of the killers, however, come from the smaller and more extreme movements outside the mainstream of Al Fatah and the Palestine Liberation Organization (PLO). Nevertheless, there have on repeated occasions been violent splinter groups of Al Fatah operating in Europe. The most violent was Black September between 1970 and 1974, operating under the direction of Yassir Arafat's second-in-command and chief of intelligence, Abu Iyad. Yassir Arafat was equivocal in disowning them saying that, while he deplored violence, he could understand the feelings of some young Palestinians when their fury at the injustices suffered by their people became too much to bear. Black September were responsible for the massacre of eleven Israeli athletes at the Munich Olympics in 1972 and for over fifty other incidents in Europe, the Middle East and Africa.[1]

More recently, four terrorists from one of the smaller groups remaining loyal to Yassir Arafat, the Palestine Liberation Front (PLF), attracted some attention with a maritime hijack. Under the direction of Abu'l Abbas (PLF Secretary-General) they hijacked the Italian cruise ship *Achille Lauro* in the Mediterranean in October 1985 and murdered an elderly Jewish American passenger, Leon Klinghoffer, who was confined to a wheelchair, presumably to terrorize other passengers into submission. This operation threw a revealing light on Arab terrorist methods. The four terrorists were very young (one had to be tried in a juvenile court). Their task was to wait until the ship reached an Israeli port, where they were to go ashore and do maximum damage before becoming martyrs. They were surprised by a steward while cleaning their weapons in their cabin, having omitted to lock the door. They were panicked into hijacking the ship, but then realized that this would have alerted the Israelis before the ship came in, so they abandoned that plan and sailed somewhat aimlessly to and fro until Abu'l Abbas (who had briefed them to board the *Achille Lauro* in Genoa with their instructions, but was not on board himself) ordered them to bring the ship to Port Said and surrender to the Egyptians. He appears to have done this on the instructions of a somewhat shocked Yassir Arafat, who negotiated for them to be flown back to freedom in Tunisia. In the event, the aircraft was intercepted by US fighters and forced to land in Italy, where Abu'l Abbas was, to the fury of the Americans, allowed to go free, though his four young terrorists were arrested and later sentenced to imprisonment by the Italians.[2]

Mainly, however, Al Fatah has fought as a more or less conventional militia in the civil war in Lebanon since 1975, killing many more other Arabs than Israelis, and suffering corresponding casualties largely at the hands of the Shia and Christian militia and the Syrian Army. Since 1987 Al Fatah has been the prime organizer of the *intifada* ('shaking off') in the occupied West Bank and Gaza strip, encouraging Palestinian children to throw stones at Israeli troops to provoke them to open fire.

Al Fatah is by far the biggest constituent of the PLO, though many other smaller movements are members, albeit in a rather sporadic manner. The PLO's main function is not military but political and financial. In these fields, Yassir Arafat's success reflects his genius in harnessing the support of able people to advance his aims. In the political field he has secured the support of a majority of Third World governments in the United Nations (though this is also partially due to the intensity of their desire to embarrass the USA, and Israel as its client state). On the financial side, the Palestine National Fund (PNF), directed by Jawid Ghossein, has mobilized Arab bankers and numerous other advisers to build up assets for the PLO estimated to be $5 billion, with an annual income in excess of $1.25 billion.[3] More than half of this comes from dividends from investments all over the world. If all other sources of income (e.g. contributions from Arab oil states) ceased tomorrow, the PLO's assets and income would be more than adequate to continue its activities indefinitely, and would still be larger than the total budget of many Third World governments.

With such assets, and such power for political activity and propaganda, Yassir Arafat realizes that terrorist operations directly attributable to Al Fatah, especially in Western Europe, are likely to be counter-productive. This does not, however, stop the PLO from providing financial backing for other constituent members and, possibly, for 'unofficial' splinter movements, as in the past.

Apart from those mentioned above (Al Fatah and the PLF), there are four other currently active movements which remain part of the PLO and generally (though certainly not always) loyal to Yassir Arafat: the Popular Front for the Liberation of Palestine (PFLP) and the Democratic Front for the Liberation of Palestine (DFLP), which have in the past conducted international terrorist operations; and the Palestine Communist Party (PCP) and Arab Liberation Front (ALF) which have not.

Movements which are now hostile to the PLO and are based in Syria include the Popular Front for the Liberation of Palestine – General Command (PFLP-GC), As Saiqa (virtually part of the Syrian Army), Palestine Popular Struggle Front (PPSF), Fatah-Provisional Command (F-PC) and Fatah – Revolutionary Council (F-RC or Abu Nidal Group). F-PC aims to make The *intifada* more violent in order to sabotage any negotiated settlement between the PLO and Israel.

Those which have used the most violence in Europe – the PFLP, PFLP-GC, and the Japanese Red Army (JRA), which has based itself for some years with the PFLP – are discussed in the next section, and the Abu Nidal Group separately later (pp. 21–2).

The PFLP, PFLP-GC and the JRA

After the 1967 Arab–Israeli war, the Arabs lost all their contiguous frontiers with Israel except that with Lebanon. Egypt, Jordan and Syria were all insulated from Israel by the occupied territories of Sinai and Gaza, the West Bank and the Golan Heights. This caused great frustration, and led a number of other Palestinian movements to start international terrorist operations in Europe as they could not get at Israel. One movement, the PFLP, which later split and then split again, was from the start paramount in these attacks and one of its splinter groups remains so to this day.

The PFLP was formed in 1967 by Dr George Habash, and carried out the first Palestinian hijack – of an El Al aircraft taking off from Rome in July 1968. Other Jewish targets (including El Al aircraft on the ground) were attacked in Athens, Zurich, London, Brussels, Bonn and The Hague in 1968 and 1969 and there were several more hijacks, though El Al security became so effective that the PFLP increasingly picked aircraft of US and European airlines. These included the hijack of US, British and Swiss aircraft to Dawson's Field in Jordan in September 1970.[4]

Dr George Habash explained that one death in London or New York brought more publicity for his cause than one hundred deaths in Israel. By 1972, however, he had changed his view and decided that international terrorist acts were counter-productive. The commander of his military wing, Dr Wadi Haddad, disagreed, and broke away with a splinter group, though he still used the same title. Operating from Baghdad, he directed a large number of terrorist operations until his death from cancer in 1978. For some years he ran a Commando in Paris, led by the Venezuelan terrorist Carlos.[5] For some of his operations (before and after his split with Habash) he was assisted by a group of fanatical terrorists of the Japanese Red Army (JRA) who threw in their lot with the PFLP after fleeing from Japan. This group was led by Fusako Shigenobu, whose husband Tsuyoshi Okudaira led a particularly bloody operation on behalf of the PFLP in 1972. Boarding an Air France aircraft refuelling in Rome, he and two other Japanese took guns and grenades from their baggage on arrival at Lod Airport and massacred twenty-six fellow passengers (mainly Puerto Rican pilgrims on their way to Bethlehem) in the baggage reclaim hall. Okudaira shot himself to avoid capture. The only survivor of the Japanese terrorists explained the operation by saying that the Palestinian cause was ideal to exploit for world revolution but that 'the Arab world lacks spiritual fervour'.[6]

The JRA participated in a number of other operations in Europe and, though quiescent after Haddad's death, they re-emerged on the international scene in 1986 for abortive operations in the run-up to the Seoul Olympics in 1988. Shigenobu and her comrades are still believed to be in the Middle East and may well reappear in Europe.

In 1974 another splinter group broke away from the PFLP – the PFLP-GC. This was and still is led by Ahmed Jibril, a Palestinian who served for a time as an officer in the Syrian Army and believes that the Palestinians must rely on military rather than political action. The PFLP-GC rejects Arafat's willingness to do a deal which recognizes the continued existence of Israel, and is aligned to Syria. It maintains an army several hundred strong, organized on militia lines, which has carried out a number of daring (though usually suicidal) raids into Israel. That is its primary activity. It has, however, also carried out operations in Western Europe.

It recently captured the world's headlines when a number of its members were arrested in Germany in possession of bomb-firing mechanisms operated by barometric altitude fuses, shortly before an identical fuse mechanism detonated a bomb in baggage which had been loaded in Frankfurt on to a Pan Am flight. This bomb killed 270 people when it exploded over Lockerbie in December 1988. The PFLP-GC was almost certainly concerned (in co-operation with Iran) in that operation. The probable reasons why it did not admit responsibility for it are that at least one of its members was still in custody in Germany, and possibly also because of the world-wide revulsion at the scale of the massacre.

The Abu Nidal Group

The Abu Nidal Group is probably the most violent of the small groups which broke away from Al Fatah. Abu Nidal (his real name is Sabri al Banna) was, with Yassir Arafat, a co-founder of Al Fatah in the early 1960s, when he was about 25 years old. By 1973 he had become disenchanted with Arafat's readiness to recognize, even if only temporarily, the existence of Israel. He declared himself the true leader of the armed struggle and set up a rejectionist movement – Fatah-RC – in Baghdad. In 1974 he dispatched a team to assassinate Arafat in Damascus, but it was captured, and Al Fatah in turn sentenced Abu Nidal to death *in absentia*.

In 1976 Abu Nidal launched a series of operations using the title 'Black June', condemning Syrian intervention in Lebanon. From his Baghdad base, he dispatched hit squads to assassinate 'moderate' PLO representatives in many countries, including Britain, France, Kuwait and Portugal. In 1982 three of his men attempted to murder the Israeli Ambassador in London, Shlomo Argov, which precipitated the Israeli invasion of Lebanon; his three terrorists were all arrested and convicted and were found in possession of a long hit list of other targets, including the new London representative of the PLO.

Abu Nidal was believed to have at that time about 100 dedicated followers, who had volunteered for martyrdom. He appeared to be willing to send them out in the role of 'hired assassins' to raise funds. By November 1983 the Iraqis were finding his uncontrolled and unpredictable operations an embarrassment, so they arrested him and delivered him under guard to Damascus. During the first six months of 1984 he carried out another fifty attacks, and Syria then began to become embarrassed. Abu Nidal moved on to Libya in mid-1985 and seemed at last to have found in Gadafi a sponsor after his own heart. In November 1985 he mounted the hijack of Egyptair Flight 648 from Athens. It landed in Malta where, in a bungled rescue attempt by Egyptian commandos, fifty-six passengers were killed as well as four of the five hijackers. On 27 December there were almost simultaneous attacks on El Al and TWA check-in desks at Rome and Vienna Airports. In Rome, four terrorists opened fire with Kalashnikov automatic weapons, indiscriminately killing thirteen and wounding seventy before the airport police, in co-operation with Israeli guards, killed three of the terrorists and wounded and captured the fourth. In Vienna, three terrorists killed three passengers and injured thirty before one was killed and the other two captured. The surviving terrorists from the two attacks gave a lot of valuable information about their training and organization. Abu Nidal appears to have had a logistic support centre in Italy, from which weapons were issued to the terrorists only a day or two before their attacks. Italy at that time was holding twenty-four Arab terrorists in prison, and the government set about tightening the very lax controls on Arab immigrants and 'tourists', and on the large number of foreigners in the country, particularly from North Africa.

Since then, the Abu Nidal Group has appeared in a number of countries and had, for example, an office in Warsaw in 1987, which left in 1988. There have been reports of individual Abu Nidal terrorists in Brazil, Colombia, Costa Rica, Peru, Venezuela and the USA. There has also been evidence of links with the JRA in Lebanon. They are suspected of participation in various terrorist attacks on US targets in Europe but it is not clear whether the participants were hired out or whether Abu Nidal was directing the operation. He moves his headquarters frequently.[7]

On 2 September 1989 five suspected members of the Italian Red Brigades (BR) were arrested in Paris, armed and with plans for operations in France, including the assassination of a senior Italian foreign ministry official, probably in co-operation with the German Red Army Faction (RAF). Documents were also found linking them with Abu Nidal. Acting on this information, Italian police next day arrested an Abu Nidal suspect, Khalid Thamer, in Rome, along with another BR suspect, Caterina Calia. This confirmed not only the Abu Nidal Group's active contacts in Western Europe and Italy in particular, but also the growing co-operation of EC police forces under the TREVI agreement.[8]

Abu Nidal is now in his 50s. There have been suggestions of ill health and frequent unconfirmed reports of his death also of internal feuds and assassinations. Whether or not his group continues to operate as such, the circumstances of its formation and development are typical. Angry Arabs with his kind of ruthlessness can always recruit and inspire supporters, and will strike out internationally when they are frustrated in the Middle East. Europe must be prepared for more Black Septembers and Abu Nidals in the future.

Other Arab terrorists operating in Europe

Other Arab terrorists will continue to operate in Europe for a number of reasons, chiefly (like Abu Nidal) because of frustration with their inability to further their aims elsewhere. These have thus far included hit squads from Hezbollah, the Abdallah group, groups from North Africa and freelance terrorists who may operate with any of the others.

Hezbollah ('the army of God') grew out of the dispatch from Iran of about 1,000 Revolutionary Guards to help the Syrian Army to check the Israeli invasion of Lebanon in 1982. They were based with the Syrian Army in Baalbek in East Lebanon, where they were also joined by members of Dawa, a fanatical group of fellow Shia Muslims from Iraq. Their primary role was to recruit, motivate and train Lebanese Shia Muslims from West Beirut and South Lebanon to carry out suicide attacks on Israeli targets and on the French and US contingents of the Multinational Peacekeeping Force (MNF) in Lebanon and on the French and American Embassies in Lebanon and Kuwait. They made spectacularly successful attacks on these in 1983, which killed over 350 French and American victims and resulted in the withdrawal of the MNF in 1984. Equally spectacular was the hijack in June 1985 of TWA Flight 847, which had taken off from Athens. After they had murdered one American passenger they landed in Beirut, where they held 108 US passengers and crew as hostages to secure the release of over 700 Shia militia prisoners by the Israelis; the hijackers went free.[9]

Hezbollah's operations in Lebanon have been amongst the bloodiest, and certainly the most successful (in terms of political concessions extorted) of all terrorist operations. Though the attacks were carried out in the Middle East, their victims and their targets for extortion were US and European. The same applies to the seizure of individual US and European hostages in Beirut, about twenty of whom are still held. Hezbollah is believed to have extorted large ransoms and political concessions for the few so far released (French, German and US); they secured for their sponsor, Iran, substantial consignments of arms during the Gulf War.

Hezbollah have occasionally sent hit squads to attack US and European targets in France and Germany and they are believed to have been sponsored by Syria. Two of these provoked the US bombing of Libya in 1986 which, even if the target should have been Syria, led Gadafi to restrain his active sponsorship of terrorism, at least temporarily. But the bombing also did much to reduce Gadafi's unpopularity with other Arab states, and to encourage Arab unity.

Other Arab groups, usually *ad hoc*, have been formed for specific tasks such as the seizure of the Iranian Embassy in London in 1980, almost certainly sponsored by the Iraqi government. Others have included the North African group now believed to have been responsible for the murder of ten French victims in a series of bomb attacks in Paris in 1986 (see pp. 61–2). Captured documents have revealed links between these and freelances like the Hamadei brothers (arrested in Germany); also with the Hindawi brothers, one of whom (Nazir) was arrested in London after an abortive operation in which Syrian complicity at Embassy level was specifically proved (see p. 91). The Christian-born Marxist Georges Abdallah and his family from North Lebanon operated also in France (see p. 61). Abdallah is currently serving a life sentence there, but the rest of the family have probably returned to Lebanon for fear of arrest, or perhaps as part of a deal. These groups and their operations will be discussed in subsequent chapters (4, 5 and 7) on France, Germany and Great Britain.

Groups like Hezbollah and the others, in view of their sometimes spectacular political success, are likely to continue to seek US and European targets, both in the Middle East and in Europe.

Latin American and Chinese drug traders

The most likely form of violence to come from Latin America will be criminal violence arising from the narcotics trade. If effective police or social measures curtail the drug trade on European streets, rival gangs may increasingly turn to violence in competing for the market, or may attempt to terrorize police, juries and potential witnesses in order to save themselves from a decline in profits or from conviction. This would be classed as crime, but the techniques, and the effects on European societies, would be more akin to those of political terrorist movements.

The growing activities of the Triad Secret Societies from Hong Kong in organizing the heroin trade in Europe, especially in London and Amsterdam, may lead to exactly the same thing. The ubiquitous drug trade is discussed in later chapters (pp. 108–11 and 184–5).

Foreign terrorists in Europe in the future

It is virtually certain that Palestinian and other Islamic groups will continue the kind of terrorism which they have practised in Europe in the past. The groups will change, but the aims, targets, tactics and techniques, advanced by technological developments (see Chapters 11 to 13), are likely to remain much the same because they have produced spectacular short-term dividends, such as the withdrawal of the MNF from Lebanon and the enormous publicity gained by the hijacks. They have achieved no long-term dividends: Lebanon remains in chaos and the Israelis remain in occupation of all Arab Palestine. But it is the short-term ecstasy which motivates the teenage martyrs whom the hard-headed leaders send to their death. The hit squads may be sent to Europe by large armies or militias (like those of the Palestinians and Hezbollah) or by governments, especially by Syria and Libya, possibly also by Iran and Iraq, and by other countries if revolutionary regimes were to seize power there. (Few people predicted the devastating effect on world peace of the coming of Khomeini in 1978–9.) Other groups may be independent or semi-independent, like the Abdallah or Abu Nidal groups. Whatever their sources, however, the terrorist groups which are sent to operate in Europe will themselves probably be small in order to maintain clandestinity, and will base themselves either in safe houses provided by immigrants or other sympathizers, or in small hotels and bed-sitting-rooms where they are unlikely to attract attention.

Other foreign groups fighting their own battles on European streets, or hitting European targets to coerce European governments or corporations have included Armenians (attacking Turkish targets), Bulgarians (government hit squads attacking dissidents or defectors), Croats (Yugoslav targets), Iraqi diplomats (shooting at Iraqi dissidents), Israelis (government hit squads assassinating Arabs), Libyans (government hit squads under Embassy protection murdering anti-Gadafi Libyans) and Sikhs (murdering Hindus). Militants from French colonies in the Caribbean and the Pacific have also attacked targets in France. The great majority of their victims have also been foreign, though sometimes, like the Iraqis and the Libyans, they have killed French and British police officers while shooting at their own people.

Experiences suggests that terrorists of this type, usually in very small groups, will continue to do these kinds of operations in the future. Some will reflect existing conflicts likely to continue, as, for example, in the Middle East, India, Turkey and Yugoslavia. Others will spill over from other foreign conflicts (internal or international) which cannot yet be foreseen but might include Ethiopa, the Sudan, Somalia, Sri Lanka and possibly Afghanistan. It is just conceivable, though unlikely, that Latin American nationalists, such as Argentines frustrated by their inability to annexe the Falkland Islands, might operate in Europe. Wherever they may come from, the pattern of their attacks is likely to be similar to those in the past, aimed to produce maximum impact by a small group at low risk.

West European nationalist groups will probably continue to operate on occasions outside their own countries and when they do they must strictly be regarded as 'foreign terrorists'. Neither the Spanish nor Northern Irish conflicts are likely to be permanently resolved for some years, any more than the Arab–Israeli conflict. It must be expected, therefore, that ETA will continue to operate in France and that the IRA will base active service units in Belgium, France, Germany and the Netherlands to attack British targets. These operations are discussed in the subsequent chapters about these countries.

Chapter three

Italy

Right- and left-wing terrorism

Of all the countries in the EC, Italy probably offers the most valuable lessons in the fields of terrorism, violent crime and the countering of them. The four giant criminal networks are notorious: the Sicilian Mafia, operating nation-wide with links all over the world, increasingly in the business of drug trafficking and money laundering; the rival Neapolitan Mafias, Camorra and New Camorra; and the Calabrian 'Ndrangheta. Their activities overlap national politics, local government, commerce, industry and terrorism, and they themselves apply terrorist tactics in some ways more vicious than most political terrorists. And Italy has had to cope with the highest level of political terrorism outside Northern Ireland and Spain. It has recently shown signs of tackling and weakening the Mafia, and it had by 1986 reduced both right- and left-wing terrorism to a point where they ceased to be politically significant. The methods they used were frequently criticized on ethical grounds, but they undoubtedly saved hundreds of lives from then onwards. Whether they are regarded as a triumph of pragmatism or as an example of shameless corruption of the judicial process, they are certainly worth studying in preparation for 1992.

Between 1969 and 1987 there were 14,599 terrorist incidents recorded in Italy, of which 359 caused death or injury. A total of 419 people were killed and 1,182 were injured (see Table 1). Of the 359 attacks involving death or injury, 267 (74.5 per cent) were attributed to left-wing terrorists, 27 (7.5 per cent) to right-wing terrorists, and 65 (18 per cent) to Arabs and others. But in those 27 attacks the right killed more victims than the left – 193 compared to 145. Of the 193, 85 were killed by a single bomb at Bologna railway station, and 52 in four other indiscriminate bomb attacks in public places. The victims of the right-wing bombs were all just members of the public who happened to be in those places at the time. The left were much more selective: for example, from the time of their first murders in 1974 until 1987, the Red Brigades killed sixty-eight

Table 1 Political terrorism in Italy, 1969–87

Year	Total attacks	Involving death or injury	Deaths	Injuries	Remarks
1969	398	3	19[a]	88	a includes 17 killed and 88 injured by a bomb in a bank
1970	376	2	7	50	at the Piazza Fontana, Milan attributed to right-wing
1971	539	2	2	–	terrorists
1972	595	3	5	2	
1973	426	5	40	61	
1974	573	7	26[b]	199	b includes 8 killed and 94 injured by a bomb in the
1975	702	14	10	7	Piazza della Loggia, Brescia, and 12 killed and 105 injured
1976	1,353	13	10	6	by a bomb in the Italicus train passing through a
1977	1,926	45	13	34	tunnel between Bologna and Florence; both attributed to
1978	2,379	67	35	54	right-wing terrorists
1979	2,513	66	24	101	
1980	1,502	48	125[c]	236	c includes 85 killed and 177 injured by a bomb in Bologna
1981	634	34	25	16	railway station attributed to right-wing terrorists
1982	347	17	23	42	
1983	156	11	10	3	
1984	85	6	20[d]	134	d includes 15 killed and 134 injured by a bomb in the
1985	63	11	20	146	Rapido 904 train passing through the same tunnel,
1986	24	3	2	2	between Bologna and Florence, attributed to right-wing
1987	8	2	3	1	terrorists
Total	14,599	359	419	1,182	

Source: Alison Jamieson. *The Heart Attacked.* London. Marion Boyars. 1989. pp. 19–25

people; these included thirty-six members of the security forces (including bodyguards), seven company executives, six judges and four prison officers.[1]

About ten right-wing or neo-fascist movements have formed, split, merged and reformed since 1965. Four are still in being but, apart from the train bomb in 1984 (see Table 1), terrorist operations have been rare since 1982–3, when over 200 arrests were made as a result of information from right-wing defectors (*pentiti*: see pp. 42–3)[2]

There was an even larger number of left-wing extremists groups using a varying degree of violence. The most significant and enduring were the Red Brigades (*Brigate Rosse* – BR) and they will be the main focus of this study. Of the others, only one, *Prima Linea* (Front Line – PL) used comparable violence, and then only for a much shorter period from 1977 until the early 1980s when it, too, was decimated by arrests.

The Italian political environment in which they worked was one of the most chaotic in Europe. BR were able to achieve a peak of terror in 1977–80, kidnapping and murdering Aldo Moro, who had five times been Prime Minister and was in line to become President. This, however, shook the system sufficiently for it to pull itself together and make an effective response.

The anatomy of the Italian state

Thanks largely to the number of small parties produced by its system of proportional representation, Italy had forty-five changes of Prime Minister between 1947 and 1989, so the average duration of a government was six months. But it was more like a game of musical chairs than a battle between parties. The largest party was invariably the Christian Democratic Party (DC), which was continuously in power, but usually in coalition with between one and five of the smaller parties. The Communist Party (PCI), the second largest, was never in any of these coalitions but it did, on a number of occasions, co-operate in deals to keep the DC in power, and it always supported the democratic process. Except for one (Craxi, a Socialist) all the seventeen men who held office as Prime Minister were from one or other faction of the DC. Five of them held it many times: De Gasperi (five), Fanfani (six), Moro (five), Rumor (five) and Andreotti (six). Only one had all his administrations in succession – De Gasperi (1947–53). By contrast, Fanfani's six turns totalled forty-six months spanning thirty-three years (1954–87). Andreotti became Prime Minister for the sixth time in July 1989, having first held office in 1972.[3]

This chaotic political charade had two main results. The fabric of the country, including the (also fairly chaotic) bureaucracy, the local governments (some of the best of which were Communist ones), the

Prefects of provinces, the judiciary, commerce, industry and agriculture, all became wholly accustomed to operating without taking much notice of the central government or expecting much from it. The black economy thrived and, although it bypassed the tax system, it filled the yawning gaps which would otherwise have appeared in the supplies of everyday goods in the shops. Italy would have ground to a halt without it. The second thing which kept Italy going, in default of any consistent or continuous influence by ministers, was an 'old boy network' of relationships between politicians going in and out of office and friends in other fields, notably in industry, commerce and the security services, especially the intelligence services. There were also more structured behind-the-scenes groupings, such as the P2 Masonic Lodge, which was seen as a sinister force behind a number of scandals involving at various times all the organs of the state including judges, senior policemen and intelligence chiefs. On top of this the Mafia and other large criminal organizations also exerted a massive influence by their power to intimidate the highest and lowest in the land. Corruption was widespread. As a result of all these things the Italian public did not, and still do not, feel any affinity with the state or trust it. They despise it, and get on with whatever they want to do.

The judicial process was incredibly ponderous (it was radically altered in September 1989 to follow more Anglo-Saxon principles). It began, as in many other European systems, with an investigation by an 'instructing judge' or examining magistrate, and thence through three levels of courts – Assize, Appeal and Cassation, the latter only considering points of law. If any if these was unsatisfied with a conviction, the whole case had to be tried again. Clever lawyers seeking to maximize fees, coupled with the intimidation of witnesses and juries, could extend the process to ten years or more, at the end of which a person held in custody all that time might be acquitted.

The police service is fragmented between the Carabinieri, under the Ministry of Defence; the State Police, consisting of small semi-independent forces each responsible to the Prefect of one of the ninety-five provinces, but under general supervision of the Minister of the Interior; and the Finance Police responsible to the Ministry of Finance for revenue duties and currency controls, which brings it right to the centre of countering terrorism and crime in matters such as drug-smuggling, control of currency for ransom payments and laundering of illegal money.

The intelligence service is also split between the military (SISMI) and political and subversive (SISDE), responsible respectively to Ministers of Defence and the Interior, loosely co-ordinated by an Executive Committee (CESIS) chaired by the Prime Minister. It was disrupted by frequent reorganization in the 1970s.[4]

The miracle is that despite the appalling levels of crime and (for nearly twenty years) of terrorism, Italy has managed to remain largely free of major public disorder, with a growing economy. This must be put down to the resilience of individual Italians and their ability to carry on with their own lives, legal or otherwise, without much regard to 'the authorities'. Apart from the changes in the judicial system (whose effects it is too early to predict), the system seems likely to continue much the same after 1992.

The origins of the Red Brigades (BR)

The Red Brigades were formed in 1970 by the fusion of a number of members of far left groups who were exasperated by the non-revolutionary behaviour of the PCI and its participation in the 'bourgeois' democratic process. This was also a response to right-wing terrorism, with its *stragismo* (slaughter tactics) as epitomized by the Piazza Fontana bombing in Milan in December 1969 (see Table 1). The right-wing 'strategy of tension' was designed to destabilize the state and to provoke repressive government by crude attempts to pin responsibility on the left wing, seemingly with the connivance of elements of the state and its security forces. (To this day, after twenty years of investigations, trials, appeals, and reversal of convictions, no one has been found responsible for that bomb.)

Of the groups which came together as the Red Brigades in 1970, one was a typical 1968 revolutionary student group at Trento University led by Renato Curcio and his wife, Mara Cagol; a second was a group of young Communists in Reggio Emilia, who had been expelled from the PCI for their extremist views and were led by Alberto Franceschini, a young engineer originally from a manual-working family; and a number of groups in Milan, many of them factory based, which included a young graduate, Mario Moretti, who was to lead BR from 1975 and is now serving a life sentence for the murder of Aldo Moro. It is worth noting that, from its inception, BR had far more connection, both in its membership and its activities, with the factory floor than its German or French equivalents (RAF and AD) ever did.

BR's earliest actions were mainly short-term kidnaps of personnel managers and others to extort concessions for factory workers, and their success in doing so earned them a considerable following on the factory floors. Their first major publicity splash came from the kidnap of public prosecutor Mario Sossi, who was released after thirty-five days of dramatic negotiation. Five days later, on 28 May 1974, right-wing terrorists killed 8 people and wounded 102 at an anti-fascist rally in Brescia. In retaliation, on 17 June BR raised the headquarters of the most right-wing parliamentary party, MSI, and killed two party workers – the first of their sixty-eight murders.

After the Sossi kidnap, the government appointed General Dalla Chiesa of the Carabinieri to direct all anti-terrorist operations. He was given 200 hand-picked men, highly trained in surveillance duties, and, since he also retained control of prison security, he was able to move stool pigeons, infiltrators and informers as needed about the prisons. As a result, his intelligence was excellent – a rare occurrence at that time in Italy. He was given a free hand, was answerable directly to the Minister of the Interior, and was not obliged to keep the judiciary informed of his activities. His powers were kept secret from Parliament for a year but, when these became known in 1975, his organization was disbanded, though he was called back to it after the murder of Aldo Moro in 1978 and masterminded the final battle-winning technique – *pentitismo* – which had more or less broken both right- and left-wing terrorism by 1982. His second tour of duty (1978–82) will be described later in this chapter.

Dalla Chiesa's methods were autocratic, unorthodox and highly controversial, but it is likely that if he had been left in the anti-terrorist appointment for as long as terrorism continued after 1974, it would have been defeated a great deal earlier than 1982.

His first major success was in September 1974, when Curcio and Franceschini were lured to a meeting with one of Dalla Chiesa's agents, a priest with a revolutionary reputation, who had let it be known through an intermediary that he wished to join BR. The meeting was surrounded and Curcio and Franceschini arrested after only token resistance. In October, Dalla Chiesa's men discovered another BR base, and kept it under observation. Robert Ognibene, another of the original BR leaders, returning to the base, walked into a Carabinieri ambush and killed a marshall before he was arrested. By the end of 1974, nine founding members of BR were in prison.[5]

In February 1975 Curcio was rescued from prison by his wife, Mara Cagol, who had concealed a pistol in the laundry bag which she was allowed to deliver to him; it was all arranged over a public telephone to which he had access inside the prison. He was rearrested in January 1976, and by then Cagol herself had been killed in June 1975 when Dalla Chiesa's men detected and surrounded a hideout to which she had taken a millionaire kidnap victim, Villarino Gancia. She and her comrades tried to shoot their way out but she became BR's first martyr.

On 22 May 1975 the Justice Minister Oronzo Reale introduced his Public Order Law 152 (now usually known as the *Legge Reale*). This was in response to the right-wing bombings in Brescia and of the Italicus train, and the first three BR murders in 1974. The Reale Law extended the power of the police to stop and detain on suspicion; to do spot checks on persons or vehicles in search of arms and explosives; and to tap telephones with written authority from a magistrate. It extended the immunities of the police and restricted the power of a judge to grant provisional liberty (bail) to persons accused of certain crimes. It forbade demonstrators to wear helmets or to conceal their faces. And it made registration of lodgers by householders compulsory.[6]

In September 1977 following repeated delays to the trial of Curcio and his comrades, the permissible duration of custody and trial could be extended indefinitely if delayed by intimidation of juries, witnesses or lawyers. (Later, in 1978, an accused person who interrupted a trial twice could be excluded from the court until the final day of the trial.) The 1977 law also permitted the provisional arrest of any person who the police believed had committed acts preparatory to armed insurrection.

Also in 1977, when Dalla Chiesa was put in charge of the prison service, a much harsher regime was imposed on high-risk prisoners. They were kept in isolation for long periods; family visits were restricted to one per month; and no personal contact was allowed, with conversations taking place through a glass screen with microphones.

Organization of a professsional terrorist movement

Reverting to BR in early 1976: after the rearrest of Curcio, there were believed to be only fifteen regular BR members still operating. Of these, Mario Moretti, one of the original Milan group, emerged as the leader, and he at once set about building a more effective organization. He was a highly professional terrorist who prepared and planned his operations meticulously. His target was 'the heart of the state' and two years later he was to pick Aldo Moro as the symbolic victim. In the intervening time, however, he carried out some very successful operations. In June 1976 BR killed public prosecutor Francesco Coco and his two bodyguards. In January 1977 they kidnapped a millionire ship-owner, Pietro Costa, whom they released early in April for a ransom of 1.5 billion lire (about £800,000). This gave them ample funds to organize the movement for their attack on Aldo Moro a year later. In the mean time they committed four more selective murders – of the president of the Turin Lawyers' Association (28 April 1977), the deputy editor of *La Stampa* (16 November 1977), a senior judge (14 February 1978) and a Carabinieri official (10 March 1978).

The organization which was to see BR through its peak years – the 'years of lead' (1978–80) – had now taken shape. At the heart of it were the 'columns', each responsible for a city or area, in which it was intended to organize mass support through a number of 'brigades'. The first column was that originally formed by Curcio in Milan in 1970; the second, also by Curcio, in Turin in 1973. Others followed in Genoa, Rome, Naples, the Veneto region and, briefly, Sardinia. Selected members of the columns also came together in specialist fronts, to organize such things as logistics, accommodation, transport, weapons forgery of documents, printing and intelligence. The leaders of the columns and of the fronts formed a strategic directorate, which elected four or five of its members to an executive committee for a six-month period. A proposal for an operation by one of the columns would be considered by the strategic directorate, who would thrash out problems of logistic support, propaganda, and so on with the fronts and, when satisfied with the feasibility, they would allocate the necessary backing and authorize the executive committee to implement it. It was this structure which successfully organized the series of some twenty-five spectacular kidnaps and assassinations from that of public prosecutor Coco in 1976 through Aldo Moro in 1978 to Judge D'Urso in 1980,[7] after which BR began to fragment into independent columns.

At their peak in 1978, the members of the columns, with the strategic directorate, the executive committee and the fronts, numbered about fifty full-time 'regulars', drawing a wage from the organization and living clandestinely, usually in groups of two or three in nondescript apartments bought or rented in cash from the Costa kidnap. It was from these fifty that almost all the armed teams for kidnaps and murders were selected.

In addition, there were some 400 to 450 'irregulars', who were not paid, doing normal jobs in offices or factories, or as students.[8] They are best described as semi-clandestine, since their work consisted mainly of propaganda and recruiting amongst their fellow workers or students, and also obtaining information to assist the columns in selecting targets and planning operations.

It was these irregulars who mainly manned the 'red brigades' themselves (though some of the regulars also worked in them). 'Brigade' was an intentionally exaggerated title. In international military parlance a brigade comprises about 5,000 soldiers, commanded by a brigadier or one-star general. A 'red brigade' usually comprised a mere four or five activists who were supposed to form the nucleus around which discontented people would rally to take direct action on the streets and, eventually, to form a 'people's army'. Some brigades did get as far as forming a number of subordinate cells, and their dream was that these four or five *brigatisti* would one day emerge as the officers commanding a brigade of several thousands of workers and students.

This fitted with Moretti's theory. The armed, fully clandestine vanguard (the fifty) had the task of attacking the heart of the state. Meanwhile, quite separately but under their guidance, the group of activists in each brigade would mobilize and prepare the revolutionary masses as a fighting Communist party. A column might perhaps run five or six such brigades in factories, housing areas, universities, and so on in its city, and would where necessary form a new brigade of a handful of activists to start work in some area in which propaganda might be fruitful or from which information was needed.

The myth of mass mobilization never materialized. In the earliest days (1970–3) when the title was coined, and the founding leaders themselves were the 'brigades', there had been some response to their leadership on the shop-floor. It looked then as if the mobilization might take off; but once the killing started, there was less mass support. The total strength of the movement – the columns, the brigades and such other sporadic cells as they formed in their areas of responsibility – never exceeded about 500, and the brigades and their cells did little more than act as propaganda voices, eyes, ears and auxiliaries for the 50 professional terrorists in the columns.

The kidnap and murder of Aldo Moro (1978)

The emergence of Moretti as leader coincided with two developments which greatly helped him. First was the removal of Dalla Chiesa and the disbandment of his very successful anti-terrorist unit in 1975. Second was the final blooming of the 'historic compromise' between the DC and the PCI, originally mooted in 1973 between Aldo Moro (Prime Minister in 1974–6) and the PCI secretary Enrico Berlinguer. As the two largest parties, they could not find any formula for a coalition but, to avoid the constant petty compromises and indecisiveness inherent in coalition with the small parties, the DC in 1976 undertook to temper its policies to satisfy the Communists in exchange for which the PCI agreed not to vote it out of power. The result of this was a minority DC government, with no coalition partners, which held power from 1976 to 1979 under Giulio Andreotti. Moro later made it clear that both he and Berlinguer had intended that this would eventually lead to government by the DC and PCI in coalition.

This 'betrayal of the masses' by the PCI was central to BR propaganda. But part of the political deal for the historic compromise was a disastrous weakening of the intelligence services. There were very strong grounds for suspicion that they not only had covered up the involvement of leading figures in extreme right-wing politics, but also had failed to press home investigations of some of the right-wing massacres such as the Milan, Brescia and Italicus train bombings. There was also suspicion that the intelligence services were being used to compile and disseminate data for use in smearing certain leading left-of-centre politicians. Though these suspicions were almost certainly justified, the government emasculated the newly reorganized political intelligence service (SISDE) without organizing anything effective to carry out its task. It remained ineffective and demoralized until after the murder of Aldo Moro by the BR in 1978. To make matters worse, under the banner of freedom of information, it became possible for both political activists and Mafia and other criminals to get a direct or indirect sight of their own intelligence files by getting an intermediary to find an examining magistrate willing to call for the person's file in the course of an investigation. It was by no means impossible to find a magistrate who could be bribed or intimidated into doing this and giving a sight of it to an equally corrupt lawyer, through whom the subject of the report would become aware of the information about him held by the intelligence services. It was then relatively easy for him to detect who the informers had been. This probably did not happen very often, but potential informers were afraid that it could happen, and were unwilling to risk it. From 1976 through the Moro kidnap until the middle of 1978, intelligence information virtually dried up. After that, the intelligence services were given the right to appeal against release of a file, and their appeal could be over-ruled only by a committee chaired by the Prime Minister. But this was too late to save Moro, or to capture any of his kidnappers until Dalla Chiesa came back on the scene in September 1978.

Moro was kidnapped at 9 am on 16 March 1978, by the Rome column of BR, reinforced by the leaders of the Milan and Turin columns, and led by Moretti in person. In the months of planning which preceded it, BR had considered three possible targets, all of them previous Prime Ministers: Andreotti, the incumbent Prime Minister; Fanfani, four times Prime Minister since 1954; and Moro, President of DC and instigator of the historic compromise and of the 'Government of National Unity' to be sworn in under Andreotti that very day.

All three potential targets had been under surveillance. Andreotti, in office, was too well guarded. Fanfani's movements were too un-predictable. Moro had a police escort but (unlike Andreotti's) neither their vehicle nor his own car was armoured; moreover, he left home at the same time almost every morning by the same route. This last was probably the strongest reason for his selection.[9]

It was a meticulously planned operation, clearly based on that of Hanns-Martin Schleyer in Germany six months previously (see pp. 48–50). Two vehicles were used to block and box in Moro's car and its escort vehicle in a narrow street. Four terrorists in Italian Airlines uniform emerged from a nearby bar and started shooting. Others joined them from various directions, and two more emerged to guard the ends of the street. All five of Moro's escort (his police bodyguards and the two drivers) were killed, but Moro was uninjured. He was bundled into a car and driven away. He was almost certainly incarcerated throughout his fifty-five days in captivity in 8 Via Montalcini, an apartment in south-west Rome occupied by Prospero Gallinari (one of the founding members who had escaped from prison early in 1977) and Anna Braghetti, using false identities as an engineer and his wife. They were his warders and were assumed to have been his killers.

About an hour after the kidnap BR made their first telephone claim. In addition to the usual flood of hoax calls, five more calls judged to be genuine came in during the day, two claiming that Moro was already out of the country. That evening the police issued a list of names and photographs of wanted terrorists. These included four of those who were later proved to have been present, with their faces visible, at the kidnap, including Moretti and Gallinari, but there was a lack of any current intelligence about them.

Later came their demand: for the release of Renato Curcio and twelve others undergoing trial for BR actions in the early 1970s. (Their trial had been repeatedly postponed during 1976 and 1977 due to intimidation of witnessess, juries and lawyers; it was due to resume, and did so, on 21 March, five days after the kidnap.)

At the start, all the political parties supported Andreotti's decision to make no concessions, though later the Socialists broke ranks and urged the 'symbolic' release of one BR prisoner 'without blood on his hands'. They presumably meant Curcio: he had personally killed no one before his capture, though the first three BR murders (in 1974) had occurred during his leadership, and he had demonstrated his approval and collective responsibility for kidnap and murder as weapons by shouting exultantly in court in 1976 when Coco and his bodyguards were murdered – 'We have executed the pig' – and again on 21 March when he tried to make a statement and managed to shout 'We have Moro' while he was being forcibly removed for interrupting the proceedings.

Parliament debated the matter only once during Moro's captivity. Policy was in fact handled at confidential meetings of the leaders and secretaries, to avoid giving away their plans to the press. The Socialists, however, gave a great deal of publicity to their advocacy of concessions. This was a source of great irritation to the DC and all the other parties and was probably a big factor in the lack of flexibility in their negotiations. They might well have played for time by showing a little subtlety as, for example, Chancellor Helmut Schmidt had done in the Schleyer case in Germany six months earlier (see p. 49). The advocates of the hardest line of all were the PCI.

With no intelligence, however, extensive police road-blocks and house searches yielded no results except to inhibit normal street crime. The police did knock on the door of the apartment used as a safe house by Moretti and his girl-friend (96 Via Gradoli, not far from Moro's family apartment) but when there was no answer they accepted the neighbours' assurance that they were 'a quiet couple', though they could have used their general authority in that area to break in. There were also some humiliating police responses to hoax calls, for example that Moro's body was in a frozen-over Alpine lake.

On 9 May after a telephone call, the police found Moro's body in the boot of a battered old car, contemptuously and symbolically parked half-way between the DC and PCI party headquarters.[10]

Emergency legislation

The prolonged trial of Curcio and his comrades, which spanned the kidnap and murder of Aldo Moro, highlighted the stress and intimidation under which judges, magistrates, juries, witnesses, lawyers, police and prison officers had to operate. It will be recalled (see p. 32) that judges, prison officers and police figured high in the list of BR murders. Judges, magistrates and lawyers (including defence lawyers) had to have full-time bodyguards and many still do to this day. Jury members travelled to and from the courts with armed escorts and, if necessary, had guards posted outside their homes. Judges and magistrates were particularly vulnerable, as it was customary for them to be readily available to the press to talk about the cases they were investigating or trying, so they had a high profile. Generally they bore the strain with great courage. This, during the years of crisis, earned them much public sympathy and respect, but after 1982 the emergency laws, which inevitably impinged on innocent people's livess, began to cause a backlash of public opinion against both the judiciary and the security forces.

It will be recalled (see pp. 31–2) that the Reale Laws of 1975, extended in 1977, has already increased police powers of seach, arrest, detention on suspicion and tapping of telephones (with written consent from a magistrate); restricted the judges' power to grant bail; and permitted judges to extend the permissible duration of custody and trial if trials were deliberately disrupted and delayed.

On 21 March 1978, five days after the Moro kidnap, Parliament passed a law which later became Law 191 of 18 May 1978. This extended the crime of kidnap to include an aggravating factor if it were 'with the aim of terrorism and subversion of the democratic order'. This was punishable with thirty years' imprisonment, or a life sentence if the hostage died. It reduced penalties for those who turned state's evidence, ceased to act in the terrorist group or assisted with the release of a kidnap victim (though the 'Penitence Law' of 1982 was to go much further than this – see pp. 42–3). Law 191 also permitted magistrates to approve telephone taps verbally, which meant that the police could put them into motion immediately (e.g. in the event of a kidnap) in the confidence that approval would come within a few minutes through the police radio network. It also permitted arrested persons to be questioned without the presence of a defence lawyer in situations of 'extreme urgency', though a lawyer had to be summoned as soon as possible. Any evidence obtained in such interrogation, however, could be used only for investigative purposes and was not valid in court. The police were authorized to hold a suspect for up to twenty-four hours if not satisfied with his identity, and they could ask a magistrate for copies of legal files (though the magistrate could refuse on grounds of secrecy of preliminary investigations). Law 191 also created new rules for the formation of juries (to counter the repeated refusal of jurors to attend 'on health grounds'); it introduced severe penalties for laundering illegally obtained money. It also made it obligatory to report to the local authorities any rental or sales agreements for property; this was to assist the detection of safe houses. As an example of this problem, three women members of the BR Rome column with no criminal records had each paid cash (presumably from the Costa kidnap) for apartments in Rome in 1977, in preparation for the Moro kidnap.

A further law was decreed on 15 December 1979 and converted into Law 15 of 6 February 1980. This became known as the Cossiga Law, after Francesco Cossiga, who had resigned as Minister of the Interior after Aldo Moro was murdered, but became Prime Minister in August 1979.

The Cossiga Law introduced two new 'aggravating factors': '*association* with the aim of terrorism and of subversion of the democratic order' and '*attack* for subversive or terrorist purposes'. Where either of these aggravating factors applied, prison sentences could be increased by half and, if the crime was punishable with more than four years in prison, no bail could be granted. Under the first of these, people organizing or directing an association which proposed such violence could get sentences of seven to fifteen years without any violence being committed, and merely participating in such an association could get a sentence of four to eight years. Under these clauses, especially after information began flowing in from *pentiti*, several hundred BR irregulars were convicted along with the regulars who had been directly involved in the killings. Also, for crimes bearing these aggravating factors, the permissible pre-trial detention was increased by one-third so, coupled with the delay and disruption already endemic in the system, this further increased the chances of some people's spending many years in prison before a definitive verdict was reached. (This last clause extending pre-trial detention time was repealed in November 1985.)

Under the Cossiga Law, the police were allowed to detain suspects and search their homes (this was repealed in 1982); they could detain and question a suspect for forty-eight hours before informing the judiciary; and they could search residential houses or whole blocks of apartments, without prior authority of a magistrate, if there were reasonable grounds for believing that someone wanted for terrorist crimes was hiding there. (The need for this power had been underlined in Germany during the Schleyer kidnap in 1977, when it was clear that the first hiding-place had been in a block of 960 apartments in Cologne, mainly occupied by students with a constant flow of tenants moving in and moving out.) The Law also required compulsory identification of anyone depositing more than 20 million lire (about £9,000) in cash.

The Cossiga Law specified reduced sentences for those collaborating with the authorities and making a decisive contribution to the reconstruction of facts and to the identification of the participants. Sentences could be reduced by from one-third to one-half, and life sentences to between twelve and twenty years. (This was a forerunner of the Penitence Law of 1982, which is discussed later on pp. 42–3.) In 1980 this incentive to collaborate was extended to the common crime of kidnap and extortion, which had the effect of reducing the very high annual rate of criminal kidnapping by 40 per cent – from seventy-five incidents in 1979 to an average of forty-five during the next four years, and lower still thereafter.

Two further laws passed at the same time facilitated intelligence-gathering by setting up a computerized data bank in the Ministry of the Interior, and improved police co-ordination by allocating a magistrate to each terrorist incident as it occurred, giving him the task of co-ordinating the activities of the Carabinieri, the State Police and the Finance Police and any other security forces involved while he investigated the case.[11]

Some of the Cossiga Laws introduced serious risks of erosion of civil liberties in the event of their being misused by unscrupulous police officers to harrass dissidents, particularly those with left-wing sympathies, which could be used as grounds for justifying arrest on suspicion of involvement in subversive activities. The balance between saving life and safeguarding civil liberties is discussed later (see pp. 153–64 and 190–6).

The return of General Dalla Chiesa

More effective in the short term than Law 191 or the Cossiga Law was the reappointment of General Dalla Chiesa on 1 September 1978 to direct anti-terrorist operations, with an initial mandate for one year, and later extended until 1982. He was, as before, given wide powers, and was responsible directly to the new Interior Minister, Virginio Rognoni.

Dalla Chiesa immediately reactivated his specialist anti-terrorist squad and successes came almost at once. In mid-September Corrado Alunni, one of Moretti's earliest colleagues in the Milan group, was arrested. On 1 October a BR base in Milan was raided and nine *brigatisti* were arrested, including two executive committee members; a mass of documentary material was also seized, including a transcript of Moro's interrogation, in which he was highly critical of Andreotti and the DC Party Secretary. Later in October, the police detected 8 Via Montalcini (where Moro had been held) and raided it, but the quiet 'engineer and his wife', alias Gallinari and Braghetti, had moved out.

At the end of Dalla Chiesa's previous tour of duty in 1975, the hard core of BR regulars had been cut to fifteen. Now it was fifty, with a much larger irregular fringe, and the highly effective organization described on pp. 32–4. It also still had plenty of money from robberies and the Costa kidnap. So he had to fight a much more difficult battle over the next three years before BR began to crumble again.

Dalla Chiesa worked full time on anti-terrorist duties until December 1979, when he was appointed to the command of the Carabinieri in Northern Italy, but he combined this with continuance of his anti-terrorist mandate operating from Milan, until his posting as prefect of Palermo in April 1982, with the task of tackling the Sicilian Mafia.[12] (It is depressing to note that the influence of the Mafia was such that he received only lukewarm support from the authorities in Sicily and was murdered by the Mafia in Palermo on 3 September 1982.)

Between Dalla Chiesa's appointment to the anti-terrorist command in September 1978 and his departure for Palermo in April 1982 (3½ years), BR committed twenty-two murders, all highly selective, and mainly of judges, police, company executives, and so on. One, however, departed from this norm: the murder of Guido Rossa, a shop-floor worker in Genoa, who was a member of his trade union and of the PCI and who had denounced a fellow worker seen distributing BR pamphlets. This murder outraged the rank-and-file of the unions and the PCI in Genoa, with its strong working-class traditions, and paved the way for Dalla Chiesa to arrest eighteen *brigatisti* there in May 1979, which virtually wiped out the BR Genoa column. Several arrests followed in Rome, including that of Prospero Gallinari on 24 September 1979.

The year 1980 was the beginning of the end for BR – and for *Prima Linea*. On 19 February Patrizio Peci was arrested in Turin and turned state's evidence, leading to eighty-five further arrests and the collapse of the Turin column, of which he was the leader. It was with Peci that Dalla Chiesa worked out the *pentiti* system which was to decimate BR, PL and the right-wing terrorist movements. On 29 April 1980 the leader of PL, Roberto Sandalo, was arrested and followed Peci's example. PL, which had committed nineteen murders since its formation in 1977, rapidly disintegrated, and its survivors merged with the hard-pressed BR. After the right-wing massacre at Bologna railway station in August 1980, right-wing *pentiti* began to come in as well. The *pentiti* system was of such significance and aroused such controversy that it will be examined separately in the next section of this chapter.

On 12 December 1980 Dalla Chiesa's campaign suffered a serious setback. The Rome column, now under the command of Giovanni Senzani, kidnapped Judge Giovanni D'Urso, who was responsible for allocating prisoners to the special high-security prisons. Senzani was a criminologist who had formerly worked in the Ministry of Justice and had first-hand knowledge of the penal system and its organization. He had joined BR in 1981 and was an ambitious man. He was keen to oust Moretti from the BR leadership, and the main purpose of the D'Urso kidnap was propaganda. The government under Arnaldo Forlani was under pressure from the judiciary, since five judges had been murdered during 1980, and conceded to almost all BR's demands. First was for the closure of the island prison of Asinara; the order to close it was given on 24 December. Second was for the publication of documents written by the 'Action Committees of Prisoners Accused of Terrorism' in Trani and Palmi special prisons, which included Curcio, Franceschini and Alunni, with the threat that their comrades would kill D'Urso unless they were broadcast by the mass media within forty-eight hours. The Parliamentary Radical Party transmitted them in their entirety from their radio station, and handed over its television time on the *Tribuna Politica* programme to the D'Urso family and, as part of the deal to save her father's life, his 14-year-old daughter was required to read a passage from the BR document referring to him as 'that pig D'Urso who deserves to be condemned'. Gaining satisfaction by publicly humiliating the child of his defeated enemy indicates the element of sadism in Senzani's personality.

D'Urso was released on 15 January 1981, four days after this television broadcast. BR – and Senzani in particular – created by this incident an impression of omnipotence and gained enormous publicity.

In April 1981 Mario Moretti was arrested in Milan, leaving the way clear for Senzani. On 27 April BR kidnapped DC regional councillor Ciro Cirillo in Naples and released him on payment of a ransom of 4.5 billion lire (£2,250,000). The ransom money was alleged to have been raised by co-operation between the DC, the Camorra and the military intelligence service (SISMI). Only one-third of it was believed to have reached BR, but Cirillo was released on 24 July. During the same period an Alfa Romeo executive, Renzo Sandrucci, was kidnapped on 2 June and was released when Alfa Romeo conceded to BR's demand to cancel a programme of 500 redundancies. These kidnaps underlined Senzani's political style in contrast to Moretti's militarism.

Senzani had issued stern threats to Patrizio Peci and the other *pentiti*, declaring them to be 'walking corpses'. On 11 June BR kidnapped Patrizio's younger brother Roberto, whom they forced to write letters begging Patrizio to recant and to admit to being a police informer before his arrest. When there was no response, Roberto Peci was murdered on 3 August.

Despite Senzani's efforts, however, the disintegration of BR continued. In the autumn of 1981, most of the Milan column were arrested. On 17 December 1981 a US NATO Brigadier-General, James Dozier, was kidnapped by the Veneto column. The police, however, detected and arrested a driver involved in the kidnap and he at once became a *pentito*. Acting on his information, the police located and raided the hideout on 28 January 1982, rescuing Dozier unharmed and arresting his captors, most of whom also became *pentiti*. Senzani himself was arrested in January 1983 in Rome.

This marked the demise of the BR as such, and two months later Dalla Chiesa was sent to Palermo. Two BR splinter groups continued to function, one following the Senzani (populist) line and the other the Moretti (militarist) line. In March 1985 the government listed 295 wanted terrorists of the left, at least 100 of whom were believed to be taking refuge across the border in France. The same document listed 1,250 leftist terrorists in prison. These, of course, included *Prima Linea* and others, as well as BR. The far right had suffered just as badly from its own *pentiti*, with 68 terrorists still at large and 350 in prison.[13]

The BR splinter groups, which later split further into four separate gangs, committed nine more murders in the seven years 1982–8. One group was largely eliminated by nearly 100 arrests in Italy, France and Spain in 1987. Though the others were also weakened by arrests, there was evidence that one of them had opened links with the Camorra, and also that they were trying to set up bases in France. They may still be able to carry out individual assassinations, but they are no longer a serious political factor and have faded into insignificance in comparison with the far greater political influence exercised by the Mafia.[14]

The Penitence and Dissociation Laws

The 'Penitence Law' (Law 304) of 29 May 1982 was introduced over two years after Patrizio Peci's arrest and expired on 31 January 1983. Up till that time all the bargains of leniency for information had been made under the existing Cossiga Law dating from December 1979, including with Peci himself in 1980 through to the kidnappers of Dozier in January 1982. They had by then become known as *pentiti*, and their defections and the resulting arrests had received enormous publicity. The purpose of Law 304 was to spell out attractive terms to the much demoralized survivors, with a limited time in which to take advantage of them. The resulting flood of information, from left and right, led to hundreds more arrests in 1982 and 1983.

The Cossiga Laws of 1979 still remain in force, though the incentives they offer are less advantageous than under the Penitence Law. They are applicable to right- and left-wing terrorism and to ordinary crime.

The provisions of the Cossiga Law were outlined on pp. 37–9. Under the Penitence Law, an accused person could be classified as a *pentito* if he or she confessed to all terrorist crimes committed and made an 'active contribution' to the cessation of terrorism. The term 'penitence' was in fact largely cosmetic. No remorse was required and the extent of the rewards or privileges granted was assessed in practice purely by the extent to which the information resulted in the location of safe houses, arms caches, etc., and the arrest of wanted terrorists.

For one thus qualified as a *pentito*, life sentences were reduced to ten or twelve years, and others reduced by one-half, and not to exceed ten years. If the contributions were considered 'exceptional' the sentence could be reduced by a further one-third. This was applied to Patrizio Peci who, in spite of admitting to eight murders, was very quickly set free. *Pentiti* were also immune from punishment for associative crimes and were given a privileged prison regime, not only to protect them, but also to enable them to be near their homes and to receive more visitors, parcels, and so on.

After his arrest on 19 February 1980, Peci immediatley declared his readiness to talk. Before he released his information, however, he prepared the ground by obtaining firm assurances of a reduction in sentence, his personal security and the chance of starting a new life in another country. He quickly built up a relationship of trust with the pragmatic Dalla Chiesa, who saw the enormous potential of *pentitismo*. It is estimated that 350 left-wing terrorists became *pentiti*, though only about 70 of these were high enough in the hierarchy to have much significant information to offer. The smaller fry therefore gained far less from it than their leaders did.

Peci did not display any remorse or claim moral justification. He described himself as 'a defeated terrorist, not a repentant terrorist'. He said that he realized that BR did not enjoy the support of the masses; that their actions were restricting the opportunities for peaceful protest; and that the armed struggle was damaging the interests of the working class.

One of his biggest contributions was his detailed account of the organization and structure of BR (see pp. 32–4) which, with the names he gave, greatly helped the build-up and interpretation of intelligence information. One of the first fruits of his information was a police raid on a safe house in Genoa whose location he had given. The four *brigatisti* inside were all shot dead. Most of those he betrayed, however, were arrested (eighty-five directly from his information) and he claimed that he had benefited them, in that they might otherwise have been killed, and that they would in any case have been arrested eventually.[15]

The total number of arrests made as a direct result of information from *pentiti* between the release of Dozier in January 1982 and the middle of 1983 was 482 from left-wing groups and 227 from right-wing groups.[16]

There were a number of arrested right- and left-wing activists and terrorists who were willing to *dissociate* themselves from violence but were not prepared to give information about their comrades or about safe houses, etc. To cater for these, Law 34, the 'Dissociation Law', was passed on 18 February 1987, applicable only to crimes committed before 31 December 1983; it ran for one month only. During this month, *dissociati* were given the opportunity to admit to their activities; to declare their definitive abandonment of the terrorist group; to renounce the use of violence as a means of political struggle; and to undertake to behave compatibly with those declarations, in prison or after conditional release. Those who did so had sentences for crimes of association reduced by half; life sentences reduced to thirty years; crimes of bloodshed with sentences of less than life reduced by a quarter; and those for other crimes by a third. *Dissociati* serving sentences of less than ten years were granted conditional liberty.

Amongst those who accepted these conditions was Alberto Franceschini, one of the founder members of BR. Imprisoned since 1974, he dissociated himself from terrorism in 1984; when the Dissociation Law came into force in 1987, he formalized this and was released.

Renato Curcio and Mario Moretti, however, are neither *pentiti* nor *dissociati*. Those who remain committed to the armed struggle are known as *irreducibili*, but Curcio and Moretti claim that they hold a '4th position'. They deny that they wish to resume the armed struggle, which they describe as 'a cycle which has run its course but which will only be properly concluded when those who gave it its impetus are out of prison'. This is hardly a convincing argument, and they have refused to make the declarations required of *dissociati*.[17]

Many consider it unjust that Curcio, who committed no murders with his own hand, should still be in prison while Peci, who admits to eight murders, is free. Curcio himself, however, rejects the notion that he has any less responsibility than those who pulled the triggers in the murders carried out under his leadership, and he underlined this in his proud and joyful outbursts in court to celebrate the murder of Coco and the kidnap of Moro.

The release of Peci was part of a deal to save lives, for which Peci received his agreed price, however morally undeserved. In terms of saving lives the Cossiga, Penitence and Dissociation Laws were effective. The figures in Table 1 (p. 27) leave no doubt about that.

There is nothing new about leniency as an incentive to give information or state's evidence. By far the most valuable sources of information in the Malayan Emergency in 1948–60 were the 'Surrendered Enemy Personnel' (SEPs), who could earn freedom very quickly. If they gave information resulting in the apprehension of a substantial number of wanted terrorists, they could also earn enough in monetary rewards to enable them to start a new life under a new name in a new country. In Northern Ireland the 'supergrasses' also yielded spectacular results until judicial unease about the reliability of verdicts based on their evidence resulted in many of the convictions' being quashed on appeal (see Chapter 6).

One of the legal hazards of *pentitismo* was that, to get worthwhile benefit from it, *pentiti* were tempted to invent or exaggerate evidence against some of the fringe members of BR, or against others who were not even members at all. Between 1979 and 1982, 15,000 to 20,000 people were arrested for left-wing terrorist crimes and about 4,000 were convicted. For some of the young and often idealistic 'associates', several years of contact in prison with professional criminals and terrorists encouraged further criminality: the more so when, on release, they were barred from public employment and not welcomed by private employers. There is now therefore a growing pool of embittered, intelligent and forcibly idle ex-convicts, ripe for recruitment as plausible criminals, with a high probability of involvement in drug trafficking.

The prolonged process of trial and the still further extension of pre-trial detection since 1980 (see p. 29 and pp. 37–9) should be partially rectified by the new system introduced in September 1989, but this will not undo the damage already done to individuals who feel themselves to have been unjustly treated during the previous twenty years.

It may be many years before the balance between the methods used to arrest terrorists and induce their betrayal of others, and the price in terms of human rights, can be finally assessed. Many innocent lives were undoubtedly saved, but the numbers killed by terrorism never approached the continual toll of murders by the Mafia. The destabilizing influence of terrorism on governments was highly publicized and therefore caused more alarm. The secret influence of the Mafia may be much greater. Attempts to apply *pentitismo* to the Mafia have been much less successful, and destroying their power and influence will be much more difficult. This is discussed in Chapter 9.

Chapter four

West Germany

The rise of the Red Army Faction (RAF)

Nazism had a more traumatic effect in post-war Germany than fascism had in Italy. The revelation of the concentration camps aroused shock and guilt. By the late 1960s Germany had (and still has) one of the most stable political systems in Europe and the economy had been rebuilt (thanks to Marshall Aid but above all to the Germans' own efforts) and was rapidly overtaking that of the rest of Europe. There were still some neo-Nazis, who occasionally used indiscriminate terrorism, though never on the scale of those in Italy. But there was no support for either Marxism or other revolutionary change on the shop-floor.

The terrorism which prompted Germany to overhaul its police intelligence and anti-terrorist measures was perpetrated partly by ultra-left movements, notably the Red Army Faction, and partly by Palestinian terrorists, especially in the kidnap and killing of eleven Israeli athletes at the Munich Olympics and an associated hijack in 1972.

The Red Army Faction (initially known by the media as the 'Baader-Meinhof Group') was born directly out of the student revolt against the Vietnam War in 1967–8. They first got themselves on the front page after Andreas Baader, his girl-friend Gudrun Ennslin and two others defiantly disrupted their trial for setting fire to a department store; and when Ulrike Meinhof, who was several years older than the others, used her position as a well-known radical journalist to gain access and organized a surprise armed rescue of Baader from custody (one policeman being seriously wounded) in 1970. In 1971 and 1972 they killed six people in bomb attacks on US military establishments, in armed resistance to arrest, and in shooting at police officers during a bank robbery. In June 1972 nearly all the leading members, including Baader, Ennslin and Meinhof, were arrested and imprisoned, these three committing suicide in prison in 1976 and 1977.

Before these suicides, another of the founding members, Holger Meins, had died in a hunger strike on 9 November 1974. His death prompted another Berlin-based group to show its hand, using the title '2nd June Movement' (commemorating the shooting of a demonstrator by police in Berlin on 2 June 1967). The 2nd June Movement and the RAF had separate origins but overlapped and later merged, so they will be treated as synonymous. On 11 November 1974 four young men came to the door of the President of the Supreme Court, Gunter von Drenkmann, delivering flowers for his 64th birthday. At that time judges were not regarded as targets, so he opened the door to them himself and was shot dead.

Three months laters, on 27 February 1975, the 2nd June Movement kidnapped the Christian Democrat candidate for mayor in the Berlin elections due on 2 March. The incumbent mayor felt unable to take a hard line with his opponent's life at stake and agreed to the release of five imprisoned terrorists serving sentences for armed robbery and similar crimes. They were flown to Aden.

Chancellor Helmut Schmidt, while accepting the inevitability of this decision, felt greatly humiliated by it and knew that giving way would encourage further terrorism. This was soon borne out when, on 24 April 1975, six RAF terrorists seized the German Embassy in Stockholm. Encouraged by Schmidt, the Swedish government stood firm while two hostages were killed in cold blood, at which point the Swedish police prepared to stage an armed rescue, but before they could go in, the terrorists made a bungled attempt to blow up the building, wounding all the ten remaining hostages and killing two of themselves. The other four terrorists were extradited to Germany and imprisoned.

Eight months later, on 21 December 1975, a mixed team of RAF and PFLP attacked a meeting of the Organization of Petroleum Exporting Countries (OPEC) in Vienna, and kidnapped eleven oil ministers (mainly Arab) and about thirty staff. The team was led by 'Carlos' (Ilyich Ramirez Sanchez), a Venezuelan terrorist who had thrown in his lot with the PFLP some years previously; it included three Arabs and two RAF/2nd June members, Heinz-Joachim Klein and Gabriele Kröcher-Tiedemann (who was one of those released in Berlin in March 1975). One Libyan oil official was killed by Carlos and two others, including a policeman, were killed allegedly by Kröcher-Tiedemann; Klein was wounded. Although this was a siege situation, the Austrian government conceded virtually every demand and, with world-wide television publicity, provided a ministerial escort and air transport to fly forty-two hostages and all the terrorists (including Klein) to Algiers, where the hostages were released on payment of a ransom (mainly from Saudi Arabia and the Shah of Iran) which some estimates place as high as $25 million.

The RAF/PFLP co-operation continued on 27 June 1976 when Wilfrid Böse and Brigitte Kuhlmann, with five Arabs, led the hijacking of an Air France Airbus to Entebbe, Uganda, where they were reinforced by three more Arab terrorists carrying heavier weapons, clearly with the complicity of Ugandan President Amin. The Ugandan Army protected the airfield and the airport terminal in which the hostages (mainly Jewish) were held. The hijackers demanded the release of seven RAF and fifty-three Arab prisoners from various countries. Israeli commandos staged a daring night landing and rescue operation in the early hours of 5 July, in which Böse and Kuhlmann and most of the Arab terrorists were killed.

These 1975–6 operations had mainly been organized by a lawyer, Siegfried Haag, aged 32. Lawyers had played a very full part in RAF activities since its foundation, and some (as in this case) had taken an active part. Haag was arrested in November 1976, in possession of many incriminating documents including what was believed to be a hit list of prominent Germans.

A third generation of the RAF then emerged to commit three sensational murders in 1977. On 7 April they shot the public prosecutor, Siegfried Buback, with his driver and bodyguard. On 30 July, in a chilling example of personal treachery, the Chairman of the Dresdener Bank, Jürgen Ponto, was shot dead in his home by an RAF gang which included his own god-daughter, Suzanne Albrecht, to whom, as a family friend, the locked door was opened.[1] The third victim was Dr Hanns-Martin Schleyer, whose kidnap and murder had far-reaching effects.

The Schleyer kidnap – peak and decline

Dr Hanns-Martin Schleyer was Chairman of the West German Employers' Association. The RAF kidnapped him on 5 September 1977 in Cologne, killing his driver and three bodyguards in a two-car blocking operation in a narrow street, which BR were to copy six months later to kidnap Aldo Moro in Rome (see pp. 35–6). The RAF demanded the release of eleven of their comrades from prison including Baader and Ennslin (Meinhof had already committed suicide).

Schleyer was held for six weeks and then murdered. Initially he was taken to one of 960 flats in a 43-storey block in Cologne. The flat, on the twenty-sixth floor, had been rented three weeks previously by a well-spoken 22-year-old girl, later identified as Adelheid Schulz, a hard-core RAF member already wanted for complicity in the murder of Ponto. She also rented a space in the basement garage with a key to the lift, which gave direct access to the twenty-sixth floor, bypassing the reception office on the ground floor. Presumably Schleyer was taken up, drugged, in a piece of furniture or a rolled-up carpet. Since some five or ten flats changed hands every week, this was unlikely to have attracted any attention. After a few days, the parking of a car with known RAF links led the police to search the block, but this took a further eight days, by which time the gang had moved to a second-floor flat in a nondescript suburban road in Liblar, ten miles out of Cologne.

Here too, the police received information from the public about suspicious circumstances, for example that the flat had been hired by a young couple three weeks earlier with rent paid in advance in cash, but never occupied, and that a furniture van had been seen delivering a single large box. By the time the police acted on these pieces of initially unconnected information, Schleyer had been moved: probably to Belgium, then to the Netherlands, and finally to France, where his body was found on 19 October in the boot of a car.

One of the reasons for the police failure to act in time was that their intelligence system was at that time based on files and card indexes. Public disgust with the RAF led to a flood of 3,826 pieces of information. Links between items (such as car numbers, addresses and events affecting them) were not immediately apparent to the staff who filed them. As a direct result of this kidnap the Germans installed their computerized intelligence data banks, which instantly drew attention to any such links (see pp. 58–9).[2]

Despite the failure to save Schleyer, Chancellor Schmidt had in fact handled the operation with great skill. While publicly declaring that there would be no concessions, he obeyed the first rule of negotiation by ensuring that the terrorists saw more value in continuing to talk than in killing their victim. He sanctioned negotiations by Schleyer's family on a ransom offer (though they had no power to release prisoners); he also sent ministers or senior officials to the kinds of places to which prisoners might be released, such as Aden, Algiers and Damascus, where they were observed by journalists who leapt to predictable (but wrong) conclusions. By these means he played for time, though sadly the intelligence system was inadequate to make effective use of it.

The case was brought to a head by the hijacking of a Lufthansa airliner from Mallorca to (eventually) Mogadishu in Somalia by four Arab terrorists, who demanded the release of the same eleven RAF terrorists and two Arab terrorists. This was once again a joint RAF/Arab operation; it was later proved by forensic evidence that all the written communications received in connection with the Schleyer kidnap and the hijack originated from the same typewriter.

After touching down in Rome, Cyprus, Dubai and Aden (where they murdered the pilot) they landed at Mogadishu. With Somali government permission the German rescue commando, GSG9, assisted by two members of the British SAS (Special Air Service Regiment) with special equipment, assaulted the aircraft killing three of the hijackers, wounding and capturing the fourth, and rescuing all the hostages.[3]

On hearing the news, Baader, Ennslin and one other RAF prisoner committed suicide, two of them using pistols alleged to have been smuggled into the prison by their lawyers. On 19 October the body of

Dr Schleyer was found (after a telephone message) in the boot of a car near Mulhouse in France.

This was the last murder committed by the RAF for seven years, though they made several unsuccessful attempts. They did, however, kidnap a rich 74-year-old businessman in Vienna, Walter Palmers, and extorted a ransom believed to have been between $2 million and $3 million from his family. All their communications were worded to give the impression that this was a non-political criminal extortion, but later a number of people were arrested in possession of arms, and money traceable to the ransom payment. All had RAF connections. One was Gabriele Kröcher-Tiedemann, who had taken part in the OPEC hostage seizure in Vienna in 1975. She was arrested in 1978 while attempting to cross the Swiss border with some of the Palmers ransom money and imprisoned in Switzerland.

The purpose of this kidnap was almost certainly to replenish RAF funds. In fact, due to the greatly improved police intelligence system, the forty-four RAF activists still on the police wanted list in 1978 needed all their efforts simply to survive in small groups, harried from safe house to safe house, always organizing the next one in readiness and carrying out enough small-scale robberies to subsist. There was a steady toll of arrests, and the survivors spent most of their time in neighbouring countries (especially France and Belgium, where they hoped that police pressure would be less). In 1978, presumably using money from the Palmers ransom, three of those wanted for the Schleyer murder were spotted hiring a helicopter and doing some target reconnaissance over NATO bases, but they aborted the operation when they realized they were under surveillance and went back underground. On 25 June 1979 they attempted to blow up the NATO Supreme Commander, General Alexander Haig, near Brussels, but their bomb exploded after his car had passed. On 31 August 1981 they wounded twenty soldiers and civilian employees with a bomb at the NATO Air Force base at Ramstein, and on 15 September they fired an anti-tank rocket projectile at the car of General Kroesen, Commander of the US Army in Europe, but it hit the boot of the car, causing only minor cuts to the General and his wife.

In December 1984 the RAF began an 'anti-NATO offensive in conjunction with the French AD (Action Directe) and Belgian CCC (Combatant Communist Cells – see Chapter 5). It started with their imprisoned members going on hunger strike, and a joint RAF/AD communiqué announcing a war on NATO on 15 December. On 18 December an attempt to bomb a NATO school in Oberammergau failed but on 1 February 1985 they shot and killed Dr Zimmerman, an armaments supplier. On 7 August 1985 they kidnapped and murdered a young American soldier solely in order to steal his identity card, with which they gained entry to the US Air Force base near Frankfurt, where they set off a car bomb, killing two American civilians and injuring eleven passers-by. During 1986 they murdered an industrialist, Dr Karlheinz Beckurts (9 July), and a senior Foreign Office official, Gerold von Braunmühl (10 October), bringing their murders in 1985 and 1986 up to six. After a two-year lull, they re-emerged in September 1988 in an unsuccessful attempt to kill a senior Finance Ministry official, Hans Tietmeyer. By that time most of the AD leaders had been arrested in France, and the impetus of the offensive appeared to flag, but on 30 November 1989 the RAF re-emerged to murder the Chief Executive of the Deutsche Bank, Alfred Herrhausen, using a large IRA-style remotely controlled bomb, which was attached to a bicycle parked on the roadside near his home in Bad Homburg.[4]

The RAF hard core now numbers about twenty. Many of these live outside Germany but can move back freely across EC frontiers. A dozen years of harassment by the German police and computerized intelligence with its EC data links have made them experts at clandestine survival and they remain well able to carry out professional selective murders like those in 1985-6. In addition to the hard core, the RAF have about 200 'militant activists' and a fringe of about 400 sympathizers who provide logistic support (safe houses, transport, etc.). The militant activists concentrate on bomb damage to the 'Military Industrial Complex' (MIK), a term first coined at the time of the Beckurts murder in July 1986. RAF militant activists attempted about ten major bombing and incendiary attacks during 1984-6, in one of which their own bombers was killed.

The RAF has repeatedly demonstrated its ability to survive set-backs and to revive (e.g. in 1972-4, 1975-6, 1977, 1985-6 and 1989). Since late 1970 the number of RAF members in prison has substantially exceeded the hard core, but it will never be wise to assume that they are defunct. A longer-term weakness, however, is that they have lost most of their student support to the Revolutionary Cells.

The Revolutionary Cells (RZ) and Autonomous Groups

The Revolutionary Cells (RZ) were initially in 1974 a 'tendency' within the RAF, but they broke away and by the early 1980s had built up a hard core of about 300 in independent cells, each from three to eight strong, supported by a fringe of some 2,000 active sympathizers.

The RZ differ from the RAF in that they believe that killing generally alienates the public, and that the traditional revolutionary structure (like that of the RAF and the Italian BR – see pp. 32-4) with its hierarchy, directives, couriers and safe houses, is vulnerable to interception, penetration and encouragement of informers (like the Italien *pentiti*) by the police.

Each Revolutionary Cell is therefore autonomous. Its members are all 'irregular', that is part-time guerrillas, mostly students or young intellectuals, occasionally living in 'squats' or communes, but more often living at home with middle-class parents, who know they spend a lot of time with 'left-wing friends' but have little idea, or prefer not to know, what they get up to. There are no full-time clandestine 'regulars', no central or regional organizations (such as the BR 'columns'), no directives, no documentary plans or target lists, no couriers and no safe houses. It is therefore very difficult for police intelligence to spot them, put them under surveillance, or recruit informers amongst them. They have a female branch 'Red Zora', which conveniently uses the same acronym, RZ.

RZ targets are similar to those of the RAF militant activists – NATO or the MIK. With no central guidance, the cells pick their own targets, getting their ideas from news reports or in the fringe press about firms undertaking defence contracts, or with 'imperialist' connections, for example dealing with Israel or South Africa 'exploiting' Third World Countries, or (in the case of Red Zora) exploiting women. In August 1987, after arson attacks on nine branches of a clothing corporation employing several thousand workers in Sri Lanka and South Korea, for example, the corporation gave way to the RZ demand to re-engage workers recently dismissed, and to pay higher wages.

The 'Autonomous Groups' (AG) have an even looser organization then the RZ. AG cells come together for a one-off operation and then disperse. Some individuals no doubt meet again when one of their number suggests an attack on some target, but they avoid any kind of consistent cell membership. They are therefore even harder to detect. They attack the same kinds of targets (though perhaps with more accent on infrastructure) and have roughly the same ideology as the RZ.

In 1986, the peak year of the RAF/RZ/AG assault on NATO/MIK targets, the German police recorded 464 criminal acts regarded as politically motivated, of which 90 per cent were carried out by Autonomous Groups. Of the 464, 318 were classed as 'terrorist crimes', of which 55 per cent were attacks on corporate targets (mainly banks, construction plants and defence industries). Most of the rest were on the infrastructure, notably energy, transport and communications.[5]

Attacks on property are now accepted as an occupational hazard by these types of industries or utilities. The cost of damage is generally covered by insurance (though this does mean higher insurance premiums). There are therefore no catastrophic losses and, though there is a possibility of injury, there is little threat to lives, so the 'terrorist' effect is small. The attacks do, however, have some effect in coercing firms to change their policy (e.g. not to accept defence contracts or to trade with South Africa), and are a considerable load (spread by insurance premiums) on the German economy. The ease with which bombs or incendiary devices can be placed, and the high yield at low risk to the perpetrators, may lead to a growth in this means of expressing dissent and influencing policy in Europe in the 1990s.

Neo-Nazi terrorists

The National Democratic Party (NDP), equivalent to the Italian MSI (see Chapter 3), attracted some electoral support in the 1960s but rapidly declined in the 1970s. By 1974 the government listed thirty-four neo-Nazi groups with about 1,350 members, 230 of whom had expressed willingness to use violence. Their violence rose to a peak in 1980 and 1981, when thirty-six people were killed, seventeen of them at the bombing of the Munich Beer Festival (*Oktoberfest*) in October 1980; these were also the only two years in which the number of right-wing violent offences exceeded one hundred, about half of these being criminal damage.

Their targets have mainly been foreign workers and immigrants, US 'occupation forces', and Jews. In the latter capacity they and the left shared an unholy alliance with the Palestinians. The patterns of age, sex and education of right-wing and left-wing terrorists were very different. Of the right, 51 per cent were under 25, but they were led by 45 per cent who were over 35; 97 per cent of left-wing terrorists were between 25 and 50. Only 10 per cent of the right were female compared with 33 per cent of the left. Only 10 per cent of the right had a university education, but 42 per cent of the left had.[6]

Since 1982, right-wing violence has declined and enjoys very little public sympathy. A revival is unlikely except as a reaction to some future government failing to keep left-wing, environmentalist or immigrant violence under control.

Foreign terrorists in Germany

Many foreign terrorists have tried to fight their battles on German streets, most often killing one another and seldom killing Germans. In Germany, Turkish targets have been attacked (by Armenians), Yugoslav targets (by Croats), Ethiopian (by Eritreans), British (by IRA), Bolivian (by Bolivians), Soviet (by Ukranians), Spanish (by Basques) and Zairean (by Zaireans), to name a few. But, as elsewhere, the great majority of attacks, several every year since 1969, have involved Palestinians. One of these (on a discotheque in Berlin on 5 April 1986) provoked the bombing of Libya by the US Air Force.

The bloodiest attack was in December 1988, when a Pan American aircraft blew up in mid-air over Lockerbie in Scotland, killing 270 people; it was considered almost certain that the bomb had been placed in baggage loaded in Frankfurt and checked through London to New York. Shortly before this incident a Palestinian cell (PFLP-GC) had been arrested in Frankfurt in possession of barometric fuses concealed in a tape recorder, seemingly identical with the one used in the bomb. Evidence later emerged confirming links between the PFLP-GC and Iran; also between Iran and a number of Islamic fundamentalists amongst the large Turkish 'guest-worker' community in Germany. Suspicion grew that the bomb, made by PFLP-GC, was inserted into the baggage by one of a group of Turkish airport workers who had access, or by another Turk who had succeeded in masquerading as one of the authorized Turkish workers and carrying his pass. Whatever the final explanation may be, it is likely to confirm that people from several countries, and the Khomeini government in Iran, were involved.

In June 1989 a raid on the flat of a Lebanese Shia student in Darmstadt revealed that he had sent a coded letter to Beirut, with photographs of seven Israeli targets and a list of twenty bars, etc. frequented by Americans. This, too, was consistent with Iranian Islamic involvement. Following these attacks, the Attorney-General declared in his biannual report in the summer of 1989 that foreign groups had replaced the RAF as the major terrorist threat to German security.

But the two incidents in which foreign terrorists had the greatest influence on German anti-terrorist policies had occurred seventeen years earlier – the kidnap and murder of eleven Israeli athletes at the Munich Olympics and an associated hijack to Zagreb a few weeks later. On 5 September 1972 eight Palestinian terrorists broke into the quarters of the Israeli Olympic team in Munich armed with sub-machine guns. The unarmed Israelis resisted fiercely and two were killed before the other eleven were taken hostage. The kidnappers demanded the release of 236 Palestinian prisoners by Israel, and Baader and Meinhof by Germany. Negotiations proceeded all day and the Germans agreed to a demand to take the terrorists and their hostages by helicopter to Munich Airport, where a plane would be waiting to fly them to Cairo; secretly they arranged for the helicopter to take them to the military air base, where a civil airliner would be waiting, and to stage a rescue as they crossed the tarmac to the plane. The Palestinians, however, suspected that something was afoot. The German police, using single-shot snipers' rifles from the control tower, opened fire. The terrorists threw a grenade into the helicopter where the hostages were, killing them all, and during the exchange of fire, five terrorists and one policeman were killed. The other three terrorists were arrested.

To secure the release of the three surviving terrorists, the Palestinians hijacked a Lufthansa aircraft taking off from Lebanon on 29 October and directed it to land in Zagreb, where they demanded that the three survivors should be sent to join them. This was agreed with surprising alacrity and the three went on to a heroes' welcome in Libya.[7]

As a result of this débâcle, the German government tightened its immigration procedures, and formed the professional rescue commando, GSG9, which was to perform successfully at Mogadishu five years later (see pp. 49 and 122).

Government, police and intelligence

Unlike Italy, Germany has enjoyed continuous political stability since its first democratic election in 1949. This has been largely due to its proportional representation (PR) system, which not only ensures that the strength of the parties in the *Bundestag* precisely reflects the total number of votes cast for each, but also has the vital proviso that a party must get at least 5 per cent of the vote to qualify for any seats at all. This has kept out the splinter parties which plague so many PR systems. Until 1986 there were in effect only three parties, though now the Green Party has secured enough votes to win seats and makes a fourth. One result has been that virtually every government has been a coalition of either Centre Right or Centre Left, and Germany has avoided the see-saw between two doctrinaire parties which was so damaging to Britain in the 1970s.

The governments of the eleven states (*Länder*) of the Federal Republic have more autonomy than most of their European equivalents. There is, for example, no federal police force as such. Each state police force has its own criminal investigation department. The federal criminal investigation department (the *Bundeskriminalamt* – BKA) can be ordered by the Minister of the Interior to investigate serious cases. After the Schleyer kidnap in 1977, the BKA was increased from under 1,000 to over 2,500.

A central pivot of the domestic intelligence system is the Federal Office for Protection of the Constitution (*Bundesamt für Verfassungsschutz* – BfV). This is a civil department, roughly equivalent to the British Security Service ('MI5'), whose relationship with the Police Special Branch is similar to that between BfV and BKA. BfV intelligence officers do not wear uniform or have police powers, and when their information justifies arrests they refer it to BKA. Unlike the British, the BfV operates openly in that its directors are accessible to politicians and journalists and make public statements when necessary. Its intelligence officers handling informants on the ground, however, have to operate secretly and anonymously since, if they were identified, criminals and terrorists could put them under discreet surveillance and thereby get leads to the informers.

The Federal Intelligence Service (*Bundesnachrichtendienst* – BND) deals with international intelligence and counter-espionage, as 'MI6' does in the UK. Like the BfV, the directors of the BND operate relatively openly, and are subject to oversight by a multi-party Parliamentary Control Commission (PKK) established in the late 1950s. All PKK sessions are secret, and they normally deal only with the directors of the intelligence services, though individual intelligence officers can be asked to attend PKK secret sessions if the directors agree. Individual members of the PKK are selected by majority vote in Parliament (a power challenged and endorsed in the courts) and this has successfully averted the risk of 'subversive' members getting on to the Commission. Since there is great sensitivity to the risk of fascist or Marxist infiltration, shared by the Christian Democratic (CDU), Social Democratic (SPD) and Liberal (FDP) parties, the PKK confidentiality is unlikely to be betrayed.

There is a central police surveillance system (*Beobachtende Fahndung* – BEFA) which, after the Schleyer kidnap in 1977, received the funds it needed to set up its computerized data bank in Wiesbaden, to which all federal and state intelligence services and all state police forces have access. This access has since been extended to certain other European police forces. This system has been outstandingly successful in revealing links between apparently unconnected data. Anxiety about the possible erosion of civil liberties inherent in this capability (e.g. by 'trawling' for information amongst people not previously under suspicion) is discussed later in this chapter under 'Anti-terrorist laws and civil liberties' and in Chapter 14.[8] There is, however, no doubt that the prevention of any RAF murders from 1977 to 1984, and the arrest of most of the RAF hard core, owes much to the efficiency of the BEFA intelligence system.

The Berufsverbot

When Konrad Adenauer was elected as the first post-war Chancellor of the Federal Republic of Germany in 1949, both his party, (the CDU) and the opposition (SPD) shared a determination to prevent either fascist or Communist extremists from destroying their infant democracy in the way that Hitler had destroyed the Weimar Republic in the 1930s, and the Communist Party had snuffed out parliamentary democracy in Czechoslovakia in 1948. The Nazi Party had been born out of the private armies (*Freikorps*) which ranged the streets in 1919 and attempted a *putsch* in 1920. When the Nazi Party itself took shape with the support of General Ludendorf, Hitler attempted another unsuccessful *putsch* in 1923. From 1927 to 1933 the Nazis, like the Czech Communists in 1947–8, sought to achieve their aims by public disorder and disruption of the administration and economy, so that the people, fearing a collapse of public order and a breakdown of the means of livelihood for their families, accepted a totalitarian alternative. Adenauer was determined to save Germany from a repetition of this.

One of the Nazi/Communist techniques had been to infiltrate their people into key positions in the bureaucracy ready to accept orders to act when the time came to spring the trap. With 10,000 refugees coming from East Germany every year, it was extremely easy for the Communists to insert suitably qualified people amongst these to seek government appointments in West Germany.

In 1950, therefore, the *Bundestag* and all the eleven state governments adopted a decree requiring that loyalty to the democratic Constitution must be a condition for holding public service appointments. It listed a number of political parties whose philosophy specifically rejected elected parliamentary government, including the Communist Party (KPD) and various right-wing parties adhering to fascist or National Socialist philosophies. Ministers were instructed to check that none of the staff in their departments who was involved with any of these parties should be allowed to remain in office, and applicants for entry to public service should be questioned to ensure that they too fulfilled this requirement. The order banning the employment of a person in public service was known as a *Berufsverbot*.

This law has been strongly criticized,[9] especially from the left, but in the first twenty-five years of its application (1950–75) fewer than 100 public servants had been deprived of their jobs by a *Berufsverbot*. On occasions it has been stupidly applied (when, for example, a train driver was dismissed because he was a member of the Communist Party), highlighting the need for a more flexible definition of 'public service'. And, of course, there is no way of knowing how many applicants for jobs were rejected on similar grounds, because there are many other factors taken into account in choosing one applicant rather than another. There is therefore some justifiable uneasiness that the law can give rein to prejudices.

Despite the *Berufsverbot*, it was estimated that 4,000 East Germans had penetrated the West German government by 1975, and a number of notorious examples came to light, including trusted members of the Chancellor's personal staff. The accession of President Gorbachov has not as yet terminated the activities of Soviet and East European spies in the West and, though he may well wish to curb them, he cannot check the momentum of the KGB overnight. When there is clear evidence that they have been curbed, the *Berufsverbot* may no longer be needed, and it has in any case been more flexibly applied in the 1980s than in the 1950s.

Anti-terrorist laws and civil liberties

As with the anti-subversive *Berufsverbot*, German anti-terrorist laws, coupled with the police powers derived from them and from the improved intelligence machinery, have had to steer a course between popular demand for firm action and political and intellectual concern for civil liberties – led by lawyers.

This conflict was confused by the fact that lawyers played a major part in the founding and activities of the RAF. Horst Mahler founded the group and defended its members in court before himself participating in a number of armed robberies before his imprisonment in 1971. When Baader, Meinhof and Ennslin were in prison in 1973, evidence was found that the offices of some of the lawyers representing them were being used as communication centres to and from those in prison and outside and with foreign terrorist groups. Throughout their trial in 1975–7, the lawyers did their utmost to disrupt and delay the proceedings; when Baader and his companion Raspe shot themselves in prison in October 1977, the accepted conclusion was that their pistols had been smuggled into them (presumably to facilitate an escape) by their visiting lawyers, using their privileged access.

For these reasons, judges were empowered to bar lawyers from the court if they deliberately disrupted judicial proceedings, if they were suspected of being actually involved in the crime for which their client was being tried, or of planning a future crime. Provision was made in 1976 for controlling written communication between prisoners and their lawyers' and in 1978 for preventing physical contacts when it was judged that these would increase the chance that a prisoner would escape, that is for interviews to be conducted through a glass screen with microphones. This was precipitated by the smuggling of pistols to Baader and Raspe.[10] Similar measures also proved necessary in Italy (see Chapter 3).

In 1978, after the kidnap and murder of Dr Schleyer, additional powers were given to the police in dealing with certain specified terrorist crimes. They were permitted to search all apartments in a block if they suspected that terrorists or hostages were there. They were empowered to set up road-blocks, to establish the identity of people passing through, and to arrest anyone refusing to co-operate in establishing identity.

The BEFA computerized data bank at Wiesbaden, introduced at the same time (see p. 56), greatly facilitated and speeded up routine police detective work (for example a telephone number or car number can be fed into any of the system's terminals and within a few seconds it will be revealed whether that number has ever appeared in any other context). It has also, however, facilitated two other techniques, not in themselves new or disturbing, but which could become so if the full volume and speed of the system were applied without proper safeguards. These are the *Schleppnetzfahndung* (trawl net search) and the *Raster-fahndung* (scanning search).[11]

The trawl net search was used (without the computer) in the Schleyer case in 1977. The BKA investigated thirty or forty envelopes posted in Paris, in which copies of the first ultimatum had been received by government offices, newspapers, the family, and so on. The envelopes had been sealed with saliva from different people but the stamps showed saliva from only one person. All the stamps were traced to a stamp machine in the Paris Gare du Nord and all the letters had been posted at 6.30am. The BKA concluded that all the letters had been taken by a courier in the night train from Cologne to Paris and posted there on arrival. With the aid of the railway office, they checked the names of all those aged between 25 and 35 who had been on that train. Amongst them was a known terrorist on the wanted list.

This gives no cause for concern in itself, but under a law enacted in 1986, police at a road-block obtaining data for identification (which could include saliva and other body fluids containing the DNA molecule, which is as unique as fingerprint) may now store the data if the facts justify belief that an evaluation may lead to the arrest of criminals or the solving of a crime. The data may not be passed on except to the prosecuting authority, and the police can use this power only with the written permission of a judge (or, in an emergency, of the prosecutor's ofice); the authority is valid for three months only. If these safeguards were not strictly enforced, the available volume and speed of recording and accessing data could lead to masses of information being held about people under no suspicion at all, and of its being passed to people who have no right to it.

The scanner search can be 'positive' – that is trying to match known personal characteristics of a wanted person – or 'negative' – that is eliminating innocent people. In 1979, when the Wiesbaden computer was in operation, the BKA had evidence that there was an RAF safe house somewhere in Frankfurt, but they had no idea where it was or who was in it. They thought it unlikely that a wanted person using a false name would pay an electricity bill by cheque, so they first asked the electricity company for the names of all those who had paid bills in cash: there were about 18,000. The next stage was to find which of these names was legal, since a legal name would reappear in other institutional lists such as holders of property, health insurance, fire insurance, state grants, and so on. Cross-checking of these revealed clearly that only two names were false. One proved to be that of a drug dealer, the other that of Rolf Heissler, wanted for the kidnap of Schleyer. When they went to his apartment, Heissler drew a gun and was arrested.

Like other European countries, Germany has introduced data protection legislation (1977). The *Bundestag* in 1981 authorized a broad census to create a data bank of personal details, mainly for social planning (housing, education, and so on) but this was declared by Germany's

Constitutional Court to be unconstitutional. It was amended, but the court still permitted the trawl net and scanner search procedures, including the recording of personal data in road checks. Machine-readable identity cards and Euro-passports were also approved (though at the time of writing they have not yet been issued).

There has been a tendency to use the data bank to pick out people who seem the most likely to commit crimes or to engage in terrorist activity, so that they can be checked more rigorously than others whose data suggests that they are law-abiding. This, too, could prove a danger area for civil rights because of the risk of quite innocent peoples being smeared, harassed or discriminated against.[12]

In 1986 Chancellor Kohl's CDU/FDP Coalition government introduced new legislation to widen the application of anti-terrorist laws to incorporate the growing menace of bombing and fire damage to property (especially the 'MIK' and the infrastructure) by RAF 'militant activists', the RZ and the AG (see pp. 51–3). Dangerous acts against rail, boat and air traffic, destruction of important work materials and disturbance of public works were all classed as terrorist offences. Maximum sentences for offences classed as 'terrorist' were doubled. A law was also passed for reduced sentences or pardons for offenders who gave evidence against their colleagues (though pardon was excluded for murder).

In 1987, however, legislation to make it a criminal offence for demonstrators to conceal their identity or carry offensive weapons was vetoed by the FDP members of the coalition. This illustrates one of the anomalies about the German proportional representation system. Except for the four years (1957–61) when the CDU had an overall majority, and another three years (1966–9) when the CDU and SPD formed a 'Grand Coalition', the FDP has held the balance of power, with an average of only 8 per cent of the vote, sometimes falling perilously close to the minimum of 5 per cent. Thus it is these 8 per cent of the *Bundestag* who are FDP members who decide whether Germany is to have a CDU or SPD government, and have had the power to veto any legislation they do not like. They have generally used this power responsibly, knowing that they would probably be squeezed below 5 per cent at the next election if they did not. One beneficial effect of this has been that no government, CDU or SPD, has ever strayed very far from the centre, which probably reflects the wishes of the electorate, and which has been a major factor in Germany's post-war success story.

Chapter five

France, Benelux, Denmark and Ireland

Foreign terrorists in France

About 100 people were killed in France by terrorists between 1976 and 88, over half of them by foreign terrorists. Thus, though lethal domestic terrorism has been amongst the lowest in Europe, lethal foreign terrorism has been the highest. One factor in this has been the historical French sympathy for people claiming to be 'freedom fighters', because of their own experiences in 1789, 1848, 1871 and most recently in the Resistance to German Occupation in 1940–5. France has a tradition of offering asylum, and is currently host to 150,000 political refugees as well as about 1,000,000 post-war immigrants from former colonies. This has also led to a liberal attitude to immigration controls on the frontiers.

As a result the Armenian Liberation Army (ASALA) has chosen French soil for many of its attacks on Turkish officials and institutions. Iranians have attacked Iranian *émigrés*. It is typical of France that Khomeini took refuge there before ousting the Shah, upon which the Shah's last Prime Minister (Bakhtiar), his Chief of Staff (Ovesi) and then two years later Khomeini's dismissed President (Bani Sadr) all took refuge in France and were all targets of attack by would-be assassins, presumably sent by Khomeini.

A particularly vicious network of Arab terrorist movements, believed to have been sponsored by Iran and led by North Africans from former French colonies, carried out a series of bombings in March and September 1986, claimed by the Committee for Solidarity with Arab and Middle Eastern Prisoners (CSPPA). CSPPA was built around the Lebanese family of Georges Abdallah who, in September 1986, was serving a four-year prison sentence and awaiting trial on two further charges of murder. In a campaign for his release, six bombs were set off between 8 and 18 September in crowded public places in Paris, killing 10 people and wounding 170. Abdallah was sentenced to life imprisonment in February 1987 but by then the network had been largely broken up as a result of German co-operation and new French laws and police powers (see pp. 64–7).

Other Arab groups operated jointly with French terrorist groups of both far right and far left against Jewish targets. 'Rejectionist' Palestininans also killed at least seven main-stream PLO officials in France during the 1980s. Although no one claimed responsibility for them, it must be assumed from the nature of the targets that Arabs were involved in nearly all the fifteen deaths which resulted from a rash of terrorist incidents in a four-month period in the summer of 1982.[1]

Action Directe (AD)

The most important of the indigenous French terrorist groups is Action Directe (AD). This was founded in 1979 and carried out about fifty terrorist attacks, mainly in Paris, before its principal leaders were arrested, along with about thirty more of its hard-core members, in 1986 and 1987. Its two founders, Jean-Marc Rouillan and Nathalie Menigon, had in fact already been arrested in September 1980 in a shoot-out with police in Paris but in 1981 the newly elected Socialist President Mitterand ordered their release as part of an amnesty for 'political prisoners'. Had they remained in prison, AD might well never have developed so, bearing in mind their own known operations and those in which they co-operated with foreign terrorists, the decision to release them may have cost many lives.

AD appeared to have three main motivations in its target selection: support for the Palestinians and Iranian-sponsored factions in Lebanon; anti-imperialism, both US and French; and an obsession with computers as the main tool of capitalist-imperialist domination. At its peak it had perhaps seventy or eighty regular members, split between two main groups. Within these groups the control and organization of individual cells was by a lateral linkage rather than a hierarchy, but the impetus relied a great deal on Rouillan and Menigon in Paris, and André Olivier and Max Frerot (their explosives expert) in Lyon.

In late 1984 Rouillan forged a link with the RAF in Germany and the Combatant Communist Cells (CCC) in Belgium, to form an anti-NATO Alliance. CCC was in fact an offshoot of AD, and had succeeded in stealing a quantity of explosives from NATO establishments in Belgium, some of which was detected in RAF and AD bombings. CCC led the way with eight bombs against NATO and associated corporate targets in October 1984, and another twelve thereafter in which they killed two people.[2] On 16 December 1985 their leader, Pierre Carette, was arrested and the movement did not reappear.

AD and the RAF issued their joint declaration of war on NATO on 15 January 1985 and, as described in Chapter 4, the RAF killed six people in 1985–6. AD followed a similar pattern: they murdered a French major-general, René Audran (25 January 1985), attempted to kill a French industrialist, Guy Brana (16 April 1986) and murdered the Chairman of Renault, Georges Besse (17 November 1986).

On 3 December 1986 the trial began in Paris of Regis Schleicher, for the murder of two policemen in 1983. Schleicher set out quite blatantly to intimidate the jury from the dock with 'the spectre of proletarian vengeance' from AD if they were to find him guilty. Within five days, five members of the jury had absented themselves 'for health reasons' and the trial had to be postponed. This led the newly elected Prime Minister, Jacques Chirac, to introduce trial without jury for terrorist offences, as will be described later (see pp. 64–6).[3]

Meanwhile the AD leader of the Lyon group, André Olivier, had been arrested on 28 March 1986. On 21 February 1987 Rouillan and Menigon were arrested along with two others, and then Max Frerot on 27 November 1987. In February 1988 thirty members of AD were sent to prison for sentences of up to thirteen years; on 14 January 1989 Rouillan, Menigon and two others were sentenced to life imprisonment for the murder of Georges Besse in 1986. On 29 June Olivier, Frerot and one other were sentenced to life imprisonment for two murders, two others to eighteen to twenty years, and a further fourteen to shorter suspended sentences.[4]

About thirty lesser members of AD were still at large but the police knew who most of them were. A revival of AD as such is unlikely, but similar movements are likely to emerge, pursuing anti-NATO and other political and environmental issues, and seeking co-operation with the wide range of Arab and other immigrants and refugees who wish to fight their battles on French streets.

Separatists and others in France

Most of the damage to property in France has been inflicted by separatist movements, notably the Corsican National Liberation Front (FLNC), the Breton Revolutionary Army (ARB) and the French Basque separatist group Iparretarrak. Also operating in France has been the Spanish right-wing Anti-Terrorist Liberation Group (GAL), which pursues and murders Spanish Basque 'political refugees' who cross into the French Basque country.

Since 1976 the FLNC set off numerous bombs to destroy French banks, tourist installations, etc. in Corsica; also, less often, bombs in mainland France to try to sicken the French public of continued involvement with Corsica. The peak was over 400 bombs in 1987. In May 1988 a truce was declared on the promise of the French government to discuss greater autonomy for Corsica. Sporadic small bomb attacks continued, however, and in August 1989 the FNLC gave warning of continued direct action against property development for the tourist industry in Corsica and against officials and landowners who co-operated in this. Though much damage has been done, however, very few people have been killed by FLNC bombs.[5]

The ARB has set off several hundred bombs aimed at French targets in Britanny since 1966 but has so far killed no one.[6]

Most of Iparretarrak's prominent members have now been killed or captured, including their leader Philippe Bidart on 20 February 1988. Only a small number of activists remain at large, though they can still carry out isolated attacks. GAL has been less active since Prime Minister Chirac tightened up on giving sanctuary to Spanish Basque terrorists (see Chapter 8).[7]

There are also occasional bombings by Caledonian and Caribbean separatists. Other small organizations occasionally using terrorism in France include the left-wing Black War (attacking South African targets); also two right-wing groups, the Charles Martel Club and the French Commandos, attacking Jewish and immigrant targets.

As in Germany, so in France, property damage has caused little political or public alarm. It is murders, and especially selective murders like that of Georges Besse, which have prompted changes in the law; those murders have almost all been committed by foreign (mainly Middle Eastern) terrorists and Action Directe.

Anti-terrorist legislation

When the newly elected President Mitterand released Jean-Marc Rouillan and Nathalie Menigon in 1981, he also included several hundred other prisoners in his amnesty, some of whom had been terrorists and who no doubt reverted to terrorism. In the summer of 1982, when fifteen people were killed in terrorist attacks in four months, he tightened the laws on immigration and sale of weapons and appointed a Secretary of State for Public Security.

The main anti-terrorist laws, however, were introduced by Prime Minister Jacques Chirac in 1986–7, heading a Conservative administration 'cohabiting' under the strange French Constitution with the Socialist President Mitterand. This legislation was provoked partly by the co-ordinated AD/RAF/CCC anti-NATO campaign with its selective murders, but mainly by the six bombs set off by Arab terrorists in Paris in September 1986, which killed 10 people and wounded another 170. These bombs went off between 8 and 18 September, while the legislation was being enacted.

Law 86-1020 of 9 September 1986 specified trial without jury for certain specified offences under 'special circumstances'. Rather than introduce a new definition of 'terrorist offences', these were categorized as:

1 Offences against the person, including murder, assassination, serious bodily injury and abduction.

2 Attacks on property which, due to proximity to people, created a public danger. These included destruction of monuments or public utilities by explosives or arson; destruction by explosives or incendiaries, or breaking into houses to intimidate magistrates, jurymen, lawyers or witnesses; aggravated theft or burglary by two or more persons at night or with violence; extortion; and the use of any means to derail or provoke collision of a train.

3 Offences in which evidence suggested the preparation and execution of an offence. These included conspiracy; production or possession of murderous devices or incendiaries or biological weapons; possession of a depot of arms of certain specified categories, or carrying or transporting them.

The 'special circumstances' under which these offences required trial without jury were when they related to an individual or collective enterprise having as its purpose a grave disturbance of public order through intimidation or terror.

In these circumstances, instead of trial before a normal court of three judges and nine jurors, terrorist offences are tried by a special court comprising a President and six Assessors, all professional judges. (British readers may envisage 'judges' to be senior and long-experienced former barristers, so it must be added that in France and many other European countries, a large number of young lawyers appointed as examining magistrates are qualified as professional judges and are available to act as assessors.) Courts of this type were already used to hear cases involving secrets concerning national defence, and had earlier been available for trials in the 1950s and 1960s in which juries were being intimidated by the violently nationalist OAS (secret army organization).

Provision was also made to reduce sentences for terrorists prepared to renounce their former activities and help the authorities. If information is given before the event which would enable the authorities to prevent the crime and identify the others involved, the informer may be exempted from punishment – though not if the crime has already been committed and resulted in death or maiming.[8]

After the collapse of the trial of Regis Schleicher in December 1986 due to intimidation of the jury, Parliament passed an amendment to make these laws applicable retrospectively to acts committed before 9

September 1986, and the trials of both Schleicher and Georges Abdallah were conducted without juries in February and March 1987.

Police powers were also increased. Where a crime is being actually committed or has just been committed, the police have power to prevent people from leaving the scene of the crime, to require anyone they believe may possess relevant information to attend a police station, and to take them into custody if there is incriminating evidence or if they wish to establish a person's identity.

In the summer of 1986 it had already been enacted that every French citizen and foreigner had to produce means of identification if asked by the police, who could act at their own discretion and did not have to produce grounds for suspicion. If a person refused to co-operate, an examining magistrate could order the taking of fingerprints or photographs, and further non-cooperation could lead to a fine or imprisonment.[9]

All foreigners other than those from EC countries and Switzerland were required to have visas. From July 1987 an old law was reactivated to expel seventy-one Spanish Basques from France and an amendment provided that 'in a case of great urgency' a person who presented a 'threat to public order' could be expelled solely on the authority of the Minister of the Interior without going through the legal processes of deportation or extradition.

On 8 April 1987 the German and French governments (and also the German and Italian governments) signed bilateral agreements to exchange police liaison officers to provide information about terrorism and other serious crimes.

These institutionalized an already thriving co-operation. On 16 January 1987 the German police at Frankfurt Airport had arrested Mohammed Hamadei (later convicted of murder and participation in the hijacking of the TWA aircraft to Beirut in 1985) and, ten days later, his brother Abbas Ali Hamadei. From material found in possesion of the Hamadei brothers, the French police were given the address of a Tunisian restaurant in France. The French Surveillance Service (DST) tapped the telephones of this restaurant, and were able to arrest three terrorists red-handed in possession of twelve litres of liquid explosive (methyl nitrate – the same type as found in Mohammed Hamadei's baggage in Frankfurt), and later arrested five more terrorists. Some of those captured gave information under the new French '*pentiti*' legislation leading to capture of members of a second network. These two networks were believed to be those which had carried out the bloody Paris bombings in September 1986 in the campaign to release Georges Abdallah; the arrests presumably accounted for the lack of an expected violent response to Abdallah's conviction and life imprisonment in February 1987. The information from the Germans is also believed to have assisted in the arrest of Rouillan,

Menigon and other AD leaders in the same month.[10] This virtual elimination of both AD and the CSPPA and North African group provided full justification for the French anti-terrorist legislation of 1986–7, which thereby probably saved many more lives.

The German participation also provided proof of the special value of *bilateral* police and intelligence co-operation. This was largely a product of the TREVI agreement in 1976, which will be discussed under European co-operation in Chapters 10 and 17.

Belgium

The Combatant Communist Cells (CCC) were mentioned as participants with the RAF and AD in the anti-NATO alliance (see pp. 50–1), when they set off twenty bombs, killing two people, in 1984–5. They were an offshoot of AD, and ceased activity after the capture of their leaders. The Revolutionary Front for Proletarian Action (FRAP) was equally short lived and has not appeared since 1985. A former Prime Minister, Paul Vanden Boeynants, was kidnapped on 14 January 1989, and a claim was made by a hitherto unknown 'Revolutionary Socialist Brigade', but the claim was almost certainly cover for a criminal group to confuse the police. The hostage was released a month later on payment of a ransom. A few foreign terrorists (mainly Arabs and Yugoslavs) have tried to settle their scores in Belgium.[11]

Otherwise, Belgium has been used as a haven by other terrorist groups, especially from France and Germany, to evade police pressure at home. It was believed that, ten days after his kidnap in Cologne, Dr Hanns-Martin Schleyer was taken into Belgium by the RAF in September 1977.[12]

Belgium has also been used as a base, along with France, Germany and the Netherlands, for IRA active service units (ASUs), which have murdered a number of off-duty British soldiers and airmen serving in Germany. On 30 June 1988, acting on information, the police arrested an alleged IRA 'godfather', Patrick Ryan, believed to be acting as quarter-master for the IRA ASU. He was arrested in the home of an IRA sympathizer; the police seized a quantity of bomb-making equipment and manuals and a large sum of foreign currency. The British authorities provided substantial evidence in support of a request for extradition, whereupon Ryan began a hunger strike. The Belgian authorities hastily deported him to the Republic of Ireland, who were somewhat embarrassed but, because they thought that the massive publicity would deny him a fair trial in Britain, released him on bail saying that, given enough evidence, they would charge and try him in the Republic – an alternative to extradition allowed in the Anglo-Irish Agreement. (In the event the Irish Attorney-General announced eighteen months later that he would not be prosecuted after all as the evidence provided by the British was inadequate – see p. 83.)

Because of its freedom from terrorism, Belgium has done little to combat it. It is, for example, unique in Western Europe in having no electronic surveillance systems, and it has very lax laws for gun control. These factors have made it very attractive to European terrorists as a rest-and-recreation ('R and R') area, or (as in the case of the IRA) a secure base from which to mount operations in neighbouring countries. It has been easy for them to get in and out of Belgium and to stay there undetected.

This has caused a great deal of resentment amongst other European police officers, many of whom suspect that the Belgian government prefers to turn a blind eye to this to avoid becoming involved in terrorism itself.

The Netherlands

The Netherlands has had more than its share of attacks on British targets by the IRA, including the murder of three off-duty British servicemen on 1 May 1988 (one of the incidents for alleged involvement in which Patrick Ryan was arrested in Belgium – see previous section).

The Dutch have a few extremist movements, and many dissident 'single issue groups'; none has used lethal violence, but some of them may have assisted the IRA with safe houses, and so on. The only domestic terrorism was in 1975–8, by immigrants from the South Moluccan Islands in Indonesia, demanding that the Dutch government should influence the Indonesian government to grant the islands independence. South Moluccan terrorists hijacked a train in 1975 and a few days later seized the Indonesian Consulate in Amsterdam. In 1977 they hijacked another train and a school; in 1978 they seized a local government office building, holding its staff as hostages. In all, they killed seven of their hostages, and six of the terrorists were killed when Dutch Marines rescued the hostages from the second train.[13]

This, however, was twelve years ago. A new generation of South Moluccans has grown up, with only hearsay knowledge of Indonesia or the injustices of which their parents complained. This younger generation is generally rather sullen and withdrawn, not only unwilling to accept the Indonesians' offer to welcome them back to their islands, but also unwilling to accept Dutch citizenship or to integrate into Dutch society. They have a high level of unemployment and many turn to drugs. Their smouldering resentment would provide combustible material if a charismatic leader were to emerge, but there is no sign of this happening at present.[14]

On the criminal side there have been a number of sensational kidnaps and extortions by product contamination (including Heineken beer).[15] Thanks to these incidents, the Dutch have developed an extremely efficient government crisis management organization and an excellent police force with a good anti-terrorist intelligence section. The Dutch Marines have a well-trained anti-terrorist rescue force (BBE), which proved itself in the South Moluccan incidents described.[16] The security at the Dutch airport, Schiphol, is amongst the best in the world.

The judicial system has needed no special amendment because it is already well suited to dealing with terrorism. No Dutch courts have juries, all the courts using professionals both as judges and assessors, similar to those in the French special anti-terrorist courts (see pp. 64–5).

The Dutch have been relatively free of terrorism, not because they prefer to ignore it (as the Belgians do) but because their security forces, intelligence services and other government organizations have a proven record of standing up to it, and a success in doing so which is an effective deterrent.

Luxemburg, Denmark and the Irish Republic

Luxemburg and Denmark are virtually free of political terrorism. The only political terrorism in the Republic of Ireland is that arising from the conflict in the North. The IRA have done a number of bank robberies in the Republic and have carried out short-term abductions and kidnaps, mainly to raise funds.[17] One bomb attack in Dublin was attributed to Protestant terrorists from the North and it is possible, though unlikely, that there could be further attacks of that type if Protestant terrorists think that they would thereby coerce the Dublin government into taking stronger action against IRA terrorists operating from across the border. If Ireland were united, of course, both Protestant terrorists and the IRA would continue their sectarian conflict with even greater intensity, which is one reason for every Dublin government's insistence that they do not want reunification without the consent of the majority of the population in the North. The organization and techniques of the Protestant terrorists and of the IRA are discussed in the next chapter.

Chapter six

Northern Ireland

About 2,800 people, out of a population of 1.5 million, have been killed in the twenty years (1969–89) of fighting in Northern Ireland. This is by far the highest rate of killing in political violence for any country in Europe, and exceeded in only a handful of Third World countries. In the same period, 107 people have been killed by terrorists out of 53 million people on the island of Great Britain. All the 107 were in England (none in Scotland or Wales); none of them was killed by indigenous British terrorists. Eighty-nine were killed by Irish terrorists, and eighteen by Middle Eastern terrorists; all except one of the eighteen were Arabs, Iranians and Israelis, the one being a British policewoman helping to protect the Libyan Embassy from anti-Gadafi demonstrators.

These 107 deaths place Britain roughly on a par with France and Germany. But the predominance of Irish terrorism, both in Northern Ireland and Britain, makes it logical to examine Northern Ireland first. To understand the intractability of the problem, a page of ancient history may help. The history will continue to exert its malign influence after 1992.

The origins of the IRA

The British Isles were known by the Romans as Great Britain and Little Britain. Though the Romans, Anglo Saxons, Norse and Danes drove the indigenous Celts to the northern and western fringes of Great Britain, none before the Normans gained a permanent foothold in 'Little Britain', which remained Celtic and became known as Ireland or, in Gaelic, Eire.

In 1155 the Pope declared Ireland subject to the Norman King of England and so it remained for nearly 800 years, but the main English and Scottish settlements began in the early seventeenth century. Risings against them were brutally repressed by Cromwell, and British rule was firmly established by the victory of the Protestant King William III at the Battle of the Boyne in 1690. The history of the next 230 years was of a constant fight by the descendants of the native Irish to retain their lands *and their Catholic religion* against the descendants of the Protestant settlers. Many of these were absentee landlords, and bitterness became intense during the mid-nineteenth century, when they turned their backs on the plight of their Catholic tenants during the disastrous potato famine. Large numbers of Catholics emigrated to the USA, carrying their hatred of the British into what became a very large Irish American community.

Most of the settlement was in the North; in 1922, anxious to be rid of the problem, the British agreed to a partition of Ireland. The six counties of the North, having a majority of Protestants, chose to remain part of the United Kingdom. The remaining twenty-six counties, over-whelmingly Catholic, became the Free State and then the independent Republic of Ireland. In the Act of Partition it was laid down that if the Parliaments of the North and South voted to unite they would be united; but the Northern Parliament never looked like voting that way.

The Irish Republican Army (IRA) led by Michael Collins had fought a long guerrilla campaign against the British, and a militant faction of it never accepted partition, so the new Free State was born into a civil war. Within a year, the IRA had murdered their own Prime Minister, the same Michael Collins, who had signed the Partition Treaty with Britain. Since then, the IRA has been proscribed by all the main Irish political parties and the IRA has remained constantly at war with whichever party is in power in Dublin. Dublin has had to have trial without jury for terrorist offences since 1962 and membership of the IRA carries a prison sentence in the Republic. The IRA's political party, Sinn Fein, at the most recent elections, attracted 9 per cent of the vote in the North but only 1.5 per cent of the vote in the South.

When the present violence began in 1969, the breakdown of the population was as shown in Table 2.

Table 2 Population of Ireland

| | Percentage | | Catholic | Population | Total |
	Catholic (%)	Protestant (%)	Catholic (millions)	Protestant (millions)	Total (millions)
North	33	67	0.5	1.0	1.5
South	93	7	2.8	0.2	3.0
United	73	27	3.3	1.2	4.5

Thus the Catholics (descendants of the natives) were a minority of 33 per cent in the North. If, however, Ireland were united, the Protestants (descendants of the settlers over 300 years) would be in a minority of 27 per cent. That is why the Protestants, whenever they vote, vote over-whelmingly on one issue – to remain separate. Moreover, the children are educated separately, either in Catholic Church schools or in the state schools, which are mainly Protestant because few Catholics send their children to them. Both communities stick to their religion, not for doctrinaire reasons, but as a label of identity. As well observed by Bernadette Devlin, a Catholic activist: 'The people of Northern Ireland are not Christians; they hate each other in the name of Jesus Christ.'

The IRA Campaign, 1969–89

There have been outbursts of lethal violence in Ireland at intervals over nearly 400 years, and the current outbreak began in 1969 as a result of attempts by the Prime Ministers of South and North (Sean Lemass and Terence O'Neill) to open a dialogue. Both communities in the North sensed that this could start a gradual drift towards union. Catholic activists organized demonstrations to move things faster; Protestant activists tried to break them up. The disorder got beyond the power of the police, the 3,000-strong Royal Ulster Constabulary (RUC), to control.[1] In August 1969 the British Army was called in and was initially welcomed by the Catholics, but within a year the honeymoon was over.[2]

As a background to the campaign, in which mistakes were made by both sides, the breakdown of the number of killings over the past twenty years is shown in Table 3.[3]

The IRA, despite using much Marxist rhetoric, were essentially a right-wing nationalist movement using violence to create a state of tension on the lines described in Chapter 3 for the right-wing terrorists in Italy. They began a large-scale indiscriminate bombing campaign in public places, exploding thirty-seven bombs in April 1971, forty-seven in May, fifty in June and ninety-one in July. Since people dared not give information, arrests and convictions were few. There was at this time an elected Northern Irish Parliament at Stormont, reflecting, as always since 1922, the permanent Protestant majority, with a Protestant Prime Minister. Fearing a Protestant backlash over the bombings, he persuaded the London government to agree to a mass arrest of IRA suspects and their internment without trial. On 9 August 1971 342 suspects were arrested. This was the government's first major error. Police intelligence was inaccurate and the 342 arrested included a large number of innocent people. Though they were soon released, the damage was done. Most of the population in Catholic areas knew who were IRA activists and who were not, so internment caused a great deal of resentment and a swing of Catholic sympathy to the IRA.[4] Encouraged by this, they intensified their campaign; killing reached a peak of 467 in 1972.

A great deal of autonomy had since 1922 been delegated to the Stormont Prime Minister, but ultimate responsibility for internal security and for the use of the British Army remained with London. Brian Faulkner, the Stormont Prime Minister in 1972, argued that he could not govern the Province unless he took over control of internal security

Table 3 Killing in Northern Ireland

Year	Army	RUC (regular)	RUC (reserves)	UDR	Civilian	Total	Monthly average	Killed on roads during year
1969	—	1	—	—	—	13	—	257
1970	—	2	—	—	23	25	2.1	272
1971	43	11	—	5	116	175	14.6	304
1972	103	14	3	26	321	467	39.0	372
1973	58	10	3	8	171	250	20.8	335
1974	28	12	3	7	165	215	17.9	316
1975	14	7	4	6	216	247	20.6	313
1976	14	13	10	15	245	297	24.7	300
1977	15	8	6	14	69	112	9.3	355
1978	14	4	6	7	50	81	6.8	288
1979	38	9	5	10	51	113	9.4	293
1980	8	3	6	9	50	76	6.3	229
1981	10	13	8	13	57	101	8.4	223
1982	21	8	4	7	57	97	8.1	216
1983	5	9	9	10	44	77	6.4	173
1984	9	7	2	10	36	64	5.3	189
1985	2	14	9	4	25	54	4.5	177
1986	4	10	2	8	38	62	5.2	235
1987	3	9	7	8	66	93	7.7	214
1988	21	4	2	12	54	93	7.7	178
1989	12	7	2	2	39	62	5.2	200
TOTAL	422	175	91	181	1,905	2,774	11.5	5,440

Note: The 'civilian' figures include terrorists. It is not always certain whether or not a civilian victim was a terrorist, especially victims of sectarian murders, e.g. of a Catholic whom Protestant murderers *accuse* of being an IRA terrorist. The best guess is that 440 were terrorists. If so, of the 2,774 killed up to the end of 1989,

    15% (422)   were British
    16% (477)   were locally enlisted soldiers (UDR) and police
    16% (440)   were terrorists (400 Catholic and 40 Protestant)
    53% (1,465) were innocent civilians (mostly killed by IRA bombs).

including the British troops, but London would not agree to this, so he resigned. The Stormont Parliament was prorogued and, since March 1972, Northern Ireland has been governed by direct rule from London.[5]

Thanks to better intelligence and tactics, the killing was cut to about half during the next four years, 1973–6, and an attempt was made in 1973–4 to reinstate the Stormont government, but with a power-sharing administration made up of Protestant (Unionist) and Catholic (Nationalist) ministers in proportion to the population. This was endorsed by a successful parliamentary election in 1973 and the power-sharing Cabinet was formed, but militant Protestants staged a strike of public utilities which brought it down in May 1974. Since then the Protestant politicians have consistently refused to participate in power-sharing, and London, with the experience of 1971–2, has set its face against ever again using British money or British soldiers to underwrite a sectarian Protestant government, so direct rule has continued.[6]

The improving performance of the police and intelligence services enabled the British government to hand back the prime responsibility for security from the army to the RUC; from 1977 onwards the killing rate has averaged fewer than 100 per year for twelve years, which is less than half the average of road deaths, and about one-sixth of the homicide rate per thousand of the population in big American cities (including Washington, DC). But it has thus far proved impossible to reduce it appreciably below this. In a few small areas, including parts of West Belfast, Londonderry and South Armagh, the army is still seen on the streets in support of the RUC, but elsewhere the RUC maintains order without any such help. However, the terrorist killing rate remains the highest in Europe.

IRA organization and tactics

The 'Official' IRA in 1969 was very run down, and politically rather than militarily oriented. Exasperated by its failure to protect the Catholic housing areas in Belfast and Londonderry from being attacked by Protestant mobs, a group of militants formed the new 'Provisional' IRA in 1970. This was a misleading title. It was, in fact, a reversion to the traditional militarist IRA, organized in brigades, battalions and companies, each tied to a particular area, for example the Belfast Brigade, the Andersonstown battalion, the Ballymacarrett Company. In certain tightly knit Catholic slum districts in Belfast and Londonderry (such as the Ardoyne in Belfast, about half a mile square) virtually all the inhabitants actively supported the IRA. Any who did not found it safer to move out.

A company was organized and led by a cadre of officers, for example the commanding officer, the adjutant, the intelligence officer and the quartermaster – a key man, who kept the guns, ammunition and explosives. This team of officers knew all the young men in their district, whom they used as a pool of 'volunteers' from whom they could call out suitable men trained for the job in hand, ranging from shooting to bombing, to petrol bombing, to throwing rocks at the police. The girls were mainly used as auxiliaries, for example as spies (sometimes Mata Hari style, seducing gullible British soldiers) and look-outs, or to take a sniper his rifle in his chosen fire position in case he was stopped by police and searched on his way there. Trained snipers were valuable;

the girl, if caught, would get a light sentence. And the tradition was for every house in the street to leave the front and back doors open, with sandwiches and a flask of coffee on the table, so that a lad on the run could be sure of sanctuary whenever he needed it.

This structure was at best only semi-clandestine. Almost everyone knew who the officers were, though it was more than their lives were worth to talk about them. But by 1978, with greatly improved RUC and army intelligence, too much was leaking out, and the IRA had to draw in their horns. They did so by adopting the fully clandestine organization which they had always used when operating in England or against British targets in Germany, where the population was hostile. The hard core formed a tight secret cell on traditional revolutionary lines – the 'Active Service Units' (ASUs)

The ASUs varied in strength, usually between five and twelve. For delicate operations they called on the pool of volunteers less and less. For most armed attacks – bombing, mining, mortaring a police station, ambushing a patrol, etc. – five or ten people were enough, with little support needed from auxiliaries, male or female. In recent years virtually all the lethal acts of terrorism have been done by the hard core of the ASUs themselves. When they have had a disaster (such as when eight men raiding a police station ran into an SAS ambush at Loughgall in 1987) the ASU has been virtually wiped out.

After about ten years it is quite common for IRA men to 'retire' from active service to logistic and (increasingly) political work. The IRA's political party, Sinn Fein, is open and legal and puts up candidates for election both in the Republic and in Northern Ireland. Many of the Sinn Fein leaders have an IRA background. Their chief, Gerry Adams, had a great reputation in the 1970s and was alleged to have been the Commander of the Belfast Brigade and later Chief of Staff of the IRA .

The British government has always, rightly or wrongly, accepted the legality of Sinn Fein, hoping that eventually the hard core of the IRA may see a better avenue for progress towards their aim by mobilizing and expanding the 9 per cent vote they attract in the six counties (now very concentrated, resulting in a comfortable majority in small areas such as West Belfast and South Armagh). No doubt with similar motives, the then Secretary of State for Northern Ireland, William Whitelaw, released Gerry Adams from prison in 1972 as one of the members of a team to negotiate a cease-fire. (Like most such truces with terrorists it achieved nothing, and was merely used by the IRA to recover strength and build up supplies.) By 1987–8, however, Gerry Adams showed strong signs of wishing to pursue the political road, openly condemning a number of 'neo-Nazi' style indiscriminate bombings – like that at the Remembrance Day service for the war dead at Enniskillen on

11 November 1987, when eleven members of the public (no soldiers) were killed. Adams seems unlikely to prevail, however, over the IRA's militarist wing, especially since Sinn Fein's humiliation in the 1989 General Election in the Republic of Ireland, when they attracted no seats and only 1.5 per cent of the vote, even less than in the previous election. His political campaign, in their eyes, will never get anywhere and, if he is too outspoken about counter-productive violence, he must be aware that they might kill him as they killed their most successful leader, Michael Collins, in 1922. He also faces the risk that he might so frustrate the dedicated gunmen that they break away and join the small but vicious rival movement, the Irish National Liberation Army (INLA).

By 1990 the hard core of the IRA comprised about eighty, organized in about eight ASUs, with other ASUs in England and in Belgium/France/Germany/Netherlands, targeting British soldiers. Above them were a larger array of 'godfathers' with an active IRA past, some elected as Sinn Fein local councillors or, in the case of Adams, to the Westminster Parliament (though he does not take his seat). Supporting the hard core are some 200 in a fluid pool of volunteers and auxiliaries.

Most of their money comes from racketeering (about £5 million a year), extortion and bank robberies. Only a small proportion (probably less than £100,000 a year) comes from Irish American sympathizers, now that most of them have become aware that it is spent on guns and explosives, not on blankets and soup kitchens. Colonel Gadafi has long boasted of sending arms and money to the IRA. In more recent years he has dispatched enormous consignments of arms and the powerful, almost odour-free Semtex explosives to the Republic of Ireland. Despite some large finds in both the South and the North, the IRA probably has a bigger reserve of weapons, ammunition and explosives than it has ever had, and certainly enough to meet its needs for some time to come. Thus far, however, the IRA does not seem to have got involved in the drug trade.

Extortion is mainly in the form of protection money, or 'revolutionary taxes'. Employers, especially in the construction industry, are told how much they must pay to be left in peace. Typical taxes are £5,000 a year per building site, or between 1 and 2 per cent of the value of the contract. This is often paid as a 'subscription to welfare of prisoners' families'. Failure to pay may be punished by sabotage, threats to harm the contractor's family and, ultimately, murder. Money is also sometimes extorted as payment for the mythical services of a bogus 'security company'. If the contractor pays up, it is very difficult for the Inland Revenue to prove precisely what services he did or did not receive.

Another rich source of money is the monopoly of IRA-owned or IRA-licensed taxis in West Belfast. The IRA own the only two large taxi firms in the area, and will also on occasions issue licences to approved independent taxi-drivers, at a price. They have bombed and burned the buses off the streets where these taxis operate, and any unauthorized driver can expect short shrift. The IRA also own an array of estate agencies and drinking clubs. Also many bars have, say, five gaming machines, one of which is tacitly left for the IRA to collect the takings; this is often the agreed way for a bar to pay its protection money, provided that the takings remain high enough. Sinn Fein also run bookshops and newsagents, which mesh conveniently into their propaganda distribution.

The most lucrative racket of all, practised by both the IRA and Protestant paramilitaries, is income tax fraud, especially in the construction industry. The starting-point is that, because it would be impossible for the Inland Revenue to collect tax from the thousands of individual casual workers, taken on for a day or a week on a site, the contractor is required to deduct 25 per cent tax when he pays them. To save him from massive paperwork, the contractor can apply for a tax exemption certificate and pay a lump sum for all the deducted tax at the end of the year. In the building trade, however, much of the work is sub-contracted and sub-sub-contracted. The main contractor sub-contracts the work on a site and the sub-contractor then sub-sub-contracts to firms of plumbers, electricians, etc. All that is needed are forged tax exemption certificates down the line. The IRA have the machinery to provide these, so they collect the 25 per cent instead of the Inland Revenue. If the contractors are challenged, they can plead that they had no way of telling that one of the certificates passed up to them was forged. If the Inland Revenue try to investigate the morass of paper, they may find at the bottom of the chain a small sub-sub-contractor who has 'gone out of business' or in some other way cannot be traced; as a result, they find such investigations are not cost-effective.

The sums involved in the 1970s were small, but when Sinn Fein began to stand for election they needed much more money; by 1986 their total tax fraud proceeds amounted to millions, though each individual fraud might still be less than it was normally cost-effective to investigate. But because of its security implications, the Inland Revenue and the RUC are trying to pursue it more effectively.[7]

Another racket, at the bottom end, is for individual casual workers to be ordered by the IRA to draw unemployment benefit as well as their hourly wages, and to contribute accordingly; this again is usually on the basis of a contribution to a welfare or Sinn Fein campaign fund, but refusal to pay leads to a more compelling demand.

Communal strife in Northern Ireland is deep rooted. If there was a chance of a gradual rapprochement in the second half of the 1960s, that has been swept away by the bitterness of twenty years of conflict in which the Protestant paramilitaries have been almost as violent as the IRA. Though a united Ireland would be in everyone's interest if it were peaceful, the forcing of the Protestant 27 per cent of the population of the island (see p. 71) into the Republic against their will would present problems beyond the Dublin government's ability to handle; they are well aware of this and repeatedly reaffirm that they do not want it. An independent Ulster would become a bigoted and repressive Protestant state. The consequent sympathy for the IRA as protectors would bring a massive surge of support from the Catholic minority, and from the Republic and the Irish Americans: the result would be civil war. No solution other than continued direct rule is likely for many years to come; the best hope must lie in keeping the violence in bounds until enough of the people get sick of it.

Emergency legislation in Northern Island

In the peak year of violence in 1972, intimidation of witnesses and juries became so intense that the process of law became unworkable. One example should suffice. A bus driver whose bus was hijacked and burned made a statement to the police: a number of IRA men were arrested and charged. In accordance with the law, a copy of his statement was given to the defence counsel. The night before the trial, IRA gunmen shot the bus driver dead in his home in front of his children. The judge accepted the written deposition as evidence, and convicted the accused (of the hijacking but not, of course, of the murder). Nevertheless, in those circumstances few people were willing to give evidence or, if they could not evade jury service, to convict.[8] (Compare the case of Schleicher in France, p. 63)

In 1972 a senior judge, Lord Diplock, was sent to Northern Ireland to assess the situation and, as a result of his report, the government initiated the Northern Ireland Emergency Provisions Act 1973. This Act introduced trial without jury for Scheduled Offences (i.e. Terrorist Offences) before a single judge, in what were colloquially known as 'Diplock Courts'. Where witnesses gave evidence personally, they were screened from the view of the accused and of the public (though sometimes their voices were recognized and denounced: 'We know who you are, Paddy O'Brien'). The court could accept written statements where witnesses 'could not be produced' because they were 'dead, ill, out of the country or cannot be found'. Statements by the accused under interrogation were admissible unless he convinced the court that they were extracted by torture, inhuman treatment, and so on. The court could accept verbal statements if witnessed by two police officers. If arms, ammunition or explosives were found in houses or vehicles, the onus was on the occupant to prove innocence. There were increased powers of search, entry, arrest and seizure of property; soldiers could detain suspects for up to four hours before handing them over to the police without having to state a reason. Police or army officers could order a crowd to disperse if necessary, and there were increased penalties for riotous behaviour.

The Scheduled Offences (SOs) included a number which already existed, for example murder, manslaughter, arson, bodily harm, assault, malicious damage, causing or attempting to cause explosions, possessing explosives, possessing, making or adapting arms, robbery and aggravated burglary, intimidation, and the making, possession or use of petrol bombs.

The Act also introduced a number of new Scheduled Offences. Six paramilitary organizations were proscribed, both Catholic and Protestant, including the IRA and the Ulster Volunteer Force (UVF). Provision was made for the Secretary of State to proscribe others, and these later included the Irish National Liberation Army(INLA). Membership of any of these proscribed organizations became an SO. It also became an SO to dress in such a way as to suggest membership, to spy in aid of terrorism, and to escape, attempt to escape, or help or harbour an escaper.

The great majority of convictions in the Diplock Courts were obtained by statements by the accused, including verbal statements, and by the evidence of police or army officers. Most of the court proceedings comprised legal arguments about whether signed confessions or evidence of police or army officers (such as verbal statements or possession of arms) were admissible. The Diplock Courts were widely criticized by friends of the accused, by Sinn Fein, by politicians, lawyers and civil rights activists in Northern and Southern Ireland, and in foreign countries, especially the USA. No one claimed that the Diplock Courts were as fair as normal courts, in which witnesses appeared before a jury and faced public cross-examination. But where (as also in Italy and France) intimidation was used for the calculated purpose of making that form of trial unworkable, the alternative was to substitute other forms of trial or accept abandonment of the rule of law in combating politically motivated violence. This balance will be examined in a wider context later in this book.

In November 1981 there emerged the equivalent of the Italian *pentiti* – the 'supergrasses' (English criminal slang for star police informers). Christopher Black, one of an ASU operating from the Ardoyne, the hardest hard-core area in West Belfast, was arrested. He was already well known to the RUC, having been released earlier that year after five years in prison for an IRA armed robbery, and he took part in a number of operations with the Ardoyne ASU from June 1981 until being caught again on one of them on 21 November. During two days of silence under interrogation he reflected on the certainty of another long sentence in prison, where he had already spent five of his twenty-seven years of life. On the third day he proposed a deal – that he would talk and give evidence in exchange for safe passage to a new country for himself and his family and immunity from prosecution.[9]

The idea spread rapidly. Other potential supergrasses under interrogation were promised a new life under a new name in a new country, with private education for their children and a pension for life – and, if they wished, elocution lessons to remove their Northern Irish accents.[10] No new laws were required because leniency for turning Queen's evidence has long existed in British law. Supergrasses from all sides – IRA, INLA, UVF and other Protestant paramilitaries – offered their services.

The IRA and INLA reacted with alarm, and tried kidnapping fathers or wives, but this backfired as these were usually loyal members of the republican community. Carrying out the threat to kill or harm them for a betrayal over which they had no control would have seemed grossly unfair to their neighbours. Far more effectively, the IRA themselves offered an amnesty, initially through the families, but then they announced it publicly in March 1982, promising the supergrasses a safe passage to the Republic of Ireland as soon as they left prison on condition that they retracted. Large numbers of them did retract, and eventually only ten cases came to trial.

On Black's testimony, thirty-eight alleged IRA men and women were tried in a Diplock Court in 1983. Black gave evidence convincingly and in impressive detail. Twenty-two were convicted, but they appealed. In eighteen cases there were no corroborating witnesses or other evidence and no self-incriminating statements. The Appeal Court decided that, since the sole evidence was from a man with a strong personal interest in getting the accused convicted, these eighteen convictions were 'unsafe' and they were quashed.

In all, 54 per cent of those convicted in the ten cases which came to trial were found guilty on only one person's evidence; the great majority of these verdicts were quashed on appeal.

The British Appeal Court Judges had a difficult dilemma. In some cases they may well have personally believed that the evidence was true, and must have been aware that, to release hard-core IRA members on to the streets – simultaneously giving a huge boost to IRA morale – would result in more lives' being lost; but they had to balance this against the preservation of the British legal tradition of weighting justice in favour of the accused. They came down on the side of that tradition. Over 400 people were killed in the next four years and it can be argued that at least half of these might have been saved – perhaps many more if the IRA had been crippled. The Italian judges, faced by the same dilemma, took the opposite view; figures in Italy suggest that hundreds of lives have since been saved, and still are being saved, but it is too early to say whether there has been long-term damage to confidence in Italian justice. Certainly the IRA will despise British justice all the more; the judges and the profession of law as a whole may feel that the principle was paramount.

There was also considerable judicial and public concern about the Diplock Court verdicts' being arrived at by a single judge. This concern was particularly expressed in the Republic of Ireland, where trials without juries for terrorist offences had since 1962 comprised three judges. This concern had dogged the otherwise thriving co-operation between Dublin and London, and between the Irish Gárda Siochána (police) and the RUC on the border. Extradition agreements and cross-border jurisdiction (trials in one country for offences in the other, and exchange of witnesses) were constantly being improved, whether the Fine Gael or Fianna Fáil party was in power. Dublin governments all knew that the IRA was as much of a menace to them as to the North, and that the biggest single barrier to reunification was its continued violence. But Southern Irish judges and politicians are uneasy about the fairness of Diplock trials, and often seek for procedural or other pretexts to avoid handing over Irish citizens to them, even if they are known members of the IRA. Dublin Prime Ministers of both parties have repeatedly urged Westminister to follow their example in using three judges or a judge with two assessors. But British governments have consistently refused, believing that assessors would be as vulnerable to intimidation as jurors, while three judge courts would put a severe strain on the British judiciary since all qualified judges are experienced barristers of middle age or older, with no equivalent to the pool of young 'investigating judges' in Italy or France. Moreover, the bodyguarding of so many former judges for many years after duty in Northern Ireland would throw a heavy load on the police.

Other legislation includes laws to assist conviction and to deter intimidation, extortion and racketeering. The revision of the Prevention of Terrorism Act in 1989 introduced the power to seize racketeers' assets anywhere in the UK, whether in banks or in other means of holding them, such as property, stocks and shares or the assets of small companies. To facilitate this, provision was made for giving the police greater powers of access to financial and business records; pooling of information held by the police, Inland Revenue and social security services; empowering police to require suspected racketeers to account for substantial assets; and imposing penalties on people who knowingly pay money to proscribed organizations or their fronts.

There is also provision for enhanced compensation and security for victims who give information. Security companies are now required to register and to submit a list of employees, whom the police have power to vet. Many bogus security companies acting as cover for extortion of protection money have closed down. There is improved control of drinking and gaming clubs. And there is a demand for modification of the 'right to silence' to empower courts to take account of refusal by an accused person to answer questions. Some of these points are further discussed in Chapters 14 and 17.

The Anglo-Irish Agreement

On 15 November 1985 the British and Irish Prime Ministers, Mrs Thatcher and Dr Garret Fitzgerald, signed the Anglo-Irish Agreement. This was a formal and binding Agreement with the declared aims of 'reconciling the two major traditions in Ireland . . . and improving co-operation in combating terrorism'. Throughout, these two traditions were referred to as 'Unionist' and 'Nationalist' – not Protestant and Catholic. The first article was unequivocal:

The two governments
(a) affirm that any change in the status of Northern Ireland would only come about with the consent of a majority of the people of Northern Ireland;
(b) recognize that the present wish of a majority of the people of Northern Ireland is for no change in the status of Northern Ireland;
(c) declare that, if in the future a majority of the people of Northern Ireland clearly wish for and formally consent to the establishment of a united Ireland, they will introduce and support in the respective Parliaments legislation to give effect to that wish.

The Agreement established an Anglo-Irish Intergovernmental Council and Intergovernmental Conference, which would meet regularly to prevent discrimination and improve human rights, police co-operation, including exchange of information, liaison structures and technical co-operation; harmonization of law, including extradition and extra-territorial development; and economic and social development.

It was agreed that the UK government might devolve certain matters to a local Northern Irish government; that the Irish government might make proposals relating to Northern Ireland but not on matters devolved to the local government; and that the UK and Irish governments each retained full sovereignty and responsibility within its jurisdiction.[11]

No Irish government had ever gone so far in acknowledging formally in writing their acceptance of British sovereignty in Northern Ireland, its inviolability until a majority of the inhabitants *there* wished to change it, and that at present there was no such majority wish.

Unfortunately, however, Protestant leaders in the North voiced violent objections to the Anglo-Irish Council and to the right of the Irish government to make *proposals* about Northern Ireland (though there was nothing in the Agreement to suggest that such proposals must be accepted, and the sovereignty of the UK government was confirmed). Their total lack of response and refusal to co-operate may have been mainly responsible for Dr Fitzgerald's narrowly losing the next General Election in February 1987. So, probably, was the British government's adamant refusal to consider Dr Fitzgerald's pleas to change from single- to three-judge courts, which resulted in a number of cases in which Irish judges found procedural means of blocking extradition on the grounds that the accused would not get a fair trial. The stridency of the indignation of the British government and press rekindled much anti-British feeling amongst the Irish electorate and made them think that Dr Fitzgerald had been too trusting of his bigoted and cantankerous neighbours.

Charles Haughey of Fianna Fáil – the heirs of the party which had opposed the original terms of partition – had taken the line while they were in opposition that Dr Fitzgerald had given away too much. Once in power, however – and with a minority government at the mercy of the Dáil – he realized that the majority of the Irish public disliked Sinn Fein and the IRA far more than they disliked the British response to the Agreement, so he announced that he accepted it and would do his best to implement it.

Friction continued, however, especially in the autumn of 1989, when it became clear that a number of lists or photographs of IRA men on the wanted list had been leaked by members of the security forces (mostly locally recruited part-timers) to Protestant paramilitaries. These lists, and especially the 'mug-shots', were relatively easy to copy, since they were widely issued to soldiers and police officers on duty at vehicle checkpoints or doing searches, and there had been frequent allegations of leakage in the past. The crisis came, however, when the Protestant terrorist movement boasted that they had used them to identify and murder a Catholic in his home on 25 August 1989. (Two soldiers and a taxi-driver were charged with this murder in September.)[12] Since such a boast would obviously have the effect of curbing this source of information, it can have had only one object – to infuriate the Southern Irish government and public in order to poison the Anglo-Irish Agreement. This was borne out by a flood of similar claims by anonymous Protestants, sending copies of lists and photographs to British and Irish newspapers. This, unfortunately, coincided with the Irish Attorney-General's announcement in October 1989 that Patrick Ryan, whose extradition to Britain had been refused in June 1988 on the grounds that he would instead be prosecuted in the Republic (see pp. 67–8) would not, after all, be prosecuted as the evidence was regarded as insufficient. This caused outrage in Britain, where it was not surprisingly alleged that this was a 'reprisal' for the leaks of wanted lists – an accusation hotly denied in Dublin. But the two things together did advance the cause of more Protestants working to sabotage the Anglo-Irish Agreement.

Nevertheless, between most ministers, officials and police officers on the ground, Anglo-Irish co-operation remained better than it had ever been, bearing in mind the painful history of Anglo-Irish relationships, the bigotry amongst those trying to wreck the Agreement on both sides of the border, and the inevitably of politicians both in Dublin and Belfast having to take up postures before their own electorates when feelings were aroused. Along with the trade across the North–South border and the Irish Sea, and the Irish need for job opportunities in Britain, the common revulsion against the IRA is probably the strongest factor drawing the two nations together.

Chapter seven

Great Britain

Indigenous terrorism in Great Britain

There has been only one indigenous terrorist movement in England since the Second World War. This was the short-lived Angry Brigade, which set off twenty-five small bombs in 1970–1, killing no one. (They probably did not intend to kill anyone.) There were eleven of them, almost all university students, coming into terrorism by precisely the same route as Curcio and Cagol in Italy, and Baader and Ennslin in Germany. They took part in demonstrations in 1968 which achieved nothing, so the demonstrations became violent in 1969 and potentially lethal in 1970–1. As in Germany and Italy, this first generation was quickly arrested but, in contrast, there were no second or third generations of terrorists in Britain. In Germany the political system anchors the SPD and CDU to the Centre, so they both shun extremists as an electoral millstone. So do all the political parties in Italy, including the PCI. Disillusioned activists therefore suffer intense frustration, which fuels their escalation of violence. In Britain, however, there is plenty of scope for left- and right-wing extremists not only to join the main political parties – Conservative, Labour and Liberal Democrat – but also to influence them. In the Labour Party, for example, Trotskyists of the Militant Tendency have been able, by sheer hard work and dedication, to influence and sometimes dominate the constituency parties and the youth organization. For the more intelligent graduates, this offers far more scope for achieving their aims than violence on the streets escalating to bombing and selective terrorism.

There has been no terrorism at all in Scotland or Wales. The nearest approach to it has been minor damage by Scottish Nationalists (sabotaging oil pipelines, for example, in protest at 'English exploitation of Scottish oil') and Welsh Nationalists (burning down holiday cottages or second homes to deter English visitors). The number of saboteurs involved has probably been fewer than ten in either case and no lives have been put at risk. The IRA have not operated in Scotland or Wales.

The IRA in England

IRA and INLA murders in England since 1969 have been few (eighty-nine) compared with those in Northern Ireland but, like terrorist killings in Italy, Germany and France, they have had a political effect out of proportion with their numbers. The IRA also judged, rightly, that one bomb in England would get more publicity than a hundred in Northern Ireland. They were, however, disappointed that their bombs did not induce political and public opinion to want to get out of Ireland; it seemed, on the contrary, to harden the public's resolve, like the German bombing of London in the Second World War.

The first IRA bomb in England, in February 1972, was placed outside the Officer's Mess of the Parachute Regiment in Aldershot. It killed no parachutists – the victims were a gardener, five cleaning ladies and a padre. This was the sole venture of the Marxist 'Official IRA' (see p. 74) in England before they eschewed violence and, in due course, became the Workers Party. A few of their most violent members later formed the INLA and in 1979 murdered a British MP, Airey Neave.

The Provisional IRA's first foray was in 1973, when a complete ASU, eleven-strong, came across in different ferries from Ireland with four cars, with their explosives already concealed under the boot. They set their bombs with delay fuses at various points in London. Two were defused and two went off, killing one bystander. Ten of the gang were arrested on board an aircraft about to take off for Ireland.[1]

Thereafter, the IRA decided that it was better to locate 'sleepers', to be resident in England, to select targets, and then to brief and stage-manage bombing teams sent over from Ireland. This resulted in about twelve more bombs, mainly in London and Birmingham during 1973.

In February 1974 they placed one of their most lethal bombs in a suitcase in the baggage compartment of a coach on the M62 motorway, which killed twelve people. Thereafter they established two more normal ASU structures, one in Birmingham and one in London. Each had a hard core of four or five, and made up the numbers with others recruited locally or coming over from Ireland.

One, based in Birmingham, set off a number of bombs in the summer of 1974 before police raided two of their safe houses containing bomb-making equipment and arrested five of the bombers. They did not, however, catch the leader of the ASU, who quickly rebuilt it with local recruits (there is a large Irish community in Birmingham) and felt ready to resume operations in November, but he was over-hasty. In the first operation, the bomber himself was killed by a faulty clock-delay mechanism. The second operation comprised two large bombs placed in crowded basement pubs on Thursday 21 November in Birmingham. Due to muddle and incompetence, the planned telephone warning did not get through. Quite indiscriminately, 21 people were killed and 162 wounded. They were mostly young people who had just drawn their weekly pay (Thursday is pay-day). The reaction, in Britain, Ireland and overseas, was predictable, and resulted in the immediate enactment of effective emergency legislation – the Prevention of Terrorism Act, which is described later (pp. 92–4). The five convicted of placing the bombs travelled together in a boat train for Ireland which left a few minutes before the bombs went off, and were arrested as they tried to board the boat in Heysham. Following leads from their statements, four others were arrested in Birmingham, including the cell leader. All were convicted.[2]

In all, during 1974, there were forty-one IRA bombs in England, nineteen of them in Birmingham, fourteen in London and eight elsewhere. They killed forty people.[3] The London ASU was established in August 1974 with a hard core of four, with others co-opted as necessary. They carried out a sustained series of bombings, which killed thirteen people, during the rest of 1974 and through 1975. The four were eventually arrested in December 1975 after a siege in Balcombe Street.[4]

IRA bombing continued sporadically, though never on the same scale as in 1974. Their most spectacular operation was in October 1984, when they attempted to blow up Mrs Thatcher and her entire Cabinet. This operation illustrated some of the strengths and weaknesses of the IRA operating in England. Mrs Thatcher became the IRA's prime target in 1981 when she stood firm against a hunger strike in which ten IRA men in prison died before they called it off. They decided that the best place to kill her would be at the Conservative Party's annual conference. Traditionally the hotel where the party chiefs stay is accessible to party activists and the press. In 1982 a suitably dressed IRA reconnaissance team mingled with them at the Grand Hotel in Brighton to get the feel of the Conference. The assassination had been planned for the 1983 Conference in Blackpool, but after a reconnaissance early in the year, they decided to postpone it until 1984, when it was to be in Brighton again.

The bomb was placed by Patrick Magee, an experienced IRA man who had been imprisoned in 1973–5 and had been one of a team planting sixteen bombs in London and other cities in England in 1978. Magee booked a room in the Grand Hotel for three nights on 15–18 September 1984. He specified a front room with bath overlooking the sea (he chose room 629 on the sixth floor) and checked in as 'Roy Walsh', giving a South London address and disguised with an unaccustomed beard. Assisted by a visitor in his room, he unscrewed the panel behind the bath, inserted 20–30 lbs of explosive wrapped in several layers of cellophane to mask the vapour, and set it with a commercial video-timer to go off at 2.54 am on Friday 12 October, the final day of the conference, when he judged that Mrs Thatcher was certain to be there.

He presumably chose a sixth-floor room in the correct belief that the less prestigious rooms up there would be less thoroughly searched than the suites on the first and second floors. He also knew that the bomb was likely to bring the masonry of the upper storeys crashing down through those below – which it did. In fact, it brought down a heavy chimney stack which fell through to the basement. No Cabinet members were killed; five other people were. Mrs Thatcher (who was still at her desk), after a quick brush-up, was facing the television cameras downstairs within a few minutes, totally unruffled, and the transmission of these interviews around the world enormously boosted her prestige – not what the IRA intended.

The police checked the register of recent occupants of room 629 and soon eliminated most of them. On the registration card completed by 'Roy Walsh' they found finger- and palm-prints matching those of Patrick Magee.[5] By January 1985 they had no doubt at all that Magee had planted the bomb but they had wind of another ambitious operation being planned, so they kept him under surveillance. On 15 June 1985 they watched him check into the Rubens Hotel in London. When he left they searched his room and found a bomb under the bedside cabinet with a precise long-delay timing device and an anti-tampering mercury tilt fuse.

On 22 June the police followed Magee to Glasgow with another well-known IRA man – Peter Sherry – where they saw them meet the leader of the ASU – Gerard McDonnell, equally well known to them – and two women in a flat. Judging that the operation was about to begin, they moved in and arrested them. It transpired that the operation was to comprise sixteen bombs going off on successive days at holiday hotels, mainly in seaside resorts. The first was to be on 19 July at Brighton, the others in Dover, Ramsgate, Blackpool, Eastbourne, Torquay, Great Yarmouth, Folkestone, Margate, Southend, Southampton and Bournemouth, plus four in London.[6]

The strength of these operations lay in their long and meticulous planning, and the sophistication of the technology. The weakness lay in the IRA's having to use their limited hard-core members, now mostly known to the police, to carry out their operations personally, and exposing themselves to surveillance. The main lesson is to underline the importance of being able to establish people's identity, by challenge or (as in Magee's case) retrospectively.

In August 1987 a man and a woman acting suspiciously, close to the home of the Secretary of State for Northern Ireland, Tom King, were questioned by police. They initially acted co-operatively and took the police to a camp site where they were supposedly taking a holiday. Here the police found a third man, who was also detained. They were searched and found to be in possession of a detailed list of addresses and car registration numbers for Tom King and a number of other targets, also a very large amount of currency and other evidence. They thereafter made no statements to the police or at their trial, at which they were sentenced to twenty-five years in prison for conspiracy to murder.

The interesting fact in this case is that none of the three had any record of IRA connections. All came from the Republic, two of them from respected middle-class families. There was evidence of a fourth man in the camp, but he was not there when they called. From this evidence the police think that they know who he is, and that he is a more typical IRA operator. He has twice narrowly evaded capture on other operations. But the story does suggest that the IRA may be using 'clean' people, unlikely to arouse suspicion, for the reconnaissance and early planning of their operations.

Meanwhile, the IRA, lacking success in attacks on combat troops in Northern Ireland or on well-guarded targets, continued to make sporadic attacks on soft targets in England and amongst off-duty soldiers and their families in England and in Germany. Reference was made to some of these in Chapters 4 and 5, such as those in which Patrick Ryan was alleged to have been involved as quartermaster. In August 1988, for example, they placed a bomb near the perimeter of the depot where army postmen are trained in North London, killing one postman in bed. In the summer of 1989 they attached a bomb under a car parked in a German street near the rented home of a married British soldier, killing him, seriously wounding his wife and narrowly missing his four young children; posing as Germans, they stopped two off-duty soldiers aged 18 and 19 in civilian clothes to ask the way and shot them in the face; four of them ran up to the car of the 26-year-old German wife of a British soldier and killed her with a long burst from a Kalashnikov automatic rifle at point-blank range. Since she was alone in the car and obviously unprotected, this seemed a particularly bestial kind of tactic. On some operations of this kind – as in the bombing at the Enniskillen War Memorial (see pp. 75–6) – the IRA have expressed regret, presumably for public relations reasons, but they did not do so on any of these occasions. The largest number of casualties occurred when they placed a bomb with a long-delay timer in the rest room of the Royal Marines Band at their Music School in south-east England in September 1989, killing eleven bandsmen. Technically the postman and the bandsmen were military men, and the German girl was married to one, but these attacks had no military value. They do, however, exemplify the IRA's terrorist philosophy of seeking maximum publicity impact at minimum risk to their own activists.

Foreign terrorists in Britain

The pattern of foreign terrorists fighting their battles on British streets is similar to that in other countries such as France, which has already been described. Palestinian extremists (especially the Abu Nidal Group) have killed mainstream PLO representatives. Libyans based in or directed from the Libyan Embassy have killed anti-Gadafi Libyans. A Nigerian team kidnapped a former minister and were caught trying to smuggle him back to Nigeria in a crate. And Bulgarian intelligence officers killed a Bulgarian working for the BBC Overseas Service, injecting poison into his leg by spiking him with an umbrella at a bus stop. Four examples, however, will be described to illustrate the wide range of such activities which may be expected.

In June 1973 the leader of the PFLP's European command, Mohammed Boudia, was assassinated in Paris by the Israeli 'Wrath of God' team. Boudia's replacement was the Venezuelan 'Carlos'. He operated in both France and Britain and moved freely between the two. He ran two girl-friends in Paris and two in London, who gave him keys to their flats. In each of these flats he normally left a locked suitcase which contained guns, ammunition, forged documents, currency, and so on. This meant that he could travel without weapons or any compromising documents (he usually posed as a Latin American travelling salesman); he could let himself in, collect his gun, do the job and return to the flat with, hopefully, a warm bed for the night. On one of these visits, he raided the London home of a distinguished British Jew, Edward Sieff, president of Marks and Spencer, whom he shot at point-blank range in the face; Sieff miraculously survived.[7] Carlos was eventually exposed in Paris when two French policemen came to one of the flats and Carlos shot them both dead, along with a PFLP courier whom he suspected of betraying him.[8] He escaped from France and reappeared later in Vienna to lead the notorious kidnap of eleven OPEC ministers, as described on p. 47.

Documents captured in Paris led the British police to his two girl-friends' London flats. Though the girls had no doubt suspected that he was up to some illegal activity, perhaps smuggling, the police accepted that they were unaware of the full range of his activities; they were sentenced to short terms of imprisonment.

On 30 April 1980 six terrorists from Khuzestan, the Arab province of Iran, seized the Iranian Embassy in London, with twenty-six hostages. The Metropolitan Police, well experienced in sieges (such as at Balcombe Street, see p. 87), negotiated skilfully for five days, during which five of the hostages who were pregnant or became ill were released. The terrorists knew that their initial demand (the release of ninety-one Arab prisoners in Iran) would not be granted but their real aim was quickly achieved: all the world's cameras and reporters converged on Hyde Park, across the road from the Embassy. The terrorists reduced their demand to one for safe custody out of Britain. When it became clear that this would not be granted, they shot one of the Embassy staff and declared that they would shoot another every forty minutes until a named Arab Ambassador came to negotiate their release. The British army rescue force (SAS) was sent in, killed five of the terrorists and arrested the sixth, and rescued all the hostages, except one more who was shot dead by the terrorists before the rescuers could reach the room in which he was being held.[9] While most of the media behaved responsibly, one television channel did not and could have prejudiced the success of the rescue. This problem, and the organization and effectiveness of the SAS and other rescue forces, are discussed later in the book (p. 122 and 197–8).

In April 1984 a group of anti-Gadafi demonstrators were gathered on the far side of the road from the Libyan Embassy in London, from which they were being kept back by British police. From an upper window of the Embassy one of the diplomatic staff opened fire with a machine-gun, wounding eleven of the demonstrators and killing a British Woman Police Constable (Yvonne Fletcher). Diplomatic relations were broken off and the British government, deciding on scrupulous obser-vance of the diplomatic immunity, escorted the entire staff to the airport, with their baggage unsearched, including the murderer and his gun (no doubt imported in a diplomatic bag).

In April 1986 a Jordanian, Nazir Hindawi, using an official Syrian passport, attempted to blow up an El Al aircraft by inserting a bomb in the hand baggage of an Irish chambermaid in a London hotel, whom he had made pregnant five months earlier. He had promised to marry her and said that he would meet her in Israel, but would travel by an Arab airline. The firing circuit was concealed in a calculating machine (which, if tested, would have worked quite normally), the plastic explosive being flattened in a false bottom of the bag. The Heathrow Airport baggage check (having only an X-ray and no sniffer) did not pick it up. El Al, however, operate a three-hour check-in process including full hand searches. One of their searchers, suspecting the weight of the bag, found the device.

Hindawi had entered the country with the full participation of the Syrian Government and Embassy, disguised as a Syrian Airlines air-crew member. When the bomb was discovered, the Syrian Embassy staff assisted Hindawi in disguising himself but he was arrested and convicted. The Syrian Ambassador and his staff were expelled.

These particular incidents have been selected to contribute to the background against which European anti-terrorist measures after 1992 will be discussed in Chapters 14, 15 and 17.

Anti-terrorist legislation

After the two IRA bombs in Birmingham had killed twenty-one people on 21 November 1974, the Prevention of Terrorism Act was enacted by the Labour government, passing though all its stages to Royal Assent within a week. Contingency legislation must clearly have been held ready in draft. The Act was made subject to annual renewal by Parliament and has been renewed ever since under every Labour and Conservative government, with only minor amendment.

The Act proscribed the IRA and a number of other terrorist organizations. Though the IRA had long been proscribed in the Republic of Ireland and had been proscribed in Northern Ireland the previous year, it had remained legal in Britain. This was preferred by the police, because they had been able to get useful intelligence leads by watching such activities as fund-raising and propaganda around the pubs in the Irish communities in London, Birmingham, Liverpool and other cities. After the Birmingham bombs, however, it was clear that the British public would no longer tolerate this (in fact, the home of one Birmingham Irishman, who had painted IRA emblems on the walls, was set on fire three times in the days after the bombing). Under the Act, it became an offence to belong to the IRA (and other proscribed organizations); to solicit financial or other support for it; to make or receive contributions for it; to arrange or address meetings in support of it; or to wear, carry or display items of dress or other articles such as to arouse reasonable apprehension that the person is a supporter of it.

Later, it also became an offence to withhold knowingly any information which might be of material assistance in preventing an act of terrorism or in apprehending or convicting anyone involved in committing, preparing or investigating such an act.

The Secretary of State had power to issue an exclusion order against any person who he believed had been concerned in the commission, preparation or instigation of an act of terrorism, either in Great Britain or elsewhere, or who was attempting or might attempt to enter Great Britain in order to be concerned in such acts. Such an exclusion order prohibited the person from entering or being in Great Britain. It would, however, not be applied to any citizen of the UK who had been ordinarily resident in Great Britain throughout the previous twenty years and was still ordinarily resident; nor to persons who had been born in Great Britain and ordinarily resident for all their lives.

This gave the power, when appropriate, to exclude a citizen of the UK resident in Northern Ireland from Great Britain. There was a similar clause under which UK citizens resident in Great Britain could be excluded from Northern Ireland. And for non-UK citizens, a third clause provided the power of exclusion from the whole of the UK.

The most controversial powers were those of arrest or detention, which could be applied anywhere in the UK but which were most commonly used by police questioning people at sea- or airports, where they could also demand evidence of identity (not required prior to the Act). Under this clause police officers could arrest without a warrant a person whom they reasonably suspected to be guilty of any of the offences set out in the Act: for example membership of the IRA, or contributing or soliciting support, etc., or withholding information; or assisting or harbouring a person they know to be subject to an exclusion order; or who is himself subject to an exclusion order; or who the police officers reasonably suspect is or has been concerned in the commission, preparation or instigation of acts of terrorism.

The police had the power to detain such persons without charge for forty-eight hours; this could be extended in any particular case by the Secretary of State by a further five days, making seven days in all. The purpose of this was that once a person had been charged (normally necessary within twenty-four hours) he could not be further interrogated on that charge. Since arrest under this Act frequently required investigation in Northern or Southern Ireland before a charge could be made, more time was often needed.[10] There have been complaints to the European Court of Justice about this but thus far successive British governments have stood firm.

When the Act was reviewed and revised by Parliament in 1989, it extended the access of police and tax authorities to bank accounts and business records anywhere in UK, empowered them to share information with each other and with the social security authorities, and to place the onus on suspected racketeers to prove that there was a legitimate source for their funds (see p. 81 in the previous chapter).

The chief complaints against the Act were similar to those against the anti-terrorist legislation in Germany: that the police misused it to 'trawl' for possible subversives; that they used it to harass people they did not like the look of; and that only a small percentage of those detained were eventually charged or convicted.[11]

The first two accusations were strongly denied by the police, and it is not easy to judge or prove whether a police officer's 'reasonable suspicions' are reasonable or not. The third accusation (of detaining many against whom no evidence for a charge was found) was rejected by every Conservative and Labour government in turn, on the grounds that it is impossible to evaluate a suspicion without asking questions: just as no one can be sure that there is not a rotten apple in a basket without looking also at a lot of good ones.[12]

There has never been any doubt – from parliamentary votes and public opinion polls – about the support of the public for this Act. They are aware that many fewer people have been killed by terrorist attacks since the Act came into force, and that many more terrorists have been caught.

Chapter eight

Spain, Portugal and Greece

The origins of ETA

ETA (Freedom for the Basque Homeland) lies second only to the IRA in West European countries in the number of political murders it has committed. There are some similarities with Northern Ireland but also some significant differences.

The Basque country in north-east Spain comprises three provinces with a large Basque majority – Guipuzcoa, Vizcaya and Alava – and a fourth province, Navarra, which has roughly equal Basque and Castilian populations. ETA claims, and operates in, all four as the Basque Homeland. The principal port and industrial city is Bilbao and the regional capital is Vitoria. The Basque region is the most industrialized in Spain (as are the six Northern counties in Ireland). The population of the region is 2.1 million (compared with 1.5 million in Northern Ireland), of which 70 per cent are ethnically Basque (compare 33 per cent Catholics in Northern Ireland). ETA's political front, HB (People's Unity) is legalized and, in the 1984 elections for the Basque Autonomous Regional Assembly, polled 15 per cent of the vote (compare 8 per cent for Sinn Fein in Northern Ireland).[1] In the Basque country across the border in south-west France there are many Basque homes which will offer sanctuary to ETA, whose campaign is directed from there (just as the IRA headquarters is in Dundalk, in the Republic). Since 1986 there has been much improved co-operation between the Spanish and French governments over cross-border co-operation and extradition (compare the Anglo-Irish Agreement of 1985). Some of the worst ETA atrocities have been in the non-Basque parts of Spain, for example in Madrid in 1986 and Barcelona in 1987; just as the worst single IRA atrocity has been in England (Birmingham 1974).

The biggest difference is that the majority (70 per cent) in the region are Basques. This enabled the Spanish government in 1977 to devolve autonomous government to a region comprising the three provinces with large Basque majorities, but excluding the equally mixed Navarra (which

ETA used as grounds for continuing their campaign). The current regional government, elected in February 1987, is a coalition between the constitutional and anti-ETA Basque Nationalist Party (PNV) and the Socialist Party (which is also in power in Madrid). By contrast, even though the moderate Catholic Party in Northern Ireland (SDLP) would form a coalition, the various Protestant Unionist parties (except for their short-lived power-sharing in 1974) have intransigently rejected any kind of coalition, on the grounds that they have an overall majority. Since no British government has, since 1972, been willing ever again to underwrite (with British troops and money) a sectarian government, there is no provincial government in Northern Ireland.

There were approximately 800 people killed by terrorists in Spain from 1968 to 1989, of which 600 were by ETA and 200 by others. Of the 2,800 deaths in Northern Ireland since 1969, about 1,700 have been killed by the IRA, 800 by Protestant terrorists and 300 by the police and the army. The annual rate of violent deaths attributable to ETA since 1976 are shown in Table 4.[2]

Table 4 Deaths attributable to ETA, 1976–89

Year	Deaths	Year	Deaths	Year	Deaths
1976	17	1981	30	1986	38[a]
1977	12	1982	40	1987	35[b]
1978	65	1983	40	1988	19
1979	78	1984	33	1989	
1980	96	1985	34		

Notes: a including 12 killed by a bomb in Madrid on 14 July 1986
b including 21 killed by a bomb in an underground carpark in Barcelona on 19 June 1987

Basque separatism has a long history. The Romans wrote of a Basque tribe with a language of its own. The origins of this language are totally different from the Roman and Asian origins of other European languages. Though Basque is not much spoken in the industrial cities of the region, many of those in rural areas do resolutely cling to it, and to their ethnicity. All through Spanish history, they have constantly campaigned for independence though, since industrialization has created powerful commercial links with the consumers of their products in the rest of Spain, the majority (those other than the 15 per cent who voted for HB) are content to settle with autonomy within Spain rather than independence.

Persecution reached its peak during the Franco era – 1939–75 – when Basque language and culture were ruthlessly suppressed. This had the inevitable effect of developing a fanatical hard core of resistance and growing popular support for it. ETA was formed in 1959.

The ETA offensive

ETA's first murder was of a police chief inspector in 1968. It first seized the world's headlines in 1973, when a gigantic bomb in Madrid killed Franco's Prime Minister, Admiral Carrero Blanco. The resulting suppression and show trials gave a boost to ETA's public support.

In 1974 ETA began to split into two streams: ETA-M, which believed in a purely military strategy, and ETA-PM, which believed in tempering military activity to promote a realistic political strategy. This can be compared to the divergence between Moretti and Senzani in Italy (see p. 41) and the current divergence within the IRA (see pp. 75–6). It can be regarded as a normal tendency in any violent terrorist movement, and counter-terrorism should take it into account. By the early 1980s ETA-PM had largely ceased from violence and its members accepted 'social reinsertion' (see p. 103), most of them pursuing their aims constitutionally.[3] Hereafter, 'ETA' will refer to ETA-M unless otherwise stated.

Facing Franco's fascist regime, ETA adopted the well-tried organization and philosophy of secret revolutionary movements. Their 'praxis' was based on the 'spiral of conflict': that is Action provokes Repression which arouses Consciousness amongst the oppressed masses (i.e. Basques) arousing further Action. With each turn of the cycle, the momentum of the Action would increase. Thus, the selection of the target for Action was such as to provoke the maximum Repression.[4] A great deal of ETA's rhetoric, both then and now, has a strong Marxist flavour. They are, however, primarily a nationalist movement, in which ideology plays little part; their actions had more in common with the Nazism than with the ideological left. The Madrid and Barcelona atrocities (see Table 4) had the flavour of Birmingham (1974), Bologna (1980) and the Munich Oktoberfest (1980). They were calculated to shock. Ever since the earliest activities of Hitler's National Socialists in the 1920s, Nazis and fascists have used left-wing rhetoric. In the 1920s Mussolini and Hitler were both initially perceived as left-wing socialists (both used the title) and it was a long time before Stalin (with his 'Socialism in one country') became recognized as the most ruthless fascist dictator of all time. The motivation in all these cases was nationalist rather than ideological.

Franco died on 20 November 1975. To the astonishment of the world, there was a peaceful transition to a constitutional monarchy and the first democratic elections for nearly forty years were held on 15 June 1977.[5] It is a sad reflection on revolutionary history, from 1789 through 1917, that the liberalization of an *ancien regime* almost always sets in motion the most rapid escalation of violence by minorities hoping to take advantage of its weakness. This is illustrated in Table 5.[6]

Table 5 Violent deaths attributable to ETA terrorism, 1968–89

The Franco period, from 1968 to November 1975	43
From November 1975 to the elections in June 1977	23
From June 1977 to the end of 1989	534

As was shown in Table 4, of the 600 ETA killings in those 21 years, 239 (40 per cent) were in the three years following the transition to democracy – 1978–80. This illustrates the fundamental totalitarian nature of terrorist movements. They use violence because they know that the majority of people are too 'misguided' to elect them in a free vote.

ETA had a hard core of about 100 regular *etarras* and, with its part-time volunteers, never exceeded 500 in all. These figures are again on a similar scale to those of BR, the RAF and the IRA. They could undoubtedly arm and maintain more than 100 regulars, but prefer to keep the hard core tight and selective to minimize the chances of penetration and defection. There are, as in Northern Ireland, plenty of other young men (there are few female ETA regulars) ready to take up vacancies as casualties occur. Moreover, ETA tend to turn these 100 over more quickly than the others, the average length of armed active service being only three years.

Of those killed by ETA, 60 per cent were members of the security forces. The Civil Guards (local police) and the Basque Autonomous Police (responsible to the Autonomous Regional Government) were prime targets, the remainder being National Police and Army.

ETA's second priority was to hit the economy, both of the Basque region and of Spain as a whole. They extorted 'revolutionary taxes' with the threat of death, kidnap or sabotage of their factories for those who refused them. These revolutionary taxes made up a great part of their finance; there were a number of kidnaps for large ransoms; and the balance was made up by bank robberies. It is estimated that a movement of their size needs £4 million to £5 million a year to operate (which is roughly also the IRA's budget). The attacks on the economy of Spain as a whole concentrated on the country's biggest invisible export – tourism. There were frequent flurries of bombs in tourist resorts, built up with maximum advance publicity to arouse alarm. In the Basque region the aim was to deter foreign companies from continuing existing operations or investing in new ones. Finally, like every terrorist movement, they used murder to punish defectors and to deter collaborators and informers.

Most of the ETA leaders were securely based in the Basque region of France and the French government, in accordance with its traditions of asylum, was very reluctant to extradite them, much to the anger of

Spaniards. A growing number of other ETA activists, finding themselves under police pressure, also fled to France and continued operating from there in raids across the border. In the late 1970s, with some evidence of Spanish police connivance, right-wing terrorist groups began to pursue them and murder them in France (see next section). This alarmed the French, who began to take action to root out the cause of these battles on French soil. In the latter half of 1982 they made a number of arrests, including the ETA leader ('Txomin') and his Directors of Intelligence and Finance. Information from these arrests led the French police to a number of arms caches; they also found a list of more than ninety subscribers to revolutionary taxes, with details of the modes of collection and penalties for non-payment.[7]

The French, however, were still not willing to extradite *etarras* to Spain if they would face major charges there, and deported them instead to 'third countries' whose governments agreed to prevent them from continuing political activities. Txomin served a nominal sentence in France for possession of firearms and was thence deported to Gabon. Later he moved to Algiers, where a large colony of about forty *etarras* gathered. From there he conducted secret (but abortive) negotiations with the Spanish government, until he was killed in a road accident in February 1987 and a harder-line leader, 'Artapalo' took over.

Though still active, ETA had passed the peak. They had other troubles too: during 1983, in three separate incidents, six *etarras* blew themselves up with their own bombs, and at ETA's request the IRA sent over an expert bomb-maker to give them some training.[8]

But the government, too, was facing its own troubles.

The challenge from the right

The greatest challenge to Spain's democracy came, not from ETA, but from the relics of the fascist right wing. They were alarmed by the explosion of terrorism in 1978–80, and contemptuous of the ability of democratic politicians to contain it. On 23 February 1981 there was bizarre attempt at a military coup. Colonel Tejero de Molino, commanding 200 Civil Guards (paramilitary police), broke into Parliament in a blaze of sub-machine-gun fire and took the entire Cabinet and 300 deputies hostage. When Tejero telephoned to say that he had captured them all, General Milans del Busch used his troops to seize the radio station, and broadcast a declaration of a State of Emergency in the region. He then telephoned the commanders of ten other military districts, claiming that he was acting in the name of the King.

King Juan Carlos acted promptly and firmly. He telephoned his senior commanders in turn, disowning the coup and ordering them to do the same. He put in motion plans to storm the Parliament buildings. Within twenty-four hours the coup had collapsed.[9] This incident firmly established the prestige of the constitutional monarchy and of the King personally; it also demonstrated his commitment to democracy and his determination to defend it from whichever side it was attacked.

Meanwhile a more clandestine form of right-wing backlash was emerging. In January 1981 (shortly before the attempted coup) four *etarras* were killed and nineteen wounded by a bomb in a bar in Bilbao. Later that year, another raiding team crossed into France, killed two more in a bar in the French border town of Hendaye, and were arrested when they tried to crash through a frontier barrier back into Spain. A senior police officer in Madrid ordered their immediate release, and refused to identify them, declaring that they were paid police informers.[10]

These gangs were two of a group of independent death squads known as 'The Uncontrollables'. In 1983 they fused together, calling themselves the Anti-Terrorist Liberation Group (GAL), and their raids became more professionally organized. There was, and remains, strong suspicion of police involvement (see below) though there is no evidence as to whether this involvement received any positive or tacit approval from within the government. Between their formation in 1983 until 1986 GAL killed twenty-three *etarras*.

It was the emergence of GAL which changed the French attitude. They were not prepared to tolerate rival Spaniards shooting each other on French soil. They were also at this time having similar trouble with Lebanese, Palestinian and other Arab terrorists in Paris. In 1983–4 they tightened their migration controls across the Spanish frontier, and began to deport known ETA activists. They still had inhibitions about sending people charged with actual terrorist offences for trial in Spain, so they continued to deport these to third countries willing to accept them, such as Algeria, Gabon and the Cape Verde Islands. But many on 'accomplice' charges were extradited to Spain on the promise that they would be rehabilitated and released.

Jacques Chirac became Prime Minister of France in 1986. He quickly made a formal agreement with the Spanish government, part of which was insistence on GAL activities' being curbed. Since then, co-operation has been good, many more *etarras* have been deported or extradited to Spain, and GAL has not reappeared.

In June 1989 two senior police officers who had been serving in Bilbao in 1983 were indicted on charges of planning a bomb attack which killed an alleged ETA activist, and of using government money to set up GAL and of hiring mercenaries (usually common criminals) to carry out the twenty-three killings.[11] How far Madrid was involved in this financing, if at all, is not known.

The government's response

Ever since the restoration of democracy in 1977 the Madrid government had been taking positive steps to defuse the Basque situation. They legalized ETA's political party (HB) and they devolved very considerable powers to an autonomous regional government. This had been put to a national referendum in 1979, and, in a 67 per cent turn-out, 88 per cent voted in favour of this devolution, that is nearly 60 per cent of all those eligible to vote in Spain as a whole.[12] Thanks to ETA's ordering a boycott (backed by threats), and PNV unwisely deciding to advise its members to abstain, marginally fewer than half of the eligible voters in the Basque region turned out to vote in favour of it, though very few voted against it. This was, of course, used by HB and ETA to try to discredit the proposal; PNV must now regret their part in giving them this propaganda tool.

The government's plan rested on three main pillars: improved policing; better international co-operation (especially with the French); and social reinsertion (i.e. the reabsorption into society of ETA sympathizers and accomplices willing to renounce violence).

To improve police response they set up in 1978 a Special Operations Group (GEO), trained in anti-terrorist duties on the lines of its British French and German equivalents. This was in time to have a marked effect on reducing ETA's income from kidnap and ransom, which passed its peak in 1981. The GEO further proved itself in May 1981, when twenty-four heavily armed neo-fascist terrorists seized some 200 hostages in a bank in Barcelona, demanding the release of Colonel Tejero and three generals who were being charged with involvement in the attempted coup. The GEO mounted an assault and rescue, killing one terrorist and wounding one hostage. Unfortunately, with 200 hostages naturally seizing any available exit and opportunity to escape from the bedlam, some of the terrorists were able to mingle with them. Since they had been wearing hoods, no one could recognize their faces. Nevertheless, it was a highly professional rescue and the ten terrorists who were arrested included three with violent neo-fascist records. There was evidence that they had received large sums of money, and a suspicion that some of them were mercenaries.[13]

In 1979 Spain had adapted some of its laws and judicial processes to take account of terrorism. As in Italy and France, terrorist aims and methods were to be regarded as an aggravating factor, for which heavier sentences were given; for example, a crime normally carrying a sentence of fifteen to twenty-five years would, if the aggravating factor applied, get twenty-five to thirty years. Aggravating factors included belonging to or acting in the service of an organization whose aim was 'to attack the security of the state, the integrity of its territories or its constitutional order', or 'collaborating in the accomplishment of those objectives . . . by provoking explosions, fires, shipwrecks, derailments . . . or similar acts'.[14] At the same time, to counter terrorist propaganda, the government laid down an 'information policy' to encourage a favourable climate of public opinion, by such means as 'judicious choice of government principles, such as democracy, the danger of destabilization, the danger of losing one's fundamental freedoms, etc.' and 'reviving patriotic sentiment in the national unity of Spain'.[15]

Thereafter they continued to improve their anti-terrorist measures and legislation in the wake of the dual threat from ETA and the fascists. The powers of the Basque autonomous regional government were extended to give them greater control over regional policing, intelligence and the judiciary, including more say in the appointment of judges; also in the fields of education and culture, about which the Basque people were particularly sensitive.

In December 1984 the Socialist government reinforced the existing anti-terrorist laws to allow detention of terrorist suspects *incommunicado* for up to ten days. This, like similar laws in other countries, was criticized for eroding civil rights and for being likely to increase sympathy for the terrorists. During 1985 1,181 people were detained in the Basque country: 765 of these were charged under anti-terrorist legislation, but only 69 were sentenced to prison terms.[16] As with the British Prevention of Terrorism Act ten years earlier, the police argued that they had to look at a lot of suspects to find each one convicted. In 1987 the maximum detention period was reduced to three days, with power to extend to five days in special cases. And provision was made for leniency or pardon for terrorists prepared to co-operate in averting terrorist acts, apprehending other terrorists and materially reducing the prospects of future terrorist action.

The Civil Guard was meanwhile gaining in skills and experience, which was why they were always the main target of ETA bombing and shooting attacks. Deaths attributable to ETA fell in 1981 to less than half their 1978–80 average and have remained at that level. (See Table 4 on p. 96; this can be compared to the reduction of killing in Northern Ireland in 1977 – see p. 74.)

Nevertheless, the Civil Guard and National Police were seen by many of the Basque population as 'foreign' (i.e. Castilian Spanish) and a Basque regional police force (the *Ertzantza*) to be responsible to the elected regional government in Vitoria was formed; by 1985 it had reached 3,000 towards its establishment of 7,000 (compared with 120,000 in the National Police and Civil Guard). It was initially confined to a law-and-order role, and the anti-terrorist campaign remained the responsibility of the Madrid government. The *Ertzantza* got off to an unfortunate start when, on the eve of their deployment on the streets, ETA raided a police station, disarmed ten Basque policemen and got away with 100 weapons and police uniforms in a police landrover.[17] The Madrid government's intention, however, is to devolve as much power to the autonomous government as possible.

'Social reinsertion' has perhaps been the greatest success of all. The policy was developed from the cease-fire negotiations with ETA-PM in 1981, in which the disposal of those in prison or exile was a major discussion point. It was agreed that ETA-PM members who renounced the armed struggle could be released and re-established in society. On 30 September 1981 ETA-PM announced its dissolution and, during the next twelve months, 250 of its members had been reinserted on condition that they confined the campaign for their political objectives within the legitimate Spanish and Basque democratic institutions.

In October 1982 a Socialist government was elected in Madrid and attempted to extend 'social reinsertion' to ETA-M. Their political wing HB, however, refused to support this initiative. This has been a set-back, because HB in November 1986 won thirteen of the seventy-two seats in the Basque Regional Assembly (compared with thirty-six for the Socialist/PNV Coalition) and in June 1987 won a seat in the European Parliament. The Madrid and Vitoria governments have therefore concentrated on persuading individual ETA-M members to accept reinsertion. They put the number of ETA exiles in France at 800, of whom fewer than 200 had been actually involved in terrorist actions, the majority having provided only support services.[18]

By April 1986 about 120 of these had accepted reinsertion. On 25 April PNV and HB met to discuss methods to eradicate violence. Three hours before these talks began, ETA used a car bomb to kill five Civil Guards in Madrid, with the obvious intention of sabotaging the talks but, although HB refused to condemn the bombing, the PNV-HB talks went ahead. The Madrid government, however, declared that this action proved that political negotiation was impossible. The killing of another twelve Civil Guards by a bomb in Madrid on 14 July 1986 reinforced this view.

Prospects for the future in Spain

In February 1988 ETA kidnapped Emiliano Revilla, a Madrid businessman; he was released on 30 October for an alleged ransom of nearly £4 million. This would be enough to maintain ETA for about a year. Nevertheless, the number of ETA murders in 1988 was down to nineteen, the lowest since 1977 (twelve). The details of these (announced by the Ministry of the Interior in July 1989) give an idea of the current pattern (see Table 6).[19]

Table 6 ETA terrorism in 1988

---

243 terrorist attacks by ETA (70 per cent of the total of 343) of which there were:

        29 against security force targets

      101 against French commercial interests (car dealers, etc.)

        12 against other civilian targets

      101 against other targets (including some drug traffickers)

19 killed, including:

        10 National police and Civil Guards

         1 Basque policeman

         1 soldier

         7 civilians

92 wounded (43 in Basque country, 49 in Madrid)

193 ETA suspects arrested, 2 killed

24 ETA suspects extradited from France

Other attacks were by Catalans (54), GAL (37) and GRAPO (6) in which GRAPO (an extreme Marxist group) killed 2 (1 policeman, 1 industrialist)

In January 1989 there were further negotiations between ETA and the Madrid government. ETA demands, as in previous talks, included:

1 amnesty for all ETA prisoners and return of exiles
2 unconditional legalization of all political parties
3 removal of all Spanish security forces from Basque territory
4 improvements in living and working conditions for Basques
5 autonomy status to include Navarra in the Basque country.

These talks broke down in April and it was clear that ETA was merely using them to secure a breathing space. The police and all the main political parties opposed renewing the talks, and the government announced that it had no intention of doing so.

Murders were resumed on 8 May, when a car bomb killed two policemen in Madrid; on 24 May three more policemen were killed by a booby-trapped car bomb in Bilbao when they had been called to investigate another incident (also a favourite IRA tactic). Five thousand people demonstrated in Bilbao against these murders.[20]

There was then a lull in the run-up to the European elections in June, in which the HB held their seat, but attacks were resumed immediately after the polls had closed on 16 June. ETA killed a total of 19 people in 1989.

An early solution seems unlikely. ETA appear to be concentrating, as in 1988, on killing members of the security forces and damaging French commercial property. Like the IRA, however, they are clearly disliked by the majority of the population. But, also like the IRA, they are likely to continue their violence at least on the present scale. As the

Arab terrorists proved in France in 1986, a handful of terrorists can easily do, say, five or ten lethal attacks in a year, some of them multiple ones. There will probably always be more than a handful of ETA terrorists willing to do this and enough others waiting to take their places when they are killed or captured. These activities will lose rather than gain popular support for HB, who are therefore unlikely to exert any great influence on the political process.

The encouraging features are first, that the Basques are in a majority and most of them do support and participate in the autonomous government; second, that the Madrid government is being liberal and far-sighted in delegating real powers to the autonomous government, in respecting the Basque language and culture and in the handling of the reinsertion programme; and third, that, with French co-operation, they have eroded what was until 1983 a thriving ETA base from which to direct and launch operations.

Portugal

After a series of short-lived administrations since the Communist revolution overthrew the fascist dictatorship in 1974, the Social Democrat Party gained an absolute majority, polling over 50 per cent of the vote, in the election of July 1987. Portugal now has one of the more stable and confident governments in the EC.

Between 1980 and 1986 an ultra-left terrorist movement, FP 25, carried out a series of bomb attacks against embassies, industries and banks of NATO countries. On one occasion FP 25 set off 100 small bombs in a day (20 April 1984), and it claimed to have carried out 12 assassinations, over 200 bombing incidents and 40 bank robberies by the end of that year. It also claimed to have hatched the 1984 anti-NATO Alliance at a series of meetings with AD, RAF and other European terrorist representatives.[21]

In October 1984 Colonel Otelo Saraiva de Carvalho was arrested and charged, along with seventy-seven others, with having formed FP 25 and been involved in its assassinations and bombings. Carvalho had been at one time a national hero, having played a leading part in the 1974 Communist coup. The Communist government had in turn been toppled in 1975 and a democratic system established. Carvalho stood unsuccessfully in the presidential elections of 1976 and 1980.

His trial began on 22 July 1985 in a purpose-built court-house with bullet-proof screens and iron cages for the defendants. Just before the trial began a defector who was to be a key witness, Jose Manuel Barradas, was murdered and five other defectors had to be kept in protective custody. Other assassinations, and an escape by ten of the prisoners, further delayed the trial, but on 19 May 1987 Carvalho was found guilty of 'founding and leading a terrorist organization' and was sentenced to eighteen years' imprisonment. This was quashed on appeal on the basis of legal irregularities in his trial, and he and the twenty-eight others who had been convicted with him were released in May 1989. On 15 September 1989, however, the Appeal Court reversed this decision and his eighteen-year sentence was confirmed. He gave notice of appeal to the Supreme Court.[22]

With all its original leaders in custody, FP 25 has been quiescent since 1986. About forty of the rank-and-file are believed to be still at large; their revival depends on whether the charismatic Carvalho and other leaders are finally released and what restrictions are placed on their movements.

Greece

Greece has a long history of sympathy for the Palestinian cause and is suspected by a number of fellow EC members of harbouring (intentionally or by turning a blind eye) a secure and active base for Middle East terrorist operations. Certainly Athens airport has been notorious for its poor security and for the number of hijackers who have boarded planes there. Greece has a similarly unenviable reputation as an easy point for entry and transitting of drugs. These reputations, if they prove to be justified, have serious implications for a post-1992 EC with open internal frontiers.

The PASOK (Socialist) party administration of Andreas Papandreou was ousted in the General Election of 1989 and the succeeding Conservative-dominated coalition indicted Papandreou and others on serious corruption charges.

Whether or not Greece has been a willing or complaisant partner, she has also been a victim of Middle Eastern terrorism. On 11 July 1988 Palestinian terrorists attacked the Greek ship *City of Poros*, killing nine people and injuring nearly a hundred.

Internal terrorism has been on a small scale by movements using a variety of names – probably designed to confuse. Typical was a bomb on a tourist beach on Mililini Island on 9 September 1989. It was clearly designed to frighten away tourists and an hour's warning was given. (Two French tourists who declined to leave were slightly injured.) Other targets have reflected anti-US feeling, arising from the presence of four US military bases, and suspected US bias in favour of Turkey in providing arms supplies.

There was much resentment in the USA and Europe over the Greek refusal of an Italian request in December 1988 to extradite an Abu Nidal suspect, Abdel Osama Al-Zomor, wanted for the 1982 bombing of a synagogue in Rome, killing two people and injuring thirty-four. He was instead deported to Libya.[23]

Much will depend on whether and how well the new government tightens its frontiers and internal security, and whether it tries to change the official attitude to Middle Eastern terrorism. Even if it does, the fact will remain that many Greeks, including some in influential positions, do sympathize with the Palestinians, and have traditionally looked across the Mediterranean rather than to Europe for their friends. Greece has a history of political instability and the influence of these people may wax or wane. There is also always a possibility of another military coup, which might give an impression of short-term security but would increase dissident activities and, in the end, produce a more brittle and fragile regime.

Whatever happens, the external frontiers and internal uncertainties of Greece will constitute the weakest link in the EC's defences against terrorism, especially of the kind which is brought in across the Mediterranean by immigrants, legal or illegal, and by temporary visitors. This weakness must inevitably be taken into account in the single market's plans for protection against terrorists and drug traffickers after 1992.

Chapter nine

International crime and drug trafficking

John Simpson, the President of the General Assembly of Interpol (the International Criminal Police Organization), in a 1974 interview with *TVI Journal*, said that the most significant international crimes were the narcotics trade, white-collar crime and terrorism, and that he expected this to remain so for the foreseeable future.[1]

Terrorism and 'ordinary crime' (in the sense of law-breaking for monetary gain) clearly overlap. Several examples were given in previous chapters of political terrorists using kidnap and extortion to finance their campaign (e.g. Italy, p. 32). £25 million in ransoms launched the El Salvador rebellion in 1979–80. Terrorists regularly use the other two crimes listed by John Simpson, narcotics and white-collar crime, both to obtain and to launder their money. And international criminal gangs use terror (like the Mafia) or subsidize political terrorists (as do the drug cartels in Colombia) to further their own activities.

The International Mafia and the drug barons

The international Mafia and its associated secret societies, such as the Chinese Triads and the Colombian drug cartels, exercise a malign and pervasive influence on the political, social and economic fabric not only of the countries in which they are based – Italy, USA, Pakistan, Hong Kong and Colombia – but also of the areas in which they have subsidiaries, especially in Western Europe and the Caribbean.

The word 'mafia' in Italy is a generic term for organized crime. Certain penalties (e.g. seizure of assets) are applied by Italian law to any organization 'of a mafia kind', which is so defined when it comprises three or more members who

> make use of the power of intimidation provided by the associative bond and of the state of subjugation and of criminal silence (*omertà*) which derives from it to commit crimes, to acquire directly or indirectly the running or control of economic activities, of

concessions, grants, contracts and public services in order to realize illicit profits or advantage for themselves or others.[2]

By far the most powerful and dangerous of the Italian associations 'of a mafia kind' is the Sicilian Mafia (or *Cosa Nostra*), with its fraternal or subsidiary structures in the USA, the UK and elsewhere in the world. Controlled by a 'commission' in Palermo it comprises a network of about thirty 'families', the biggest of which is about two hundred, the average being about fifty.[3] Within the family, discipline, and especially silence, are most rigidly enforced, with a perception of certain death for transgressors or defectors, balanced against the opportunity for wealth beyond any conceivable expectation for its members from any other source and – by these same ruthless means – collective protection for those who remain loyal. There is never any shortage of recruits waiting to take the places of any *mafiosi* who are arrested or killed. The Mafia's vulnerability, however, comes from its history of violent internal rivalry between families competing with each other for lucrative areas. Its strength lies in its infiltration of politics, banking, police, intelligence and industry (especially construction and public works). Numbers of highly placed people in every one of these fields in Italy have been involved with the Mafia, as a result of succumbing to the choice of accepting money and opportunities for power rather than of living under the threat of death for themselves and their families.

Despite repeated internal blood-letting and periodic decimations of its hierarchy by convictions on the evidence of Mafia *pentiti* (see Chapter 3), the Palermo Commission, and its currently dominant 'family', the Corleonesi, have access to quite enormous reserves of wealth, dispersed in a range of legal and illegal investments, property and bank accounts world-wide which it has so far proved almost impossible for the authorities to detect or seize.

The Mafia's direct links with terrorism have been largely with far right groups, and there are strong grounds for suspecting their involvement in the bloody bomb incidents in Italy in the 1970s and 1980s (see Table 1 on p. 27). The 'strategy of tension' and the emergence of an authoritarian society, in which capitalism and crime can both flourish, are wholly advantageous to them. This does not, however, prevent them from making use of left-wing terrorist groups (e.g. in facilitating the production and distribution of drugs) when it advances their aims, which are money and power.

Mafia intimidation and assassinations at the highest levels in society make those of the Red Brigades at their peak look insignificant. For example, in Sicily in one period of 3½ years (1979–83) they assassinated the President of the Sicilian Region, the Christian Democratic Party secretary, the Prefect of Palermo, the head of the Palermo Flying Squad, the Chief Prosecutor and two Chief Examining Magistrates of Palermo in succession. Six years later (late 1989) after numerous trials and appeals, no definitive verdict had been passed on any of these murders.[4]

From 1978 to 1984 *Cosa Nostra* gained virtual control of heroin distribution from South and East Asia to Europe and the USA. They were then hit by a rash of internal wars and by a number of *pentiti*, whose testimonies resulted in the arrest and conviction of many senior *mafiosi*. This process was aided by the 'Rognone La Torre' laws passed after the murder of General Dalla Chiesa in September 1982 (see pp. 156–7). 'Association of a mafia kind' became in itself a criminal offence, and the public prosecutor had right of access to investigate the provenance of income and the tax situation of anyone suspected of Mafia association and of his family. The onus was then on the suspected person to prove that his assets had a legitimate source; otherwise they could be seized and later confiscated.

After a series of 'maxi-trials' (one with 475 defendants of whom 361 were imprisoned, 19 for life) the Italian Mafia regrouped and expanded its activities in its traditional fields of international finance and the domination of construction and public works contracts. It established a thriving UK operation under Francesco di Carlo, who covered his drug smuggling and other activities with ownership of a hotel, a wine-bar, an antiques business and a travel agency, all, no doubt, useful for money laundering. Arrested in possession of 35 kg of heroin, he was sentenced to twenty-five years' imprisonment in March 1987. In the same year British Customs and police broke up a massive operation organized by the Detroit Mafia, to use the UK as a depot and distribution areas for smuggling cocaine from Bolivia into Europe. Companies trading in computer parts were set up in London and Jersey to launder anticipated profits of $3 billion every month.[5]

Under President Zia, the heroin-financed Pakistani drug Mafias achieved a degree of influence in their society comparable to that of the Mafias in Italy and Colombia, and Mrs Bhutto has thus far had little success in breaking it. Pakistan has its own addiction problem, with more heroin addicts (700,000) than the USA (500,000). It is also the main centre for production and processing heroin from the 'Golden Crescent' (Pakistan, Iran and Afghanistan) and now provides 60 to 70 per cent of the top-grade heroin sold in the West. Production is accelerating: earnings in 1989 were estimated to be £2.5 billion, more than Pakistan's total legal exports.[6]

The other main heroin-producing area is the 'Golden Triangle' (Burma, Laos and Thailand), much of whose production is marketed through the Triad Secret Societies in Hong Kong. The Triads handle much of the heroin distribution to the West, with strong bases amongst the large Chinese communities in London and Amsterdam. In their rigid discipline, violent rivalries, tradition of silence and the ruthless elimination of their own transgressors and of those who stand in their way, the Triad Secret Societies have much in common with the Sicilian Mafia.

The cocaine trail

One of the greatest generators of terrorism and criminal violence in the world is the cocaine trade from the coca fields in Colombia to the addicts in Europe and the USA. The Colombian drug cartels, of whom the most powerful is based in Medellin, have distribution centres in London, Amsterdam and other cities. They are run on the lines of commercial multinational corporations, with corporate headquarters (usually in the Caribbean area or Central America), with their own finance, purchasing, distribution, market research and political risks analysis departments. Their London and Amsterdam operations are similarly run like multinational subsidiaries. Narcotics are very big business, with a turnover of $500 billion per year of which $300 million is profits. Potential assets (including stock in transit) are in the trillion dollar range. The cartels subsidize terrorist groups in rural areas of Peru and Colombia to keep the police away from the coca fields and laboratories. They also operate professional assassination squads, like those of the Mafia, to eliminate people who obstruct their path and to terrorize others into conforming with their wishes. The combination of this, the stick, and the carrot (from the almost bottomless availability of money for bribes) is highly effective.

The Colombian drug multinationals are likely always to be able to find some who will succumb to the threat of death or the lure of bribes in the ranks of politicians, officials, police officers, bankers, business people and judges. In view of the number assassinated, this is hardly surprising. The saying goes in Colombia that a judge has the choice between silver and lead, and inevitably some choose silver.[7]

In August 1989 the Colombian Medellin drug cartel assassinated Luis Carlos Galan, the most popular candidate for the 1990 presidential election, and the most likely to succeed the incumbent President Virgilio Barco, his closest political associate. Barco, harnessing the popular outrage over the assassination, launched massive raids on the headquarters, laboratories and other premises of the Medellin barons, arresting over 10,000 people and seizing property and equipment valued at millions of dollars, including 135 aircraft and 15 helicopters in the first week. He also used emergency powers in bypassing his Supreme Court to extradite drug runners and money launderers wanted in the USA. The barons responded by declaring total war on the government. The USA and many other countries promised aid. The Colombians achieved a major success when Jose Gonzalo Rodriguez Gacha, one of the three leading Medellin drug barons, the one most prone to violence, was surrounded by the army and killed on 15 December 1989.

This total war is likely to be very bloody. If the barons are to be defeated in Colombia it is likely that international military forces, especially naval and air, will have to assist in monitoring and curbing the drug traffic across Central America and the Caribbean. The possibility of such concerted international action, a world war on drugs, is examined in Chapter 17. Even if it were to come about, however, it would take a long time, because so long as there is a demand for a lucrative product there will be people ready to take risks to supply it.

Therefore the place at which the problem must be tackled is at the consumer end. Though drug addiction is growing world-wide, an enormous percentage of the $500 billion turnover is made up of the 20-dollar and 100-dollar bills or their equivalents paid to pushers by addicts on the streets of Europe and the USA. Certain countries, including Turkey and Japan, have contained the problem by a mixture of ruthlessness and public education. Some other countries, like Malaysia and Singapore, keep it in check with the death penalty for couriers and traffickers, but they catch only the little people.

One beguiling solution, much advocated in both the USA and Europe, is to make drugs legal but to control their distribution (like that of alcohol) and tax them heavily. The argument is that Prohibition (of alcohol) in the USA failed in 1920–33 because enough people wanted to buy it to drive up the price and create huge profits to finance the criminal under-world – as drugs are doing now. The protagonists of legalizing drugs claim that their price would fall and a large part of it would be gathered in taxes, which could be used on public education against addiction; also that quality control would be easier, and that consumption could be steered towards safer, less addictive drugs by differential taxation.[8]

The snag is that drugs are easy and cheap to produce. As was pointed out in Chapter 1, it costs only £140 to buy the raw materials to make 1 kg of cocaine in a Colombian laboratory, but the total price collected for it, split into many thousands of doses on the streets, is about £70,000, virtually all of which goes into astronomical profits for a wholly criminal hierarchy from the barons to the street pushers. The prices of legalized drugs would be controlled by market forces (with added taxation) so would fall dramatically, but the producers and the distributors, deprived of their huge profits, would vastly increase their production. There would be a limit to taxation, above which it would defeat its object by promoting a thriving black market. There would therefore be a massive increase in addiction. Legalization of soft drugs would not solve the problem: most hard drug addicts start with cannabis or amphetamines; and the pushers are now secreting quantities of crack in cannabis so that victims smoking cannabis become addicted to crack without realizing it.

Addiction to crack may become firmly rooted after only a few doses. In view of the terrible and often irreparable damage which is done to the addict, it must surely be a policy of despair to ruin the lives of hundreds of thousands more people in the hope of cutting the criminals' profits by giving them free rein to saturate the market.

The alternative is suppression: this would require drastic methods. Capital punishment is rightly ruled out in most European countries, but anyone selling or in possession of even 100 grams of 'hard drugs' has ruined or will ruin a large number of other people's lives, and deserves to be imprisoned till the end of his own life, with no provision for remission, for 'life-meaning-life'. The problem with such a sentence is that the prison staff would have no incentives with which to deter violence from desperate life prisoners and to secure their co-operation. This could be overcome by having three regimes within the prison – severe, normal and privileged. The prison staff could move the prisoners from one regime to another in order to give them the necessary powers of punishment and reward, to apply leverage on the prisoners' behaviour, to deter recalcitrance or violence, and to contain it in the severe regime if necessary. This form of imprisonment is discussed more fully in a wider context in Chapter 15 (pp. 171–2).

Addicts should not be treated as criminals but they should never be allowed unsupervised on the streets until their addiction is cured, because they will inevitably have to recruit more addicts in order to pay for the drugs they need themselves. It costs the average European addict about £100 per week to satisfy his or her addiction. Some, like the 'yuppies' who do it for kicks or to relax from the stress of their day's work in the city, are despicable. Others are pitiable, weak and inadequate, leading barren lives, and fall prey to stronger people who lure them into an escape through drugs. Initially the yuppies may finance their addiction from their incomes or minor fraud and the others by petty crime, but, in the end, both find it easier and safer to finance it by selling drugs to others. They have, in effect, a dangerous and contagious disease.

Once they are identified as addicts, therefore, they should be given compulsory treatment in clinics, in custody if necessary, until the doctors are satisfied that the addiction is broken, but thereafter they should be subjected to weekly tests so that, if ever they resume the habit, they can be taken into custody for further treatment. Addicts who proved ready to co-operate positively with the treatment could be allowed to live at home and continue to work, subject to supervision and routine tests to satisfy the clinic that they have not reverted to taking or selling drugs.

Both the clinics and the prison regimes will cost a lot, but these costs can be offset by freezing and, on conviction, seizure of all the assets of anyone arrested for trafficking in drugs. In any event, the long-term price will be greater still unless the spiral is broken.

So long as addiction continues to grow, it will continue to be a generator of violence, not only in Europe and the USA, but also in Colombia, Pakistan and other drug-producing countries. They are in the front line (fifty Colombian judges are believed to have been murdered since 1980) and European countries owe it to them as much as to their own people to cut off the demand.

Computer crime and extortion

The proceeds of computer fraud in the USA are estimated at $3 billion per year. The Stanford Research Institute has calculated that the average computer fraud in the USA costs a major company $425,000, a bank $132,000 and a public authority $220,000, and that criminal proceedings are instigated in less than 1 per cent of computer-related crimes. Courts, moreover, are lenient with white-collar offenders. The FBI estimate that only 1 in 10,000 apprehended computer criminals are currently sent to prison (the figure was 1 in 22 in 1984). US computer crime has been growing at 500 per cent each year and continues to do so.[9] The London Business School estimates British losses from computer crime to be £407 million per year; some consultants think they may be as high as £2,000 million.[10]

Most computer crime is done by dishonest employees who can defraud their institutions of huge sums of money at what they perceive to be little risk. (The figures above suggest that they may be right.) It is now well over ten years since a computer programmer in a US bank discovered the 'Salami technique'. He knew that all bank transactions were rounded off to the nearest cent. Often, however, splits and percentage increments or deductions may result in the computer's recording fractions of a cent. He programmed the computer, in rounding these off, to pay all the fractions of a cent into a secret account of whose existence only he knew. From this account he periodically transferred sums to his normal legal account. Like so many criminals he eventually gave himself away by spending too freely. By that time, the account contained $11 million.[11] But for each person convicted, there may be thousands who are not detected or not prosecuted.

There are many other ways in which skilled computer technicians can insert false programs into computers, for example by combining them with other programs so that the computer carries out its official program quite normally, while secretly carrying out the fraudster's program at the same time.

As well as for fraud, computers can be used to obtain unauthorized information, for commercial espionage or breaching national security. It is remarkably easy to hack into a computer system by remote control without access to the building housing the main computer if the hacker has managed to discover one or more codewords. With more personal computers per head than any other European country, Britain is particularly vulnerable. As well as its uses for criminal gain, the potential of hacking for reconnaissance and planning of terrorist operations is obvious. Government networks (especially in police, intelligence and defence departments) are as vulnerable as bank and other commercial systems.

Computer manufacturers, competing with each other over price, speed and user-friendliness, have been astonishingly slow in devising and building in safeguards to prevent or detect such abuses. Their major users, the big corporations (especially banks), are also the main targets, but most of them seem to prefer to accept a small drain on their profits rather than sacrifice speed and convenience (and frustrate their staff) by tighter security. They may often also prefer not to prosecute for fear that their public image would be destroyed by publicly airing their vulnerability to fraud in sensational court cases.

Computers also offer great opportunities for extortion or malicious damage. It is relatively simple to insert a virus (or rogue program) into a computer, which will automatically be passed on to the software of other computers which have dealings with the infected network. In the case of a bank this can extend all over the world. Damage may be inflicted indiscriminately; in Britain in 1989, for example, the Royal National Institute for the Blind computer picked up a virus from such a network which wrecked large numbers of software discs used for converting programs into braille. The virus programs can be in the form of a 'time bomb'. In 1985 a disgruntled employee in USA, at odds with the insurance company which employed him, inserted a virus into their computer, ready to be activated if they fired him. Two years later (1987) they did fire him, so he triggered it to go off two days after he left, when it erased 168,000 vital records from the computer. He was the first person convicted for inserting a virus (under the criminal offence of 'harmful access to a computer') but, to the fury of the banking and insurance industries, he was sentenced only to seven years' probation.[12]

The damage to banks, insurance companies, mail order firms, and so on can be catastrophic, not least because, when the virus first shows itself, hundreds of thousands or even millions of pounds may have to be spent on checking other programs to see if they are affected. One large insurance company, thanks to a hacker 'having fun', lost a set of computer files *and* the back-up copies. Restoring the information took nearly a year and cost more than £7 million with another £15 million in lost business.[13] The mere threat to trigger a 'time bomb' virus can be used to extort a ransom which a big corporation may think is the lesser of two evils to pay. Like other victims of blackmail, they seldom report it.

Other forms of extortion – such as by threat to kidnap, kill, maim, sabotage, bomb or (increasingly prevalent) to contaminate food or

115

pharmaceutical products – are also used by both terrorists and criminal extortioners. In 1988–9 an extortioner in Britain contaminated, first, pet food and then babyfood and demanded that a ransom be paid into a building society account under a false name; the extortioner withdrew the ransom in small sums from different cash dispensers all over the country. The manufacturers complied, with the approval and co-operation of the police, but it took more than a year before they caught the suspected extortioner making a withdrawal.

Laundering illegal money

Laundering illegal money so that it cannot be traced is an essential process for any criminal or terrorist who has obtained it by theft, fraud, extortion or drug trafficking, and this is an important area of overlap in which the terrorist often turns to the criminal world for professional services. Drugs provide a particularly attractive currency for laundering, with their huge value-to-bulk ratio for smuggling across borders and selling for cash.

There was, for a time, a strong suspicion of links between drug trafficking and the arms trade, with some governments' turning a blind eye to the sources of money used to pay for the arms, either because they wanted to make the sales, or because they wanted to prop up a specific Third World government for political reasons, no matter how.[14] Other big sources of illegal money include smuggled diamonds and gold, stolen goods and securities which may, in aggregate, amount to more than the illegal flow of money from drugs.[15]

Whether illegal money enters a bank in banknotes or by electronic transfer (e.g. of a ransom), the essential is to move it on quickly and cover the traces before the Inland Revenue or police investigation discover it. Professional launderers (including the Mafias) customarily operate shell companies which can account for money by recording fictitious services, or sales of fictitious goods. Mail order firms, companies claiming to provide a large turnover of fast-moving items for cash (e.g. spare parts) and vending machines provide admirable vehicles for 'constructive accounting' to conceal the collection and dispersal of dirty money. So do casinos. Who can prove how much money was scooped up by the croupier at a gaming table?

Banknotes are usually dispersed in relatively small deposits in different names (or individuals and businesses) in different banks in different cities, which are then asked to initiate the transfer of these balances in a series of electronic transactions to other accounts in home or foreign banks, and thence to others, ending up in accounts far away in the names of various unconnected individuals or companies. The hope is that bank confidentiality and the problems of international policing will make them untraceable. R.T. Naylor explains how easy it is to send 'criminal money whizzing around the world at the touch of a computer key'.[16]

Most Western banks (though sadly not all) can now be required by court order to give access to named accounts for inspection by police or fiscal authorities if there is reasonable ground for suspicion that money in them may have been acquired by criminal means. There is, however, sometimes a 'Catch 22' problem in that the police may be unable to produce the necessary evidence to convince the court without access to the accounts, and the courts may refuse to order the access without that evidence. Some banks, aware that much lucrative business may be lost if they lose their reputation for confidentiality, will do their utmost to conceal criminal transactions. In some countries, mainly in the Third World but also in some offshore tax havens which thrive on financial independence, governments and courts refuse to allow any access at all.[17]

In December 1988 the Central Banks of twelve countries, including all the 'Summit Seven' (Canada, France, Germany, Italy, Japan, UK and USA), the Benelux trio, Sweden and Switzerland, signed the 'Declaration of Basel', committing themselves to identifying their clients and sources of funds, refusing suspicious transactions and co-operating with judicial enquiries. The United Nations Vienna Convention, signed in the same month but subject to ratification, will commit those signatories who ratify it to imposing more rigorous controls to catch drug traffickers, to seizure of their assets, and to mutual judicial co-operation in prosecuting them. Ratification, however, may take some years and, even then, effectiveness will depend on how far individual banks are willing to honour their obligations at the risk of losing some of their most profitable clients. Self-interest, both for governments and corporations, is a compelling incentive for seeking loopholes.

The best solution for this may be for the same twelve countries – or at the very least the Summit Seven and Switzerland – to introduce currency controls to make it unlawful for banks based in their countries to move any money for any purpose into or out of foreign banks which do not provide effective provision for access, and which decline to subject themselves to inspection by an international monitoring organization. A total boycott by all these leading banking nations could have a crippling effect on any country, or on any of its banks, which failed to co-operate. It could also cripple some of the tax havens in small independent states, though many of them are probably small enough to subsist on rackets in conjunction with countries other than the big ones which apply the boycott. Something more than a boycott may be needed to deal with the bigger and more unscrupulous tax havens – perhaps a blockade and a threat of 'secondary boycott' of any other country's banks which deal with them. An example of this was Panama until the USA helped to oust

General Noriega, himself accused of being heavily involved in drug trafficking. A large proportion of the billions of dollars built up by the drug barons was alleged to have been banked there with Noriega's connivance, and drawn on to finance further criminal and terrorist activities. Though Panama was an extreme case, there will always be other small states, especially island states, whose leaders may be tempted by the huge riches on offer.

For these controls to work, however, it would be essential for the international monitoring organization to be broadly constituted, with its own activities internally monitored by having enough people from different countries a party to each activity to guarantee the detection of corruption or coercion.

The speed and scope of modern computer systems offer huge potential power, for detecting malpractice, monitoring and investigation, to the larger nations with an interest in international order. If the USSR and China begin to share their interest, it may become practicable and justifiable to use this power to the full.

Chapter ten

European co-operation against terrorism

Interpol

Interpol has 136 member countries. These inevitably include a large number who would never trust *all* the others with sensitive political or intelligence information, and a smaller number whom virtually none of the others would trust at all. Most, however, share a common interest in co-operation against ordinary crime, for example national police forces warning each other when a suspected criminal is believed to have crossed a border or to be in possession of forged documents.

Article 3 of the Interpol Constitution specifically bars its member countries from intervention in or investigation of military, political, religious or racial matters. Two resolutions were adopted by its General Assembly in 1984 giving guidance in the interpretation of Article 3. It was resolved that crimes committed against innocent victims or against property outside the area of conflict, regardless of their motivation, should not be regarded as political; it was also resolved that Article 3 did not debar members from sharing technical information about terrorism, provided that the information did not discriminate for solely political purposes. Members were encouraged to share information relevant to prevention of terrorism as freely as their national laws would allow.[1]

In 95 per cent of cases members would no doubt act in the spirit of those resolutions, but Interpol resolutions are not legally binding, and experience unfortunately shows that when national self-interest is involved it usually prevails; and the countries which sponsor or sympathize with the terrorists concerned would certainly not co-operate.

Interpol is, of course, very useful to police who are fighting normal crime. In the field of terrorism, however, its greatest value probably lies in the police officers' getting to know each other, thereby facilitating bilateral co-operation, which is by far the most effective kind of co-operation in sensitive matters.

The United Nations

The United Nations, not surprisingly, has proved virtually useless as a vehicle for concerted international action against terrorism. No matter how indiscriminate and how horrific the casualties, there will always be some countries which will class the act as part of a 'war of liberation' against a 'military imperialist' or 'economic imperialist' or 'neo-colonialist' or 'oppressive' government. These definitions are applied on its own appraisal by any state finding it convenient to condone a terrorist attack. Every hijacker – every political terrorist, in fact – knows that there will always be a number of sanctuaries available for him. If US or Israeli victims are involved some countries will approve any terrorist act as a matter of course. Framing resolutions in words to which no one will object produces phrases which are deliberately vague or ambiguous, and so hedged with exceptions (e.g. of 'politically motivated' acts) that they have no real meaning. After the Munich Olympics massacre in 1972, even some of the radical Arab countries were shocked by the intensity of the world's disgust, which rubbed off on the reputations of all Arab and other Islamic countries, and they agreed to participate in a study group on the prevention of terrorism. After five years of laborious discussion, it had changed its terms of reference to seeking an explanation of how certain people were driven to taking lives, 'including their own', that is to explain and (for some members) to justify terrorism rather than to co-operate in preventing or punishing it.[2]

The Tokyo, Hague and Montreal conventions

When hijacking first became a major scourge in the 1960s and early 1970s, there were three conventions which aimed to improve international response to it.

The Tokyo Convention of 1963 extended the jurisdiction of a state to its aircraft anywhere in the world, and agreed that it could seek extradition of hijackers wherever they landed. In practice, however, this could be applied only between countries which had extradition treaties unequivocally covering this crime.

The Hague Convention of 1970 extended this jurisdiction to any aircraft leased by the state, or which had landed on its territory *en route*. Signatories also committed themselves to 'extradite or prosecute' hijackers.

The Montreal Convention of 1971 incorporated attacks on aircraft on the ground or attacks on airport facilities such as would put lives at risk.[3]

All three have been ratified by more than 100 states (107, 113 and 111 respectively). All, however, leave a loophole whereby any signatory state can decline to extradite if it judges that the offence was 'political'. Moreover 'extradite or prosecute' does not mean 'extradite or convict'. No international agreement can commit the judiciary of a state to find a person guilty so, to evade the obligation to extradite, it has merely to prosecute the alleged offender and acquit.

TREVI and Bilateral Co-operation

In 1976 the countries of the European Economic Community (then nine) established a structure under the name of TREVI (a French acronym for International Terrorism, Radicalism, Extremism and Violence). The structure is directed by regular meetings of EC Interior Ministers. Under their policy guidance a number of working groups were set up, one comprising the senior permanent officials of the ministries and others charged with improving exchange of information and intelligence assessments, equipping of bodies concerned with combating terrorism and internationally organized crime. This last group therefore monitored the links between terrorism and the Mafia, drug cartels, etc. which help to finance it, and the laundering of illegal money (see Chapter 9).

Under the supervision and policy direction of these meetings of ministers and of senior officials, there were regular contacts between police and intelligence chiefs and day-to-day liaison between national police co-ordinating bureaux.[4] In Britain's case, this function is performed by the European Liaison Section of the Special Branch (the police intelligence service) at New Scotland Yard.

The principal value of TREVI is probably its role in developing personal contact and trust between individual police and intelligence officers of the (now twelve) member countries. Though meetings of all twelve are of value in co-ordination and exchange of ideas, really sensitive information will never be thrown into a pool, even of this size. (Greece, for example, has a reputation for sympathy for the Arab cause and for bad port and airport security which must inhibit total frankness on some subjects.) There can, however, be total trust in *bilateral* relationships between individual officers of certain countries (notably Britain, France, Germany and the Netherlands) who know each other personally. It was, for example, information obtained by the Germans from the Hamadei brothers in 1987 and passed on to the French Surveillance Service, which greatly facilitated the decimation of both the most vicious domestic French Terrorist Movement (AD) and the Arab groups which had killed ten French people in Paris in 1986 (see pp. 66–7). Similar personal co-operation exists between officers on first-name terms in the British Special Branch and German BKA, the British Security Service (MI5) and the German BfV, and between British and German officers respectively with their Dutch equivalents. Even within this network of trust, what is exchanged 'between, say, a British and a Dutch officer will be passed to their German colleague only if they agree that he needs to know, and vice versa. 'Need to know' is the cardinal basis of trust in all intelligence work, when the lives of informants are at stake.

Similar co-operation has had similarly beneficial results between anti-terrorist commandos. In 1977 the German GSG9 were at the side of the Dutch BBE at the train hijack near Glimmen, and were able to offer them the use of their frame charges, which happened to fit perfectly the need to blow in the door of the train for the successful BBE rescue (see p. 68). In the same year, a British SAS major and sergeant accompanied the German GSG9 in the final stages of the shadowing of the hijacked Lufthansa aircraft through Dubai and Aden to Mogadishu Airport. The SAS stun grenades proved particularly useful in the rescue, in which the two SAS men took part. Thanks to frequent training exchanges and liaison visits, they both had personal friends in the GSG9 team. (see p. 49).

This example, in fact, illustrates the breadth of the network of German–British friendships. At the height of the linked Schleyer kidnap and Lufthansa hijack in 1977 (see pp. 48–50) Chancellor Helmut Schmidt, to many peoples' surprise, found time to fulfil a long-standing speaking engagement in London. This enabled him to pay a low-profile private visit to his friend Jim Callaghan, the British Prime Minister, at which they were joined by GSG9 and SAS officers. As well as having stun grenades, the SAS knew the Gulf, South Arabian and East African area well and had personal contacts (again on first-name terms) with the Foreign Ministers of some of the Gulf States. The setting up and triumphant success of the operation therefore owed much to personal friendships covering the range from Prime Ministers to sergeants (see p. 49).

Throughout this book, there are examples of the enormous strength added by family and personal relationships within criminal and terrorist organizations. The same role can be played at every level by government and professional friendships in co-operation to defeat them. The prime dividend from the formal and institutional structures is to further these relationships and to give authority and discretion for trusted friends to work together without inhibition. The professionals always want to co-operate. It is for the politicians to provide the political will, the means and the scope for them to do so.

The Council of Europe

IN 1977 the Council of Europe adopted their European Convention for the Suppression of Terrorism (ECST). Up to 1989 seventeen of the twenty-one member countries had ratified it. Article 1 was a determined attempt to overcome the 'political offence' loophole, the signatories agreeing that, for extradition purposes, certain offences would *not* be regarded as 'political', including kidnap, attacks on diplomats, hijack, hostage-taking and endangering life by the use of bombs or automatic guns. If a state declined a request to extradite, it would submit the case to its competent authorities for prosecution. To get the Convention signed by enough members to be worth while, however, the Council had to insert two additional articles which totally defeated the object: that there was no obligation to extradite if there were substantial grounds for believing that the accused person might be prosecuted on account of race, religion, nationality or political opinion (Article 5); and that, notwithstanding Article 1, any state may reserve the right to refuse extradition for any offence which it considers to be political (Article 13).

This would mean, in practice, that no state need take any notice of Article 1 if it considered it more in its national interest to evade it. To make sure of this, Article 14 permits any signatory state to withdraw from the Convention, instantly and without notice, simply by notifying the Council of Europe that it has done so.[5] On top of this, as with the Tokyo, Hague and Montreal Conventions, a country not wishing to extradite had only to go through the motions of prosecution and acquittal to honour its obligations.

The reality of this had been illustrated in January 1977 when an Arab, wanted by both the German and Israeli governments for allegedly (some say avowedly) master-minding the Munich Olympics massacre, entered France as the PLO representative for the funeral of a Palestinian murdered a few days earlier in Paris. His name was Abu Daoud but he was travelling on a false Iraqi passport under the name of Youssef Raji ben Hanna. He claimed that the French government knew of his coming and had promised him immunity. If this was so, it did not appear to be known to the French intelligence service who, acting on a tip-off, arrested Abu Daoud at his hotel. Both the German and Israeli governments applied for his extradition but the French court released him on legal technicalities; for example they tried him under his false name and rejected the German request on the grounds that the Germans had failed to establish his identity or to provide the necessary documents. Far from giving the Germans more time to do these things, they flew him to Algiers with almost indecent haste four days after he had entered France. It was alleged that the French government was concerned about prejudicing its relations with Arab countries and that the Germans had not pressed as hard as they might lest they suffer further terrorist attacks to release Abu Daoud. Acid comments in the French press included one in *Le Monde*, that the government had 'police that is not taking orders, a judiciary that is taking orders – a sad record'.[6]

When national self-interests are at stake, even the most responsible of countries, it seems, will look for loopholes.

The Economic Summit

Reference was made earlier to the potential punch of the seven nations which meet each year for the Economic Summit – Canada, France, Germany, Italy, Japan, UK and USA. Meeting in Bonn in 1978, their Presidents and Prime Ministers, led by Chancellor Helmut Schmidt, resolved to impose a total air boycott on any country which failed to extradite or prosecute a hijacker. Under such a boycott, no aircraft operated by the offending country would be allowed to land at any airport in any of the seven countries; nor would any aircraft of any origin which had landed on its way at an airport in the offending country. Nor would any aircraft from any of the seven countries land at any of the offending country's airports.[7]

Since these seven countries operate 80 per cent of the Western world's commercial air traffic, this boycott would hit the country's airlines and its economy very hard.

The boycott has never been applied and, in cases where it might have seemed justified, there have been strong reasons for not applying it. One such case was the hijack of TWA Flight 847 to Beirut in 1985. The airport was not under the control of the Lebanese government, but of the Shia Militia, who would certainly not have negotiated the release of the American passengers and crew without the hijackers' going free. Similarly, when the hijack of a Kuwaiti aircraft ended in Algiers in 1988, the Algerian government could not have saved the passengers except at the price of giving safe custody to the hijackers back to the Hezbollah-controlled area of Lebanon.

At later summits, the seven agreed (in 1984) to co-operate over expulsion of known terrorists, including those with diplomatic status; to restrict diplomatic premises; to review arms sales to countries supporting terrorism; to scrutinize loopholes; and to take specific steps to facilitate co-operation between each other's police and intelligence services. In 1986 they strengthened these measures and named Syria and Libya as governments known to support terrorism. In 1987 they agreed to make no concessions to terrorists or to their sponsors; to improve airport and maritime security; and to extend the boycott agreed in Bonn to attacks on aircraft on the ground. This, no doubt, was a reaction to the seizure of the Pan Am aircraft at Karachi Airport on the ground in 1986, leading to the loss of many lives.

The main dividend from the summit meetings was, as with TREVI, the encouragement and authority it gave for co-operation between police and intelligence professionals. Nevertheless, the seven countries do have enormous coercive power and they have now discussed and prepared the means of applying it. It remains to be seen whether, and in what circumstances, they will have the political will to pay the short-term price of using that power, and whether they would all stand together.

Schengen and the European internal market

Under the Schengen Agreement signed in June 1985, France, Germany, Belgium, the Netherlands and Luxembourg agreed to open their frontiers with each other in January 1990, three years in advance of the European internal market to be implemented under the Single European Act (SEA) at the end of 1992. The precise details of the Schengen Agreement (like those of the internal market, which will include all the twelve EC countries), are still being negotiated. (As a result of developments in East Germany, some of the wording needed to be amended, so the full implementation was slightly delayed.) In both cases the aim will be movement of persons, goods, services and capital across each other's frontiers as freely as they move across state borders in the USA. The current regulations between the five under the Schengen Agreement, and the teething troubles of its first two years in operation, will provide invaluable experience in the run-up to the full internal market in 1992.

The essential feature is that, while internal frontiers will be open, external frontiers will be tighter. It will be necessary for all the governments to agree, for example, that if another government requests them to arrest a named individual if he or she attempts to enter or leave through an external frontier, they are bound to accept that request, and to extradite the person to the requesting country.[8]

This alone, however, will not compensate for the loss of the internal frontiers as currently the most effective places at which to spot and arrest criminals and terrorists. In Germany, for example, of 900 million people who cross the borders each year, 100,000 are arrested – half from wanted lists and half due to the on-the-spot instinct of officials.[9] The only substitute will be to give the police in each country a reliable means of checking the identity of any person – resident or visitor – any time, anywhere. At present, however, in some EC countries, citizens are not required to carry any means of identification.

The need for this power is made even stronger by the number of immigrants, foreign temporary workers and visitors in Europe at any one time. And with so many immigrant citizens in all the EC countries, it will be impossible to distinguish between citizens and visitors without asking to see some proof of identification. Technical means available or becoming available for providing means of identification, both for residents and visitors, with safeguards against impersonation, are discussed later in this book (Chapter 12).

125

In the Schengen negotiations, it proved easier to agree on the abolition of border checks of people than of some kinds of goods. Considerable difficulties also arose over harmonization of laws and practices between the five countries, especially in the fields of arms control, facilities for hot pursuit of suspected criminals and terrorists across borders, international surveillance, the linkage of national police computer data bases, police liaison and communications, judicial processes, visa requirements, work permits for aliens, long-term residence rights and social welfare facilities to which aliens are entitled.

Weapons, for example, are relatively easy to acquire and possess in France and Belgium, which worries the Dutch, who have strict gun laws. On the other hand, the Dutch are permissive about soft drugs, which worries the Germans. Laxity in either gun laws or narcotics control will also worry the British if not resolved before 1992. And unless work permits and social welfare facilities are made roughly equivalent, immigrants, no matter where they enter the EC, will flood into the country which seems most advantageous for them.[10]

Other problems will arise, such as Denmark's relations with other (non-EC) Nordic countries, the special relationship of Switzerland with its contiguous neighbours, France, Germany and Italy, and the pressure of migration from North Africa to southern European countries.[11]

These problems are examined more fully in Chapter 17.

Part III

Technological development

Chapter eleven

Computerized intelligence systems

Technical and human intelligence

Every successful anti-terrorist campaign in history has underlined the decisive part played by intelligence. Terrorists living clandestinely, whether amongst 10 million people in a city or in inaccessible jungles or mountains, are very hard to find. So are their irregular auxiliaries, living a normal life with a normal job, but working for the terrorists – or carrying out terrorist operations – in their spare time. To have any hope of finding them, it is necessary to discover some of the people who support them, or who at least live in their environment as neighbours and have some awareness of their activities. These people can be watched or questioned to gain leads towards the hard core. This was one of the secrets of the success of General Dalla Chiesa in Italy (see Chapter 3).

The initial break-in is achieved by a mixture of patient watching and surveillance to spot unusual movements and then to check them against other pieces of information. Once a supporter is recognized as such, individual surveillance will almost always lead to results.[1]

This is where the combination of human and technical intelligence pays dividends. Human intelligence is still the most important, since no machine can yet match the perception of the human brain in integrating sight, sound, memory, instincts and 'hunches' to sense that something is or is not as it should be. The intelligence analyst, however, can combine these perceptions with relevant facts from other sources, and these include the now quite remarkable ability of computers to identify relevant facts instantaneously and call up any other facts which have links with them. The products of other technical aids, such as high resolution cameras and surveillance systems, can also be fed in.

The German computerized intelligence system, developed after the Schleyer case in 1977, was described in Chapter 4 (pp. 55–60). Examples were given of the 'trawl net' and 'scanner search' in operation, whereby information about a very large number of people could be checked, either 'positively' to find one who matched known characteristics of a wanted person, or 'negatively' to eliminate them from the enquiry. As each year goes by, the police computers can do these searches faster, in more detail and more reliably, but of course they also depend on the extent of the information about individuals, vehicles, etc. in the data bank.[2]

Britain now has a similar system (with the acronym HOLMES) which can gather and display any linking facts, or confirm that there are none, within thirty seconds. This has been particularly valuable in solving 'serial' crimes, like sequences of bombs, terrorist killings, rapes or child murders. Most criminals and terrorists have a *modus operandi* in which their combination of characteristics and practices can leave a signature as unique as their fingerprints, or as recognizable as their scent to a bloodhound. Another British system can make digital records of facial characteristics on photographs (acronym FACES). A high percentage of terrorist and other crimes are committed by people about whom there is already some information in the data bank, very often including a photograph (this certainly applied to most of the hard-core terrorists in Northern Ireland, Germany and Italy). People who have witnessed an incident may be able to describe at least some characteristics of a person they saw, helped by expert questioning. Each characteristic will eliminate a large number of people recorded on the computer and it may eventually leave only a handful of 'possibles'. Presented with photographs of these, witnesses are far more likely to recognize the wanted person than when it was necessary to turn over the pages of a huge book of photographs.[3] The computer has also greatly increased the speed at which fingerprints can be matched.[4]

All of these aids to intelligence, however, are based on binary computers, that is computers which can just say yes or no, albeit to millions of questions every second. They offer, in fact, merely a much faster and more compact means of doing what card indexes have provided for nearly two centuries. On a punched card, there is room for a limited number of bits of information in the form of punched holes, perhaps a choice of 2,000 holes. Each hole indicates some personal quality, such as height, colour of eyes, year of birth, language capability, trade or profession. If a nineteenth-century personnel manager wanted, say, a carpenter who spoke French, was unmarried, in good health and under 25, he had only to put a bunch of cards through the machine (initially using knitting needles and later with jets of compressed air): the only cards thrown up would be of people whose card had a hole indicating each one of these requirements. The computer now contains vastly more than 2,000 bits of information. Today a common silicon chip a few millimetres square can hold 250,000 bits, on each of which it can say only yes or no (like the punched card) but it can say it several million times a second. (Rather quicker than the knitting needles.) If the silicon chip is part of a simple system of parallel computers, information can be scanned at up to 25 million bits a second, looking for entries in the data base which match the question. It is thus very quick to locate, say, every recorded reference to the registration number of a particular car – or even of all the cars whose number contains, say, the letters JN and the figures 25, which may be all that the witness managed to remember.

Modern computer systems (including HOLMES) can now make logical inferences and act on them without further instructions. Intensive and highly competitive research is going on to enable them to match other capabilities of the human brain – creativity, taste, emotion, conscience, judgement, instincts and hunches – all the kinds of things which add up to a quality for which we use the other meaning of the word 'intelligence'. When a computer system matches one of these capabilities (such is its ability to make and act on logical inferences), this is what we know as Artificial Intelligence (AI).

The computer and the brain

The brain of even a very stupid person can do a great many things that the most advanced computer cannot yet do. It can recognize a face instantly. It can pick out a voice amongst a hundred other voices in a crowded room and know at once whose voice it is. It can have a feeling that something is not quite right without having any idea why. The brain does this through a complicated linkage between millions of brain cells which can send millions of electrical impulses through millions of cell junctions, each sparking a response in another cell. There are, in a human brain, something like a million million (a thousand billion) such electrical contacts (cell junctions or synapses) with an as-yet unplumbed system of links. Neural research has shown that the brain operates by a series of logical inferences, each one of which may involve several thousand inter-cell reactions. Each such logical inference initiates another, in the same way as a series of successive programming steps taken by a modern computer, the answer to question A prompting question B, and so on. It is known how long it takes for the brain cell (neurone) to fire its electrical impulse. It is also known how long it takes a brain to do a 'flash' recognition of a face. There is time only for a maximum of 100 programming steps for this recognition.[5] If eventually, the complex linkages between the million million electrical contacts can be discovered, it may eventually be possible to match these programming steps in a system of 'fine-grained' parallel computers, that is a system of several thousand or even a million tiny and very simple computers linked on a single board. The research into these fine-grained (or 'neural') computers is going ahead very fast.

The most rapid progress has been in the matter of size. A computer system using thermionic valves and metal grids, as in Alan Turing's first computer in the 1940s, would have needed a factory complex the size of Greater London to house the million million electrical contacts to match those in a human brain. In the 1960s the replacement of valves by transistors would have reduced this to the size of a large concert hall. The current microprocessors could fit them all into a small room. By the end of the 1990s it should be possible to cram the million million contacts into a space the size of the human brain.

Logical inferences

A brain generally performs its most sophisticated functions – its instincts, emotions, judgements, flash recognitions, etc. – by learning from experience. It does this by its ability to strengthen the relevant synapses when a number of experiences passes a certain threshold. A slug, for example, with the simplest of brains, can be given laboratory access to a plant which tastes good but has unpleasant after-effects. After a number of experiences it learns to avoid that plant. Similarly if it encounters an obstacle it seeks a way round it – lateral thinking – and after a bit of experience it learns to avoid the original route and takes the detour from the start. A computer too can be programmed to do this kind of thing.

The more advanced a brain is, the more material it will have had programmed into it before birth. A kitten or a human baby, for example, both know 'instinctively', when they leave the womb, that food comes from a nipple to which they are guided by scent. As they grow, they are taught new skills by their mothers, as a cat teaches her kittens to hunt. A kitten separated from its mother at birth and brought up amongst rodents will never hunt such rodents, and would probably starve if released into the wild.

The purely data-based computer can be programmed to make a whole series of specific one-in-a-million yes-or-no choices, each question prompted by the answer to the last one. To approach the human brain, the next step is for it to become 'knowledge-based', that is to make logical inferences based on experience (like the slug). Each logical inference comes from a series of choices based on 'if-then' rules, leading to a *probable* conclusion, just as a toddler learns to recognize, say, a particular type of car. First, he discovers that a square box with wheels is called a car. He sees a bigger one and says 'Car' but his parents say 'No, that is a truck'. Then he sees others which are not quite the same as the family Vauxhall Astra, for example two others in the street have slightly different shapes (say an Austin Maestro and Volkswagen Golf). Unlike simple binary decisions, his recognition is a muzzy one, based on a balance of evidence and he may not always get it right. But when he does, he is rewarded by his parents' approval. Soon, as they drive along, he is pointing to cars as they pass, shouting 'Maestro', 'Astra', 'Golf', 'Sierra'. A boy or 3 or 4 years old may be doing this with total confidence long before he can read. He can also recognize that he is looking at a horse not a cow, or a duck not a goose. He could not conceivably explain how he tells the difference. He just knows.

A computer can be similarly trained to make logical inferences. Each inference may be based on 100 or 1,000 individual binary decisions, some of them grouped into key words or concepts. Current knowledge-based computers can work through 30,000 logical inferences per second (LIPS). Coming on stream now are parallel computer systems capable of 200,000 LIPS, possibly involving as many as 200 million binary decisions per second. The potential of this for police intelligence systems is obvious. And the pace of development continues. The fine-grained parallel computers now in their early stages may make even this look like an ocean liner trying to race a jet aircraft.

Perhaps another analogy will help. Take an oil painting of a mouse eating some grains of corn, with a cat looking intently at it from behind a bush, and a dog trotting along a path nearby. That picture is made up, in fact, of a number of tiny grains of pigment, each of which absorbs most of the spectrum of white light hitting it, and reflects just one colour, perhaps with tinges of a few others. Like an intersection of conductors in an old-time computer grid, it says 'no' to every other wavelength of the spectrum (red, yellow, green) but 'yes' to violet with a tinge of blue. There will no doubt one day be a high-resolution full-colour fax which could faithfully reproduce that process in its computers each end – a purely data-based operation. The human eye, however, will look at the picture as a picture and the brain will make logical inferences. It knows from experience that the cat will spring at the mouse; it also knows that when the dog sees a sudden movement by the cat it will probably give chase – probably, not certainly. Thus the brain takes in a whole story in a fraction of a second – quite unconscious that it is actually looking at a complex jumble of tiny grains of pigment, the means of communication of an idea in the mind of an artist to the perceptions and inferences of whoever looks at the picture. That is the kind of challenge facing computer science.

Expert systems

The development of knowledge-based computers able to make logical inferences makes it possible for non-professionals to have instant access to a range of expertise far beyond what any one person could master. Given a portable 'intelligent computer' a police officer investigating at the scene of a crime, for example, will be able to feed the evidence into his computer which, either from its own memory or through the links with the main computer, will at once flash on to his screen any linking data (e.g. that the car whose number he has fed in is owned by Mr So-and-so, who was involved in a previous case, and whose *modus operandi* included certain recognizable idiosyncracies).[6] It will, if appropriate, prompt him on things he should look out for. To give an idea of the scope of two such computers now in police service in Britain, there is one about the size of a pocket book or a 'Walkman' which costs less than £100 but has a memory containing the equivalent of a 300-page reference book; another, a portable desk-top computer, has inside it the equivalent of a 30-volume *Encyclopaedia Britannica*. Should this not contain all that is needed, it can, by means of a modem through any telephone line, ask whatever questions it needs to from the main computer at police headquarters. These systems will all make logical inferences, and may also be able to eliminate many lines of enquiry on which otherwise much time would be wasted.[7]

Obviously not every police officer on patrol can be equipped with such a computer. When any patrol officer sends in a report or emergency call, however, a knowledge-based computer at police headquarters could very quickly search the data base to provide evidence of links which could be sent back to the officer, or used to brief others for necessary action.

Expert systems have proved particularly useful in the medical and legal professions, especially in the USA, where doctors and lawyers receive very large fees. To save their time, patients or clients are asked routine questions by a computer, whose next question depends on the answer to the previous one. Before seeing the doctor, for example, the patient might be asked 'Did you feel a tightness in the chest? Did you feel any aches or pains in your arms? Were you short of breath? Did you detect any bubbling of fluid in your lungs when you breathed?', and so on.

The doctor would then start the consultation with some fairly conclusive evidence about the source of the trouble. Similarly the staff of a lawyer, knowing the client has come to get advice about a traffic accident, or a divorce, or a boundary dispute with a neighbour, would set the computer to ask an appropriate series of routine questions. Armed with the results, the lawyer could get straight to the heart of the case.[8]

The programming of an expert system requires a combined effort between two experts; an expert in the *subject*; and an expert in *computers*, known in this context as a 'knowledge engineer'. The subject expert (doctor, lawyer, police or intelligence officer) knows the line of questioning to pursue, and the knowledge engineer converts this into a program on the computer.

Another advantage of expert systems is that they can be constantly improved to take account of developments and experience. The British police, for example, have a great deal of successful experience in hostage negotiation.[9] Each time there is another such incident, the appropriate expert, with the knowledge engineer, can amend the program available to assist this kind of negotiation.

Neural computer systems

The neural or fine-grained parallel computer systems are developing at a hectic pace on both sides of the Atlantic. They differ from the coupling of normal computers in parallel in that they consist of a very large number of 'ultra-micro computers', each with very limited capability. These are known as reduced instruction set computers (Risc). Each one is connected to a number of others, and its own operations have a direct effect on theirs. (Some of the opportunities this can present for computer crime were discussed in Chapter 9.)

This is similar to what is known about the interaction of the human brain cells (neurones) and for that reason the low Risc ultra-microcomputers are also often referred to as neurones. Even with several thousand of them mounted on one board, they still have a very long way to go to match the brain, but computer scientists are confident that they have found the right road to get there. It is significant that psychologists are now co-operating with computer scientists in the research. The quantum leaps from transistors through personal computers to ultra-microcomputers during the last quarter-century suggest that some things now in the realms of science fiction may come sooner that we imagine.[10]

This will have great potential in the field of European anti-terrorist intelligence, with linked neural computer systems able to handle a vastly increased volume of data and to identify and recognize people or things from scanty evidence in the way the human brain does. The capabilities of trawl net and scanner searches could then also, however, have frightening implications for civil liberties unless there is a built-in monitoring system to prevent their abuse.

Chapter twelve

Identification and detection of impersonation

Identity cards, passports and visas

Access control is the most important of all the basic routine security measures, whether it is control of access to a factory, a computer centre, a high security office, an airfield or an aircraft. 'The strongest castle walls are not proof against a traitor within.' Good perimeter surveillance is best bypassed by entering the front gate by trickery, or thanks to the laxity of the security guard.

Most people in Western Europe carry at least one plastic card which is personal to them only, such as Access, Visa, bankers' card or cheque card. A large number carry passes: people working in airports, the BBC, vulnerable oil installations, computer centres, and so on. None appears to resent this; nor do people feel that their freedom is curtailed by it. Most of them probably take some pride in belonging to the club, and feel a shade superior to people with visitor's tags or temporary passes. Yet there is often strong resistance to the issue of a national identity (ID) card.

Most passes contain a photograph (usually behind heat-sealed plastic) and a signature; so do most national ID cards and passports. Passes, credit cards and ID cards almost always contain a black strip containing machine-readable electronic or magnetic data as a guard against forgery. But none of these things gives any really reliable proof that the person presenting the card is the person to whom it was issued.

The Germans carry ID cards, signed and with a photograph. The German government in 1987 prepared a scheme for machine-readable identity cards and machine-readable Euro-passports, but they have not yet been issued. When they come into use, the machine-readable strip will be able to activate the national police computer to check whether there are any recorded data about the holder.

Many sensitive establishments – and an increasing number of hotels – issue key cards, whose electronic data, when pushed into a slot, will operate the lock. Other passes are in the form of a tag, which the holders carry on their lapel; there is a reader focusing a beam across the door, which will operate the lock if the lapel tag gives the correct return signal back along the beam. The more sophisticated reader can also be programmed to record each time each cardholder goes in or out of that door. This is particularly useful in spotting anyone who is abusing the right of access, for example to operate a fraudulent program on a computer. The existence of such a system is a powerful deterrent against fraud.

A more advanced form of card is the 'smart card'. This contains its own microprocessor, with a memory that is small, but still able to record quite enough personal data to identify the holder and detect impersonation plus a lot of other information if needed. The card may be passive (reacting to a signal sent out by the reader) or active (the card containing a power source and sending out its own signal). An active smart card need be only the size, thickness and weight of the smallest calculator. A passive smart card is simply a normal plastic card, different only because it has a microcircuit printed on it, and some cost less than £2.[1]

As with the processing of intelligence data (see Chapter 11), the fast-developing neural computers may open up untold possibilities for uses in conjunction with smart cards, because of the huge volume of data they will be able to store and process, and the speed and scope of their capabilities of recognition and linkage.[2]

Anti-impersonation

If ID cards and machine-readable passports are issued by the EC governments, it will be well worth while to incorporate in them data with which to detect impersonation. The method is to measure and match some biometric characteristic unique to the person to whom the card was issued, such as digitally recorded fingerprint data. These data can be recorded on a smart card, or on the memory of the main computer, or ideally on both.

The need for this was proved in Germany in 1986, when the Red Army Faction kidnapped and murdered an American serviceman for the sole purpose of stealing his military ID card in order to gain access to a US Force base for a car containing a bomb (see pp. 50–1). The photograph and signature on a card are not reliable; guards, especially in bad light, will usually be satisfied if it appears to be a genuine card. It is also relatively easy (with the document forgery equipment which most sophisticated terrorists now have) to make a substitute photograph look quite plausible, though the terrorists did not find that necessary in this case. It would be almost as quick, and far more reliable, for the person presenting a card at the gate to place it in a slot and put the appropriate finger on a scanner to match it with the card. The terrorists might just as easily have stolen the card without killing its owner, or persuaded a disgruntled pass holder to 'lend' them his pass.

The process of enrolling an authorized person with a fingerprint-scanning access control system, and thereafter using it to monitor his entry, is very simple. To enrol, he places his finger on the scanner and, when the data have been converted into digital form, the machine inserts it into the memory on his smart card and/or into the memory of the establishment's main computer. If it goes on to the main computer, he is also given a personal identification number (PIN) so that, when he wants to gain access, he can call up his data on the memory as he places his finger on the scanner. The enrolment process takes less than a minute. The entry verification (with smart card or PIN) takes only about four seconds and can, if required, be used to operate an electronic lock.[3]

There is the theoretical possibility of a finger's being cut off from a kidnapped person and used – like the stolen ID card – to gain entry. Alternatively a plastic match could be made from a cast. In either case, however, one way to overcome this would be by incorporating a check which would operate only if the bloodstream was flowing in the finger.

The retina is as unique as a fingerprint, but needs to be read by a laser gun pointed into the eye. This meets with a certain amount of consumer-resistance, but its proponents claim that it is both quick and reliable.

Voice characteristics offer a means of speaker verification which is economical to install, and has very low false rejection and false acceptance rates. The makers claim fewer than one error in 10,000. To enrol, each individual repeats a number of predetermined words so that variations in pronunciation can be captured. To obtain entry, speakers enter their PIN and are prompted to say a word chosen at random from those recorded. This guards against abuse. If the number of authorized people is small, the PIN can be dispensed with; the speaker is then prompted to speak a number of predetermined words and the computer matches these with all the recorded profiles to see if it matches any of them. An advantage of voice verification is that the characteristics come satisfactorily through a telephone.[4]

The vein-check works on the principle that the vein pattern on the back of the hand or wrist is as unique as a fingerprint. It can be read very quickly by passing a diode across it, just as a jar of ketchup in a supermarket is identified from its bar code and charged at the check-out point.

The genetic molecule (DNA) found in all body fluids is equally unique, but at present the matching process requires laboratory tests taking several hours, so it has no application to access control, though it has proved extremely valuable in forensic tests to convict criminals (for traces of blood, semen, saliva, etc.).

The digital recording of the fingerprint or the vein pattern probably offer the most practical and reliable means for use on internationally linked police records as part of a European system. The appropriate data could be recorded on every ID card and passport. Visitors entering the EC from outside could be verified by matching their fingerprint or vein pattern to their passports; alternatively, if they are from countries like Libya and Syria, with a record of issuing forged passports, a condition of entry could be a visa card on which the data had been recorded by the EC Embassy or Consulate issuing it, provided that the Embassy had some means of vetting the authenticity of the applicant.

Eventually, if public opinion comes round to accepting the desirability of everyone carrying means of identification incorporating one of these guards against impersonation, the potential of modern computer systems (especially neural systems) is such that every citizen's data could be held on the national computer, and links between co-operating countries (the EC and its neighbours, eventually including Eastern Europe and the USSR, plus Japan, Canada, Australia, and others) could create a system approaching 100 per cent reliability *within and between those countries*. Unfortunately the countries most likely to sponsor terrorists or drug trafficking are the ones which would not participate. The only answer, for people coming from those countries, would be for visa applicants to be fully investigated before visas were issued, and for the digital data on the visa card to be transmitted and recorded on the national computer system of the country to which the visa gave entry.

The civil rights implications of identification and anti-impersonation techniques are discussed in Chapters 14 and 17.

Detecting hijackers

El Al aircraft have been the most desirable targets for Arab hijackers since 1968 but, after the first one, they have virtually never succeeded, because security is much tighter than on other airlines. After their first hijack in 1968 (see pp. 19–20) El Al put armed sky-marshals amongst the passengers, with a locked bullet-proof door sealing off the flight deck. Two attempts to hijack El Al aircraft at Munich in February 1970 were thwarted by the hijackers' being spotted by the El Al aircrew before they had boarded. The next attempt, 7 September 1970, was thwarted in the air, with one hijacker being killed and the other captured.[5] El Al now require passengers to check in at a special lounge (at all airports, not just in Israel) three hours before take off. As well as meticulous searches of passengers and baggage, they normally carry out two separate interrogations of each passenger. They say that minor discrepancies or suspicions aroused in these interrogations are more effective than any hardware in detecting hijackers. If hijackings ever become too serious to be endured, other airlines (especially US airlines, which are now the commonest targets) might have to emulate El Al, but in the intense competition for traffic they would lose passengers by demanding the three-hour check-in time. If the threat justifies it, however, it is the best answer.

In the early 1970s attempts were made, particularly in the USA, to concentrate the search effort on passengers falling into a fairly narrow profile (based on age, type of ticket, method of purchase, nationality, destination, and so on) but this appeared to have little effect. Armed sky-marshals resulted in more hijacks' being thwarted in the air but did not significantly reduce the number of attempts.

The best overall results came from the introduction in January 1973 of the 100 per cent search of passengers and hand baggage at the boardng gates, initially at US airports, but later copied elsewhere. The number of hijackings was almost at once reduced from an average of seventy per year to thirty and, by the 1980s to twenty per year.[6]

Nevertheless, rare as they are, hijacks have a political effect out of all proportion to the actual threat to passengers: witness the hijack of TWA Flight 847 to Beirut in June 1985.

Once again, computer technology may now offer two major advances in aviation security, without seriously delaying the check-in and boarding process. The first would be to require all passengers to complete a brief questionnaire at check-in, supplemented by data taken from their passports, visas and air tickets. From these sources a profile could be established including their age, nationality, domicile, where they had spent the last five nights (often required in health regulations in some countries), the purpose of their journey, where they bought their tickets, how they paid for them (hijackers are unlikely to use a cheque or credit card from which they could be identified, or traced after the hijack) and other seemingly unimportant details which, in the hands of an expert interviewer, could provide means of disclosing discrepancies. The questionnaire and the oral questioning would be done in the vicinity of the passport barrier, and experienced questioners would be able to pass 90 per cent of passengers through very quickly.

These data would be fed instantly into a computer system programmed to draw attention both to profile characteristics (which would probably eliminate 80–90 per cent of passengers from suspicion) and to possible links between apparently unconnected passengers. It can be assumed that a team of four or five hijackers would probably buy their tickets separately, for cash, check in separately, and avoid any contact in the boarding lounge, but a computer analysing other details from the papers and questionnaires might reveal at least a possibility that they were linked. Any passenger or group of passengers about whom the data or resulting links aroused any doubts could be called out of the boarding lounge and interviewed and, if need be, a more detailed search carried out. If they showed any reluctance, such as declining to agree to their papers or pocket books being searched, they could be held back for a later flight. A skilled interviewer (as the Israelis have found) would almost certainly be able to detect from people's demeanour whether it was safe or unsafe to let them board.[7]

The second possible development would be for responsible governments to agree on a scheme to issue voluntary 'International Air Travel Permits', valid for any of their airports and airlines. Under this scheme, bona-fide travellers, especially regular business travellers, would be invited to submit voluntarily to detailed vetting by their own intelligence authorities. If, like the great majority of travellers, they were quickly proved to be above suspicion, they would be issued with an International Air Travel Permit on a smart card, whose electronic data would include essential information including digital fingerprint data, all the data also being duplicated on their own national police computers, linked on demand to those of other contributing countries. Membership of the scheme would be restricted to countries which maintained a high standard of vetting and of operation of the procedures and which were prepared to make all their records and data banks available to other contributing countries through the computer links.

Travellers equipped with one of these permits would be checked through very quickly indeed, with their card and fingerprints briefly checked through the computer terminal, with need for a minimum of questioning, if any at all. Indeed, holders of such cards could be allowed later check-in times, priority reservation of seats and other incentives. Given these advantages, the great majority of travellers would submit to the vetting and obtain a permit.[8]

Other travellers, including citizens of countries not subscribing to or admitted to the scheme, would be required to check in earlier, to be subject to more detailed checks and to written and oral questioning. The scheme would thus allow the immigration and intelligence authorities to focus virtually all their investigations on the small minority of passengers amongst whom any potential hijacker or other criminal or terrorist would be found.

The initial cost of this scheme, notably for skilled personnel for vetting and the large amount of recording of data on the computer software, would be high. Applicants for cards might have to wait some time for their turn, but once they were cleared, their permits could be renewed over the years, like passports, involving nothing more than minor clerical work by post. The dividends of the scheme, moreover, would be far wider than just protection against hijacking; they would greatly increase the chances of detecting criminals, including international drug traffickers.

Chapter thirteen

Searching for guns, explosives and drugs

The challenge

Detection of guns and bombs has thus far relied mainly on two methods of metal detection: X-rays and magnetometers (in the arch familiar to airline passengers). In addition, dogs and chemical sniffers are used to detect explosives and drugs. Neutron bombardment of various kinds is currently undergoing user trials in the UK and USA; various other technologies, such as measuring dielectric properties and the use of ultra-sensitive infra-red detectors, are in the research and development stage.

Something more than metal detection is now clearly necessary. For short-range use, there is a pistol made wholly of plastic, including bullets, springs, screws, etc. Apart from the firing mechanism, many bombs need contain no metal at all. Moreover, it has now become common practice to incorporate the firing mechanism in the circuits in a normal piece of electrical equipment such as a calculator or casette recorder (recent example were given on p. 54 and 91). Non-metallic chemical methods can be used for delay fuses (for example acid eating through a membrane to initiate spontaneous combustion on contacting another chemical). And the commonest place for terrorist bombs is now in motor vehicles – under the wheel arch (tilt bombs) or in or under the bonnet or boot.

Nor can vapour detection be wholly relied upon. Plastic explosives, including Semtex, of which Colonel Gadafi bought large quantities from Czechoslovakia to deliver to the IRA and Palestinian terrorists, emit very little vapour; other explosives can be wrapped in several layers of plastic, each heat-sealed and sanitized before the next layer is added.

Operational factors also undermine the efficiency of searching of airport baggage, especially if there have been no recent hijacks. Some operators become bored and lose concentration; some passengers become exasperated with the hassle and delay. This is particularly so if there are false alarms; passengers will object strongly if a false alarm reading on their hold baggage leads to their being prevented from boarding or delayed. For this reason the US Federal Aviation Authority (FAA) has specified a 95 per cent detection probability (DP) and a false alarm rate (FAR) not exceeding 1 per cent for any new search equipment being developed.[1]

Aids to the searcher

Ears, eyes, noses, fingers and experience leading to hunches or suspicions remain the most effective weapons available to searchers, just as the brain remains superior to the computer in its sensitivity. On the other hand, a human being may lose concentration without realizing it or admitting it, while a machine can be regularly checked to ensure that it is working properly.

There are a number of aids available to supplement the senses of the searcher. Stethoscopes have long been used for detecting the tiny sounds of timing mechanisms. Mirrors and, more recently, fibre optics have been used for looking round corners, inside boxes, and so on: light or other signals bounce off the outer walls of fine glass or plastic threads like a ball-bearing bouncing along a pipe – so fine that they can bend quite sharply without interfering with the reflection. A bundle of threads in a flexible armoured tube transmits a picture from a tiny lens at the head of the tube to the operator's eyepiece or a display screen.[2]

Another aid to search, technically simple but not yet in use, is the tagging of explosives. This can take two forms: tagging for detection and tagging for identification. Both would be done during manufacture. Tagging for detection means the incorporation of an ingredient which would react to an internationally agreed form of penetrating ray (X-rays, gamma rays or neutron bombardment). Tagging for identification would involve the incorporation of 'microtaggants' into the explosive during manufacture. These consist of particles of colour-coded melamine plastic. A large number of colours can be used and are easily changed, so the number of permutations and combinations is almost infinite (e.g. three red with one yellow and four blue). Under this system the coding would be recorded each time a batch of explosives changed hands, from manufacturer to international distributor to wholesaler to retailer to user, anywhere in the world. When a bomb containing tagged explosives was discovered and defused, its origin and distribution history could be traced, greatly facilitating police investigation.[3]

There are, however, many problems. A substantial percentage of larger terrorist bombs use improvised explosives, such as the mixture of fertilizer and fuel oil, or the so-called 'co-op' mixture of nitro-benzine and sodium chlorate. Best results would therefore come from tagging factory-made detonators, detonating cord and priming explosives, some or all of which are needed in every improvised bomb.

There would be resistance from the explosives trade and non-cooperation from those countries which wish to sponsor terrorist bombs as a political weapon, such as Syria, Libya, Iran and Cuba. Most explosives manufacturers are in industrial countries which would wish to co-operate in protection from terrorism and, given a strong lead and a plan involving them all, they might be prepared to legislate to compel their manufacturers to conform. Unfortunately, however, explosives manufacture is a low-technology industry and it would be easy for the sponsoring countries to manufacture enough to supply terrorist needs. There would, however, still be some advantages in operating the scheme. If, say, 90 per cent of the explosive-manufacturing countries tagged their explosives and recorded their distribution, it would narrow the field of suspicion as to the origin of untagged explosives, or the 'missing link' if there was a break in the record of movement of a batch of tagged explosive. Diplomatic, economic and, in the last resort, military pressure could be applied to the offending country, especially if its action had resulted in large-scale indiscriminate massacre. As in so many other fields, the lead would best be taken by the 'Summit Seven' countries whose economic sanctions could hurt most, or by the twelve countries which have agreed to operate the access scheme in their banks to combat money laundering (see pp. 117–18). If, in future years, the USSR is willing to join the anti-terrorist club, such action could be very effective indeed.

Vapour detection

Dogs can recognize astoundingly small percentages of certain vapours, especially those associated with the human body, to which their noses are at least a million times more sensitive than the human nose. This is especially valuable to the police in detecting and identifying criminals and terrorists if the dog can be briefed with the scent of something they have handled or worn. Dogs can also detect explosives, cocaine, heroin, amphetamines and marijuana, and are not fooled by masking smells such as mothbals, onions, perfumes and spices. The limitation of dogs, however, is that their sense of smell can become fatigued without their realizing it. This can largely be overcome by good training and good handling, but it is not always easy for a handler to tell when his dog's senses or concentration have lapsed.

Mass spectrographic analysis is a technique widely used in seaports and airports to detect vapour and dust particles emitted by explosives, drugs, alcohol, tobacco and other contraband. The plant is quite large. Samples of air from trucks, cars or containers can be drawn directly into the machine through a long hose; or by a separate hand-held remote sampler which sucks the air through a cartridge which is then inserted in the main plant. This system can handle about twenty vehicles per hour, and can be combined with other means of search (e.g. X-rays and neutron bombardment) which simultaneously maintain the same throughput.[4]

A small sniffer, in a manpack with a hand-held probe, is the Computerized Organic Tracer (COT) which sucks in and detects nitrobenzine vapour. The Canadian EVD 1 sucks vapour into a cartridge which is then analysed in a portable (35lb) detector, taking about 1½ minutes. It detects a wide range of explosives at a vapour density of a few parts in a trillion and costs about £25,000.[5]

Then there are instant hand-held sniffers, which indicate quite low percentages of vapour either visually or by an alarm tone. Inevitably these are not as sensitive as the heavier equipment, but they are very useful for detecting bombs or drugs in cars or hidden behind partitions or furniture, for example, and for a quick check of passengers and their baggage.[6] Every piece of baggage at Singapore Airport is searched with hand sniffers before check-in, and if there is any doubt, it is opened and hand-searched in the presence of the passenger.[7]

Neutron bombardment

Thermal Neutron Activation (TNA) is currently under trial at a number of airports in the USA and Europe. The plant at present costs about $1 million. The package to be searched is subjected to neutron rays which, if they strike material with a high nitrogen content, will emit a pattern of gamma rays which will trigger an indicator or alarm. It can, however, be used only to detect quantitites of about 1kg or more of explosives; if set to be more sensitive than this it has an unacceptably high false alarm rate. There is also a possibility of false alarms if the package contains a substantial amount of other materials with a high nitrogen content, such as certain kinds of cheese.[8]

Hydrogenous Explosive Detection (HED) is a simpler and cheaper alternative, costing about £7,000. This picks up water-based materials, which includes most explosives, but it gives false alarms with other water-based materials. The technology depends on neutron emission from a cobalt source, which could pose dangers to people in the vicinity if carelessly used by an unskilled operator. The indication of explosives is given by the degree of neutron scatter. This equipment is portable, and has been used successfully in Northern Ireland for some years.[9]

There is also a hand-held portable gamma ray explosives detector which, like the hand sniffer, can be used to search behind partitions, furniture, and so on. Research is being conducted into the possibility of developing an imaging system, but this is in its early stages.

Other research

Dielectric properties refer to the ability of different materials to absorb an electric charge. There is reason to believe that explosives and other materials may each have a 'dielectric fingerprint'. A system was tested in the USA in 1977 for detecting letter and parcel bombs in US mail. Though results in the first year seemed promising, it was not proceeded with, but research is continuing and it seems likely that an effective piece of equipment will be developed.[10]

Infra-red rays are already extremely sensitive in detecting minute variations in the emission of heat from various materials. They are already used to detect the warmth of living human bodies buried in earthquakes or avalanches. If the sensitivity could be further improved, it might be possible to detect the outline of something masking the emission of heat from a body, such as a gun or other dense object concealed in the clothing. Thus far, the images have been too blurred to be of use, but there are many possibilities for heat detectors if they become sensitive enough.[11]

Multiple methods

There is no single type of detector which has a 100 per cent detection probability, bearing in mind the range of explosives and drugs to be found. To approach this probability, therefore, it would be necessary to use a number of different tests in succession. Though this would add to the cost, both of equipment and numbers of operators, it need not necessarily impose more delay on the checking of passengers, packages, vehicles or containers. If, for example, packages were passed through a tunnel containing an X-ray machine, a succession of TNA and HED neutron detectors and a vapour detector (or a dog at the end of the tunnel) packages would keep moving through each in turn: the number entering and leaving per minute would be the same as for only one. On the other hand, even if each test had only a 90 per cent DP, based on detecting different characteristics, the overall DP would be very high indeed.

Airport and airline security

The hijacking of passenger aircraft is rare, but each case of it is a gross infringement of the liberty of several score or several hundred people, often having a permanent effect on their physical and mental health. Hijacks also poison and disrupt international politics out of proportion with the scale an significance of the hijack itself. If the terrorists use a bomb, this deprives the passengers and crew of their ultimate civil liberty, the right to live: 329 indiscriminate victims in an Air-India aircraft over the Atlantic in 1985 and 270 at Lockerbie in 1988, for example. Prevention of these attacks and deterrence, detection and conviction of hijackers and bombers depends on access control of both people and material to the air side of airports and to aircraft.

Chapters 11 and 12 examined the application of emerging technology to checking the bona fides of passengers, establishing their identity, concentrating investigation on dubious ones and detecting links which might indicate a possible hijack team (see pp. 140–1). This chapter has considered the emerging technologies for detecting bombs and guns.

Combined, these could provide immensely improved airport and airline security, provided that enough of the international community showed the will to co-operate in enforcing them, or if at least enough powerful countries were prepared to boycott the airports and airlines of any others who failed to provide such co-operation.

The requirement would be the redesign of the procedures in airport terminals (initially by means of temporary barriers and partitions, to be replaced in due course by internal reconstruction) and the allocation of the necessary capital and running expenditure to instal the additional equipment and pay the extra security staff to operate it. This cost could be transferred to airport landing charges and thence to the price of air tickets, all therefore ultimately paid by the passengers whose safety is being protected. Since some airports and airlines would be tempted to undercut the competition, it would be necessary for standards to be strictly enforced by the International Air Transport Association (IATA), with common consent, as a condition of the airports and airlines retaining their operating licences.

The common standard required of airports would be on the following lines. There are three avenues for getting a bomb into the hold or cabin of an aircraft: concealed in cargo or supplies loaded by airport staff on the ramp; in hold baggage checked through from linking flights across the ramp or checked in by embarking passengers in the terminal; or smuggled in by passengers in their hand baggage. Both in hold and hand baggage, a bomb or gun may have been inserted without the knowledge of the passenger – the 'naive carrier' who is carrying a 'gift' on behalf of a chance acquaintance – or it may be in the baggage of a suicide bomber. The same precautions needed to prevent people getting bombs into the cabin should prevent them from smuggling weapons aboard for a hijack.

Ramp security should be the easiest to enforce, since it is wholly under the control of the airport authorities and of staff employed by them. First, there must be watertight control of every means of access to the ramp through maintenance areas, cargo sheds, kitchens, and so on; from the terminal buildings; and from outside the airport. Second, every one of the staff issued with passes giving such access should be security vetted and their passes should contain electronic biometric data (digital

147

fingerprint data, etc.) to prevent impersonation. (At the time of writing the Lockerbie bomb is believed to have been inserted either by a 'naive carrier' or by an impersonator amongst the Frankfurt baggage handlers.) Third, such staff should be subject to frequent spot checks, with metal and vapour detectors and hand search.

All cargo and hold baggage should be monitored by multiple means, passing along a conveyer belt with successive X-ray, dogs or vapour sniffers and neutron bombardment. It should also pass through a blast-proof vacuum chamber to trigger any barometric (altitude-operated) fuse. These would, of course, require expenditure on equipment and personnel, but need cause only negligible delay to loading and check-in procedures, since they would be in a continuous-flow system, entering the conveyor and emerging at the same number of packages per minute as if they had to pass through only one, the slowest, of the checks.

The airport layout for passenger check-in and boarding should be changed – initially with temporary partitions. Only travelling passengers should have access to the check-in desks. From the public concourse with shops, banks, etc., and counters for purchase of tickets (though not for allocation of seats), they should enter the boarding cycle with both hand and hold baggage through a passengers-only barrier on presentation of a ticket for travel on that day. Thence they would pass through a series of 'reservoirs' connected by one-way 'valves' or 'pipelines' from which there would be no exit than through the door of an aircraft for which they have a boarding pass for a specific seat (which, in theory, applies to normal boarding now).

This boarding pass and seat will be issued at a check-in desk in the first reservoir after the passengers-only barrier. At this check-in desk they will hand in their hold *and* hand baggage, all of which will then enter the conveyor to pass through the successive checks (X-ray, vapour, neutron, etc.) though probably not at this stage the barometric chamber. While their baggage is on this conveyor, the passengers will go through passport and immigration checks, in which their machine-readable passports, visas or identity cards, with fingerprint or vein pattern scanner, will establish their identity and confirm that there is no bar to travel on their national (or linked national) computer. They will then (through the next one-way valve) enter the next reservoir – a search hall. Here the passengers will pass through magnetometer arches, and both they and their hand *and hold baggage* (in their presence) will be subject to hand search, either at the discretion of the searcher or if any of the multiple checks have given rise to any uncertainty. As a possible refinement, an electronic number could be simultaneously recorded on the passenger's boarding pass and on the tags of both hand and hold baggage, so that (on the same principle where shoplifted goods can be automatically detected passing out of the door of a store) the aircraft could be held back unless all three are confirmed to have entered the passenger or cargo door. This should provide an extra check that a 'passenger' has not handed in a bag and failed to board – the commonest way of loading a bomb – though both the pipeline systems and strict documentation should prevent this in any case.

The passengers would then pick up their hand baggage, and their hold baggage would be passed for loading, passing in bulk on the way through the barometric chamber – as is already done in many airports. As with the passengers, there would be no leaks in the baggage reservoirs or piplines; an added bonus could be that the electronic tags would ensure that bags would not accidentally be loaded on to the wrong aircraft.

The passengers with their hand baggage would then enter the third 'reservoir' – a general departure loung with bars, duty-free shops, and so on. The duty-free shops should adopt a principle used in many airports, whereby the buyer signs an order and pays, but the actual package or bottle is selected and handled only by the shop staff, loaded in bulk, and handed over to the passenger in exchange for the order after arrival at the destination.

A further measure, which already gives added security at Singapore Airport, could be for passengers and their hand baggage to be subject to a final check (with discretionary hand search) on passing the valve into the fourth reservoir – the boarding lounge from which the only exit is to their particular aircraft. This would guard against their acquiring a gun or bomb from another passenger or staff accomplice who had managed to smuggle it into the departure lounge, for example amongst catering supplies or shop merchandise.

The redesign of terminals should ensure that embarking and disembarking passengers never mix, and that transit and embarking passengers meet only in the individual aircraft boarding lounge. In many of today's terminals, embarking and disembarking passengers pass on travelators in opposing directions in the same corridor; it is thus very easy for a disembarking passenger to pass or exchange a bag containing a gun or bomb with an embarking passenger *after* he and his hand baggage have been checked. This reduces the embarkation security to the level of the most insecure airport used anywhere en route by any arriving passengers. The Singapore system provides some security against this but it is in fact best if there is no mingling at all.

Even more important is to ban the practice of allowing transit passengers who are taking a leg stretch at an intermediate stop to leave their hand baggage on board. Some of the other passengers will be finishing their journey at that stop, and if one of them leaves a bag, package or coat on boad, no one is likely to guess that it does not belong to a transit passenger. This was almost certainly the means whereby a bomb was placed in the cabin of a TWA aircraft which blew up over

Greece in April 1986 on a Cairo–Athens–Rome–Athens–Cairo shuttle, killing four passengers. The only sure protection is for *all* passengers to disembark at transit stops with *all* their hand baggage and for the cabin to be checked. At the same time, the documentation should be such as to ensure that no passengers can finish their journey at an intermediate stop, leaving their heavy baggage in the hold.

Small airports and airlines, and perhaps some bigger ones, will resist introducing these measures and some will try to circumvent them to cut costs and attract passengers. It will therefore be essential for IATA to have sufficient powers to enforce them. As with other international measures proposed in this book (e.g. in Chapter 10), the best starting-point will be the Summit Seven – Britain, Canada, France, Germany, Italy, Japan and the USA. Between them they operate 80 per cent of the Western world's air traffic; a boycott by them would quickly ruin any airport or airline which, after warning, failed to achieve the required standards. Other responsible airlines – KLM, SAS, Swissair, Air India, etc. – would almost certainly support the scheme, and within a few years Soviet and East European airlines may wish to do so too.

Part IV

Public safety and civil rights

Chapter fourteen

Detection, arrest and civil liberties

Chapters 3 to 8 of this book examined some of the measures taken in European countries to make the rule of law workable in the face of planned intimidation and disruption of the judicial process, and mentioned the civil rights implications of some of these measures. The purpose of this chapter and the next is to strike a balance between public safety and civil rights. This chapter considers problems before an accused person comes to trial: detecting the offender amongst the crowd; detecting and acquiring evidence of racketeering and money laundering; corruption and intimidation; arrest, detention and interrogation; and some associated problems. The next chapter will focus on the processes of trial and sentence in the face of intimidation of judges, witnesses, juries and prison officers.

Finding the needle in the haystack

The best deterrent against terrorism and other crimes is a high prospect of arrest and conviction. The first problem is to find the terrorist or criminal. It is extremely easy for five or six terrorists to conceal themselves, either in cities or in rural areas, especially if they have some training in clandestinity. With so many immigrants in the EC, foreign terrorists can hide as easily as indigenous ones.

No one has any right to impersonate someone else but it can be argued that there is a right to conceal identity as part of the right of privacy. Has a man the right to conceal his visits to his mistress from his wife? Or a wife to conceal visits to her lover? Have people a right to conceal business activities from their competitors? Or to avoid being found out going to a red-light district?

Perhaps they do have a claim, but this claim may be outweighed by the right and duty of the police to save innocent lives by checking whether someone is a wanted person. The police are not likely to find the wanted person without checking a lot of others too. As to which right prevails depends on the situation in the country. Where the level of violence is low, as in Denmark, the right to privacy will prevail. In Northern Ireland, where nearly 3,000 people out of 1.5 million have been killed in 20 years, the balance may go the other way. In El Salvador, where 70,000 people out of 5 million were killed in 10 years (1 in every 70) it certainly will.

Have demonstrators a right to conceal their identity by covering their faces? In some European countries this is a criminal offence, because people have used demonstrations as a cover for inflicting injury, death or criminal damage. That is an abuse of the freedom of assembly. On the other hand, if demonstrators have tear gas discharged at them, they surely have a right at least to tie damp cloths over their noses and mouths.

Sir Robert Mark, probably Britain's best policeman in this century, said that 'total freedom is anarchy; total order is tyranny'.

Police power to tap telephones, tape telephone conversations and intercept mail was greatly increased in Italy in the late 1970s, subject to the authority of a magistrate. This was necessitated by the highest rate of kidnapping in the world (287 in the five years 1977–81), higher at that time even than in Colombia. If the police could tap the telephone of the victim's home and work-place within half an hour of the kidnap, they had a good chance of intercepting the first demand for money and concessions, and thereby an increased chance of saving the victim's life and catching and convicting the kidnappers. By 1984 the kidnap rate had been cut to less than half, and stayed there. So their measures did prove their worth, but to prevent abuse such powers must be tightly controlled by the judiciary and those who exercise them must be accountable for their actions.

In 1974–5 and again in 1978–82, General Dalla Chiesa was given wide powers as director of anti-terrorist operations in Italy, and was responsible directly to the Minister of the Interior, without having to report his actions to the judiciary. This was highly successful in both periods, and undoubtedly saved many lives, but it was a dangerous power to place in any one man's hands. He was an honourable man, and his success was grimly recognized by the Mafia, who were quick to assassinate him when his talents were switched to Sicily in 1982 (see p. 40). Special undercover intelligence operators acting without effective control have disturbing opportunities for abuse, and they should be given these powers only for a strictly limited period. Due to political pressure this period was too short in Italy in 1974–5, and the Red Brigades were able to revive in an ever more vicious form. It was adequate in 1978–82, when the momentum which Dalla Chiesa and his team created did carry through to the abandonment of co-ordinated murder campaigns by both left- and right-wing terrorists, though individual murders by splinter groups, like other forms of crime, can never be wholly eliminated. His greatest achievement – *pentitismo* – had its effect both in the investigative stages (in pinpointing terrorists) and in trial and conviction, so its civil rights assessment will be made in the next chapter after its use in evidence has also been considered.

In 1950 the West German government adopted the *Berufsverbot*, which bars from the public service anyone who adheres to a political philosophy aimed at overturning democracy. The justification was the experience of the Nazis' destroying the Weimar Republic in the 1930s, and the Communists' ousting parliamentary government in Czechoslovakia in 1948. As was described in Chapter 4 (pp. 56-7) the power has occasionally been used stupidly, but it has been consistently supported by both government and opposition, and has contributed to Germany's political system in the past forty years being the most stable in Europe. To ensure common-sense application, this power too must be constantly monitored by Parliament, the judiciary and the media.

If the war between the Colombian government and the drug cartels really does become total war, it may be necessary to take measures to prevent infiltration into the police and public services by corrupt officials in the pay of the drug barons. During the first week after the murder of presidential candidate Luis Galan in August 1989, the government swooped on all known premises of the Medellin cartel and arrested over 10,000 people, but only one of these was anywhere near the top echelons of the organization. The other leaders had clearly been tipped off, which tells its owns story. It was not until four months later that Jose Gonzalo Rodriguez Gacha was killed (see pp. 111-12).

The most vexed questions of all are in the field of intelligence. What personal data is it justifiable to hold? Few would question keeping data on violent criminals, rapists, child abusers or persistent swindlers and thieves in order to help the police to prevent them from repeating the crime. Should this also be applied to terrorists? For a time? Or for the rest of their lives? And what data, if any, should be maintained about people with no criminal record? If police wish to question people near the scene of a crime just committed, should they be empowered to demand proof of identity and to detain any who do not provide it (as in France)? And if data about an individual are recorded, should he or she have a right to know, or to inspect the data personally? Intelligence must have a degree of secrecy, but this must be balanced against the civil liberties of the individual.

In the context of the breath-taking pace of development (described in Chapter 11) of microelectronic means of recording, linking and accessing personal data, it will be possible, year by year, to record more and more, and process it more comprehensively and more quickly. Properly used, this can be of immense value in preventing terrorism and catching terrorists. On the other hand, if unscrupulous governments and corrupt police officers were able to abuse this power, and if they were not restrained by democratic institutions (Parliament, the judiciary and free media), this could become the greatest of all threats to democracy and civil liberties.[1]

Racketeering, laundering, bribery and intimidation

Terrorist movements in Northern Ireland (Protestant and Catholic) and in Spain get the majority of their funds by racketeering and intimidation. So do the Mafia in Italy. Their techniques were described in context in Chapters 3, 6, 8 and 9; briefly, they include obtaining money by defrauding the tax and social security departments, mainly amongst casual labour in the construction industry; by running illegal businesses; by securing a monopoly for their legal or illegal businesses by intimidating rivals (e.g. taxis in West Belfast); by extorting part of the proceeds of legitimate activities (e.g. from the proprietors of bars and gaming machines); and by extorting protection money or 'revolutionary taxes' from businessess, for example by forcing them to pay for non-existent services from a bogus security company or from a 'caterer' contracting the supply of unspecified 'refreshments'.

Italy (for the Mafia) and the UK have made laws to authorize official access to bank accounts and other financial and business records where there is suspicion that they may reveal the presence of illegal money. In the case of the UK, this has normally to be authorized by a judge though a senior police officer can authorize it in an emergency with the obligation to notify and justify his action as soon as possible. There is also pooling of information between the police, Inland Revenue and Social Security departments. The onus of proof that the money has a legitimate source lies on the suspected person.

This onus of proof is a reversal of normal British legal tradition, whereby the onus of proving that a crime has been committed lies on the prosecution. The amount of illegal money in circulation in the UK, however – from racketeering, fraud, counterfeiting and drug trafficking (approximately £1 billion a year) – is sufficient to have a significant and malign influence on inflation, as well as underwriting terrorism and crime, so the change is justified.

The next stage is to extend this access to the international banking system. A start has already been made, but the agreement so far is only amongst the most responsible countries – the Summit Seven, Benelux, Switzerland and Sweden. It would be perfectly feasible to require other banks world-wide to allow such access, given judicial safeguards, with the threat that banks which refused to do so would be compulsorily boycotted by the rest of the international banking system, enforced by government exchange regulations banning transfer of money to these banks (see pp. 116–19).

There are two dangers: first, that the power, like any of the others, might be used corruptly; second, that it might be used to catch out people for minor discrepancies in their day-to-day transactions, which could become a form of harassment. Once again, reliable and independent monitoring (probably by the judiciary) would be needed, and abuse by officials severely punished.

Dealing with racketeering and extortion is just one part of preventing or detecting the laundering of illegal money, and the need for access to bank and business records is a necessary part of dealing with other means of laundering too.

In various countries there is a requirement for anyone depositing more than a certain sum (e.g. £9.000 in Italy or $10,000 in the USA) to produce evidence of identity which is then reported to the police so that they can check whether there are any recorded data about that person.[2] No one whose activities are lawful and innocent will suffer any deprivation of civil rights from this.

Victims of racketeering, bribery, extortion of protection money and coercion to defraud are invariably threatened with dire consequences if they tell the police. One way to overcome this is for police agents with concealed tape recorders to put themselves in the way of being selected as victims, but this requires very brave men.

Arrest and detention

In the UK, detention without trial under the Prevention of Terrorism Act can be up to seven days with the Home Secretary's approval. For a brief period in Spain a ten-day period *incommunicado* was allowed, though this was later reduced to three to five days. In Italy, if the judge considered that there was a deliberate attempt to delay and disrupt the process of bringing an accused person to trial, he had the power to extend the period of custody indefinitely (see Chapters 3, 7 and 8).

All these things do erode civil liberties but they are a product of a calculated policy by terrorist and some other extreme organizations to force this erosion and to exploit public anxiety about it to the full. It is part of the technique of 'provoking repression' so strongly advocated by revolutionary philosophers such as Carlos Marighela. If they can make liberal processes of law unworkable, the choice lies between using fewer liberal processes or allowing the rule of law to collapse, (as was happening in Northern Ireland in 1972).

During the trials of leading members of the Baader-Meinhof Group, the German government was faced with defence lawyers who were actively participating in the terrorist movement by acting as a communication link between the imprisoned leaders and those outside, smuggling things in to them and disrupting and delaying court proceedings. For any of these offences, lawyers could be barred from the court and their prison visits restricted; they also had to speak to their clients through microphones without physical contact. This again was an emergency measure necessary to sustain the rule of law, and the temporary suspension of some of the normal prisoners' rights was justifiable and necessary.

Interrogation

Police interrogation in the privacy of a cell gives great scope for mental and possibly physical bullying to extort confessions, so it is standard practice for criminals and terrorists to complain that these methods were used. Apart from the obvious need to select interrogators carefully and to supervise them, the best insurance against this is for every interrogation to be taped, on audiotape in routine cases and on videotape in serious cases. Means to prevent or detect cutting or tampering with the tape must be installed, and the accused person or his lawyer must be given a copy of it. Audiotapes have been used by the British police in this way for some years now, and not only have enhanced the effectiveness of interrogation but also have greatly reduced the number of objections to it as evidence.[3]

It should completely eliminate the use of 'verbals' in evidence – that is, of verbal statements alleged to have been made by the accused in the presence of two police officers. This has never been a satisfactory means of obtaining evidence for conviction.

There must always be a 'right of silence' under interrogation, but there is no justification for banning the prosecution from exercising the right to draw attention to this silence as material evidence at the trial. This ban was a necessary precaution in the nineteenth century when criminals were often illiterate and unsophisticated, and were putty in the hands of a clever and aggressive interrogator; their only recourse was to say nothing and this was accepted as a reasonable defensive action in the circumstances. Criminals and terrorists now understand very well what is going on and many are expert in circumventing the law. A person under interrogation must certainly have the right of silence, but the wording of the caution should be changed to the effect that 'I shall ask you some questions. You are not obliged to answer, but my questions and your answers (or refusals to answer) will be recorded on audio/videotape which may be presented as evidence in court'. The judge and jury would then have the right to draw their own conclusions, especially when they see the demeanour of the accused person on videotape, as to why he was refusing to answer the questions.

There is nothing revolutionary about this. Every small boy learns it the first time he is caught by his mother at the jam cupboard. If he refuses to answer her questions, she will draw her own conclusions. And it is

158

now a vital part of democracy that we can judge our politicians by whether they evade or answer questions on television, and their demeanour under interrogation. Innocent people with nothing to hide do not need to stay silent. The conviction of four alleged IRA bombers at Guildford in 1975 was quashed by the Appeal Court in 1989 when new evidence about their interrogation came to light. Had the original jury seen these interrogations on videotape, they could have judged for themselves.

The British Prevention of Terrorism Act makes it an offence for a person to withold without reasonable excuse any information which he or she 'knows or believes might be of material value in preventing an act of terrorism, or in securing the apprehension, prosecution or conviction of a person for an offence involving commission, preparation or instigation' of a Terrorist Act. This is not restricted only to answering questions; it is also an offence simply to fail to report the information to a constable or some other proper authority as soon as possible.

This clause has been challenged at most of the parliamentary reviews of the Act on the grounds that it is unreasonable to expect someone to betray a close friend or relation, but it remains in the Act. It is uncertain whether the courts would regard a mother who declined to betray her son as having a 'reasonable excuse'. This clause is a distasteful one, but it is justifiable in a period of emergency when the alternative is to increase the prospect of people being killed.[4]

If arms, ammunition or explosives are found in a person's house or car in Northern Ireland, the occupant has the onus of proving that he or she did not know they were there. This is again a product of experience because, however flagrant the case, denial of knowledge was the invariable defence. Like other cases of reversal of the normal onus of proof, this is regrettable but justifiable when dealing with large-scale and sometimes indiscriminate murder.

It is proper that an accused person should have access to a lawyer as soon as possible but in the face of terrorism some countries have permitted interrogation without the presence of a lawyer.[5] In Italy there is a proviso that proceedings of such an interrrogation are not valid as evidence in court. This, and the use of video-cameras in interrogation, should provide adequate safeguards. If lawyers maliciously obstruct and delay the process of bringing their clients to trial, as became prevalent in Germany and Italy, the necessary emergency measures to overcome this will inevitably result in some sacrifice of civil liberties by other lawyers and their clients.

The problems of the trial itself, in the face of calculated intimidation of judges, witnesses and juries, has a chapter to itself. First, however, some other aspects of European judicial, political and security co-operation need to be considered.

European judicial co-operation

The most important international judicial problem is that of extradition. This was considered in Chapter 10 in the context of international treaties.

Another related measure, long advocated by France, is the idea of a European judicial area, in which offenders could be tried and sentenced in any EC country, calling evidence from any other country.[6] This could work satisfactorily, given goodwill, between countries with similar legal traditions like France and Belgium or the UK and the Republic of Ireland. Even in this case, political considerations can interfere, especially where one or both of the governments concerned feels electorally vulnerable and wishes to placate a marginally significant sector of its own voters. This affected the behaviour of both governments after the arrest of Patrick Ryan in Belgium (see pp. 67–83) in highly suspicious circumstances. Ryan was also wanted for offences in the UK, and the British requested extradition, but the Belgians hastily deported him to the Republic of Ireland where Prime Minister Haughey, in the run-up to a closely balanced General Election, refused to extradite him to the UK on the grounds that his government planned to prosecute Ryan themselves (though after eighteen months they decided not to prosecute). Throughout the whole affair, both governments reacted angrily, which will not make future cases any easier to handle.

This problem would be even more difficult between two countries with different legal systems and traditions, for example between one with an adversarial system and one with an accusatorial system, or one with trial by jury and one without.

Given the will to do so, an adequate degree of harmonization might lead to public acceptance in both countries of the fairness of the other's trial. In 1986 a crowd of British football hooligans caused a large number of fatal casualties at a European Cup Final at Heysel Stadium. They were extradited for trial in Belgium in 1987–8 but the British public were somewhat bewildered by the proceedings, which seemed very slow, and the general feeling was that the Belgian court had been too lenient. The British public have no more sympathy for the football hooligans who disgrace them than they have for terrorists, and in these areas there might be a good chance of harmonization. Britain's readiness to extradite football hooligans to Belgium, however, contrasted with Belgium's refusal to extradite Patrick Ryan.

A much criticized provision in the British Prevention of Terrorism Act is the power to issue exclusion orders against inhabitants of Northern Ireland entering or remaining in Great Britain if suspected of involvement in terrorism (see pp. 92–3), unless the person has been resident in Great Britain for at least twenty years or since birth. This order can be issued by the Home Office without the person's being tried or convicted. The activities of the IRA have ensured that this power is ovewhelmingly supported by the British Parliament and public. It is hard to see, however, how it can remain in force after all EC frontiers are opened at the end of 1992.

Banning political parties and terrorist broadcasts

Is it an infringement of civil liberties to proscribe a political party? Not if it actively supports and raises funds for a violent terrorist movement. On the other hand, it may be better just to proscribe the terrorist movement, rather than the political party which supports it. Both the British and Irish governments have proscribed the IRA, but in both countries its political front, Sinn Fein, is free to campaign and put up candidates for election. Its dismal performance – 9 per cent of the vote in the North and 1.5 per cent in the South – presents both governments with unanswerable evidence that Sinn Fein and the IRA have no grounds for their claim to represent the Irish public or the Northern Ireland Catholics. It can be argued that if extremists have opportunities for political activity, they are less likely to turn to terrorism. Even this can rebound because if (as with Sinn Fein) their political action gets such a humiliating public response, this will enable the militant wing of the party to claim that only violence can achieve results.

Another factor is that if the political party operates openly – issuing propaganda, running party offices and bookshops, recruiting in the pubs, and so on – this often gives leads to the police which they would not get if the party were driven wholly underground.

More controversial is the banning of broadcast interviews, with spokesmen of terrorist organizations (e.g. the IRA or INLA) or of political parties which support them (e.g. Sinn Fein). Both have been banned in the Republic of Ireland for many years, but were not banned in Britain until 1988, though in both countries journalists may report what the spokesmen said. There have been a number of past occasions when the public had been outraged by such interviews, notably in 1979, when the BBC sent a team to a clandestine location in Ireland to film a back-to-camera interview with a member of the INLA who exulted in the murder of a popular and highly respected politician, Airey Neave.

Most broadcasters claim that such a ban shows a 'lack of faith in democracy', in that most viewers will see through the terrorists' arguments and reject them; also that, if they are denied the chance of putting their case on the national broadcasting media, the terrorists will grab the news by more and more violent bombing until they get their way.

The case in favour of the ban was convincingly put by Conor Cruise O'Brien, formerly a minister in the Republic of Ireland government, in an address to the Edinburgh International Television Festival in 1989.

161

He later summarized it in an article in the London *Times* on 16 September 1989 ('Freedom to peddle murder'). He raised four arguments against broadcasting such interviews.

First, that they boost the morale of the terrorists' own supporters, who derive cheer from their 'true faith' being broadcast to an audience of millions, and do not consider whether or not the majority will reject it.

Second, that they widen the base of support for the terrorists in small but significant target areas of the population. One example was those supporters of the British Labour Party who back a 'troops out' policy and would be further encouraged to vote for it; since the Labour Party may well be elected to power, the possibility of their adopting this policy is a major encouragement to the IRA to continue their campaign of terror. Another target was the teenage children of Irish parents in Britain, some of whom already see glamour in the IRA. The sight of 'an IRA man appearing on TV – even in Sinn Fein drag – would double that glamour' and thereby attract supporters and recruits for the terrorists.

His third argument was that IRA spokesmen would exploit the very revulsion which IRA atrocities arouse – such as the brutal murder with prolonged bursts of automatic rifle fire poured into the body of a lone and unprotected 26-year-old German girl married to a British soldier, while she was parking her car in a German street in September 1989. The IRA spokesman commented 'All very sad, but if you want it to stop, support British withdrawal from Northern Ireland'.

The fourth argument followed from this. No country would permit a Mafia spokesman to broadcast a threat to murder business people who refused to pay protection money. Allowing a terrorist spokesman to do the equivalent would give him a status above that of other criminals. The terrorist organization would thereby tend to be 'decriminalized' in the public mind.

Conor Cruise O'Brien ended by suggesting a referendum on the question 'Should spokesman for terrorist or pro-terrorist organizations be allowed to broadcast?' The answer would be 'no' by a large majority, and this would refute the broadcasters' claim that a ban shows a 'lack of faith in democracy'.[7]

For both ethical and practical reasons it is usually unwise to proscribe a political party which itself acts within the law. If, however, it funds or advocates terrorism or has a policy which does not denounce it, it should not be permitted to promulgate its advocacy on the public broadcasting media, since that is likely to encourage further terrorism and put more lives at risk.

Reserve powers and legislation in draft

The British Prevention of Terrorism Act was rushed through all its stages in Parliament to become law within seven days of the killing of twenty-one people by IRA bombs in Birmingham in November 1974. It contained several drastic measures, but they have stood the test of time and have been renewed each year by whichever government was in power. This emergency legislation must clearly have been held ready in draft before the event, in something like its final form.

In Northern Ireland, internment without trial in 1971 is now generally recognized to have been counter-productive. It was discontinued in 1976 and all internees released. The power to intern, however, was retained, though it has not been used for the past fourteen years. Its retention is a wise precaution. Two sets of circumstances come to mind in which it might be necessary to invoke this power: if there were an extremely violent escalation of indiscriminate IRA bombing; or if fighting between the rival Protestant and Catholic paramilitaries were to reach an intolerable level. To disrupt and check the offensive in the first case, it might be justifiable to arrest and detain known members of the hard core of the IRA – and most of them are known, though many of them spend much of their time across the border in the Republic. In the second case, it might be necessary to arrest and detain the leading militants on both sides. These detentions could be temporary until the situation had stabilized.

The registration of lodging is another measure which may be necessary in an emergency, if there is evidence of terrorists and their cadres moving in and out of villages or of city housing areas. It requires every hotel, lodging-house, or private household to notify the police within twenty-four hours of the arrival and departure of any person who spends one or more nights in the house. This is an extension of the normal obligation of hotels to register their guests for retrospective examination of their books by police (which was how they identified and arrested the IRA bomber of the Grand Hotel in Brighton in 1984 – see pp. 87–8). Lodging registration requires notification at the time. If police on routine house calls find someone there who has not been registered, this at once leads them to make further investigations, both about the lodgers and about the household. This was often very fruitful in the Malayan Emergency in the 1950s. It was also a reserve power in Sri Lanka in 1983–8, where their Emergency Regulations were based on the Malaysian model. When Sinhalese nationalist terrorism escalated in the south of the country the government was able to authorize police officers to invoke the power in towns and villages where they judged it to be necessary.

Any government faced with a terrorist threat which may escalate is wise to have emergency legislation ready in draft to cover a wide range of powers, some (though seldom all) of which might be needed to cover the worst case. And once drastic powers have been legislated, when the time comes to relax them, it may be better to suspend them rather than repeal them. Both of these will help to avoid the dangers of rushing into legislation which has not been fully thought through.

Chapter fifteen

Trial and sentence in face of intimidation

Trial without jury

On average, of the people tried by jury in the UK after pleading not guilty, nearly half are acquitted.[1] Since no one goes for trial unless the Director of Public Prosecutions considers that the evidence is so strong that he or she is likely to be found guilty, this suggests that a large number of guilty criminals are released into society with positive encouragement (by belief that they can get away with it) to commit more crimes. This is a grave infringement of the civil liberties of the public as a whole and, in particular, of their future victims.

There are a number of explanations for this. It is a very proper principle that it is better for one hundred guilty people to go free than for one innocent person to be convicted; this has resulted in the scales' being heavily weighted in favour of the defence. This weighting evolved when most criminals were very unsophisticated. One example of it was the denial of the right of judge and jury to draw their own conclusions from refusal by the accused to answer questions (see pp. 158–9).

Modern criminals and terrorists are now highly sophisticated. It is extremely rare for an innocent person to be found guilty and even more rare for a doubtful verdict to be upheld on appeal. The criminal slang 'bang to rights' (for someone caught red-handed) indicates that in face of any evidence short of that he will have a good chance of exploiting his 'rights' and getting off. Thus the public is denied the protection of the only effective deterrent for criminals and terrorists – a high expectation of conviction if caught.

But another reason for the low rate of conviction lies in the now highly professional techniques of jury-nobbling (by bribery) and jury intimidation. Flagrant intimidation of juries in France and Northern Ireland (see Chapters 5 and 6) led directly to the suspension of trial by jury for terrorist offences in both these countries.

In fact, one of the worst deprivations of personal freedom now is for a person to be required by law to sit on a jury trying a member of either a professional criminal gang or a political terrorist movement. Where, for example, a man with a wife and children is required to face the kind of threats made in the case of Regis Schleicher (p. 63), it is unrealistic to expect him to reach a verdict of guilty if he believes that this may cost him his life, sentence his wife to be a widow and condemn his children to forfeiture of his parenthood and material support for life.

Trial by jury in its present form is therefore clearly unsuitable for trying cases against violent criminals and terrorists. The Republic of Ireland recognized this in 1962, since when terrorist offences have been tried by a court of three, a judge with two assessors. This has worked well.

In the Netherlands there is no trial by jury for either civil or criminal cases. Courts consist entirely of professionals, a senior judge presiding over a number of junior judges or magistrates in the role of assessors. France introduced trial for terrorist offences by a court similarly made up of seven professional judges after the collapse of the first Schleicher trial in 1986.

The shortcomings of the single-judge Diplock Courts in Northern Ireland were discussed on pp. 78–81. So were Britain's difficulties in having a panel of judges or assessors as in the Netherlands or France, since all British judges are experienced lawyers of middle age or older. One way round this would be to make promotion to Queen's Counsel or judge conditional on having served for, say, two years away from advocacy, working as an assessor under a presiding judge. This would not only facilitate multiple-judge courts in Northern Ireland, but also enable courts in Great Britain to sit with professional assessors instead of jurors if the judge considered that there was a risk of jurors' being either bribed or intimidated. The judge should have discretion to make this change even after a trial has started if evidence of interference with the jury comes to light, in which case the judge would require the trial to begin again in front of the assessors. This would have prevented many perverse acquittals in trials of rich criminals with a gang outside with the money or intimidatory power to put pressure on the jury. It would also have avoided the quashing on appeal of a large number of those convicted on supergrass evidence (see pp. 80–1).

Video and CCTV to protect juries and witnesses

Television technology does, however, suggest a radically new alternative approach. There is now no need whatever for the jury or the professional assessors to be in the court at all; they could do their job equally well by watching and listening on closed circuit television (CCTV). Where necessary, witnesses too could give their evidence on camera. This has already been done experimentally in some cases of child abuse, where the judge considers that the child would be too frightened to speak out in the presence of the accused person glaring across the court – often a father or stepfather, of whom the victim is terrified.

Where justice requires that the jury's anonymity must be preserved, the judge would have the power to order the jury to sit in a separate building (so that they could not be watched coming and going); or even, if necessary, in a separate town. In front of the jury would be five television screens, showing close up the faces of the judge, the accused, the witnesses in the box and the prosecuting and defending counsel.

The jury need be seen by no one. Though it is arguable that the judge should see them, it would in fact be better psychologically if there were no camera in the jury room at all. Certainly the accused should not see the jury, nor should the public, nor should witnesses. Some lawyers will claim that prosecuting and defending counsel should be able to see the jury to watch their reactions. This claim should be firmly resisted. As Sir Robert Mark pointed out in his controversial Dimbleby Lecture in 1973, there are a number of lawyers prepared to be quite unscrupulous and dishonest in their actions inside and outside the court in furthering the interests of criminals and terrorists. He quoted a case of defence lawyers' fabricating an alibi for an accused person remanded in custody by smuggling in a club visitors' book for him to sign retrospectively in prison during a privileged and unsupervised 'lawyers' visit'. This purported to show that he was in that club on the night in question, but in this case the fraud was discovered.[2] As described in Chapter 4, abuses of privilege by lawyers were even worse in Germany. Where there is a need for a jury's anonymity to be protected at all, it must be protected from crooked lawyers as much as from the accused, the witnesses and the public.

It is in fact quite unnecessary to be able to see the audience in order to argue a case. The hustings now play a very small part in electoral politics. Political leaders do their persuading by television, never seeing their audience. The competent ones quickly learn the art of speaking, not to a public meeting, but to a family of two or three sitting at home – multiplied a million times. Counsel can similarly develop the art of persuading twelve jurors or a number of professional assessors using the same medium.

In Diplock trials (and in some terrorist trials in other countries) witnesses give evidence behind a screen, and are seen only by the judge and counsel. If the threat of bribery or intimidation is severe, this protection may not be enough, and the judge should have power to order that witnesses, too, give evidence from a separate room or building. They should normally be seen on camera by judge or counsel but, if he or she thinks necessary, the judge should have power to order that the picture from the witness's camera be seen only by the judge and the jury.

167

The witness's voice must, of course, also be heard by the counsel and by the accused. If essential (though this should be only in extreme cases) the voices of witnesses could be electronically disguised.

If ever the murder of judges (already a disturbing feature in Northern Ireland and Italy) were to reach Colombian levels, where fifty judges and large numbers of public prosecutors have been murdered, it would be better for even the presiding judge and counsel to be seen only (on camera) by the jury, and only heard, anonymously, through microphones by everyone else. This extreme is more likely to be necessitated by international criminal gangs (such as the Mafia, the Triads and the drug cartels) than by terrorists, but it is a reserve power which should be kept ready for use rather than allow the rule of law to collapse.

For justice to be seen to be done, the biggest problem in this proposal would be to satisfy the public that the system was not being abused, for example by rigging the jury so that it was made up of people chosen as likely to convict. To overcome this, juries would have to be selected by an independent body, whose members would be publicly known and trusted, and appointed by Parliament. An Ombudsman should be appointed, with access both to the jury selection process and to the juries themselves should he find this necessary.

Evidence

In the previous chapter (pp. 158–9) the case was put for permitting audiotapes or, preferably, videotapes of the interrogation of accused persons to be presented as evidence in court. Every accused person has a right to silence but the public whose laws he or she is accused of breaking have an equal right, through the judges and juries who act on their behalf, to interpret that silence. A video-recording or police interrogation would be much fairer as evidence than the 'verbals' (police statements of what the accused person said) currently accepted by the courts.

The more radical use of video-cameras and CCTV to protect witnesses from bribery or intimidation was discussed above. So were possible ways of protecting the identity of assessors or juries as an alternative to the single-judge Diplock Courts.

Any of these alternatives would have enabled the supergrasses in Northern Ireland to contribute as much to the elimination of terrorism in Northern Ireland as the *pentiti* did in Italy. Few people doubt that most of the evidence given by the supergrasses was accurate, but the trials before the Diplock Courts did not satisfy the Appeal Courts that the convictions were safe. Apart from the single judge, it was considered that evidence by a single witness with a strong incentive to bring about convictions was not enough. Corroboration from other witnesses was needed, and none dared to give it, even from behind a screen.

If guaranteed anonymity from everyone but the judge and (under the proposed scheme) the video jury or assessors, witnesses would almost certainly have come forward. Many terrorists now at large would be in prison. Others would be discouraged. The great majority of the people yearn to seen the end of violence by Protestant as much as by Catholic terrorists. There are many precedents. In Malaya, it was the 'supergrasses' (surrendered terrorists) who brought about the crumble of the terrorists,[3] and in Italy it was the *pentiti*. Terrorism in Northern Ireland could have been smashed (except for isolated incidents which would occur in any case) during the past five years. At a conservative estimate, this would have saved at least 200 of the 400 lives since lost. These lives have been a heavy price to pay for the failure of the UK judicial system to find a way to harness the desire of a large number of Protestant and Catholic terrorists to get out of their movements and end the violence.

Dalla Chiesa's brilliant and pragmatic exploitation of *pentitismo* did undoubtedly save several hundred lives from left- and right-wing terrorism. Perhaps because so many Italian judges had been murdered, the courts, including the higher Appeal and Cassation Courts, had fewer inhibitions than the British equivalents, though the number of terrorist victims (other than judges) was far higher in Northern Ireland than in Italy. The morality of *pentitismo* was discussed in Chapter 3. Despite the name, repentance played very little part. There was very little remorse for past murders, nor for the betrayal of comrades. The incentive for *pentiti* was to escape from an intolerable situation which could end only in violent death or long imprisonment, and to earn their freedom some ten years earlier, while they would still be young enough to enjoy it. 'Earning' was measured by the number and seniority of the people prosecuted on their evidence, and the value of information given. Only about 70 of the 350 left-wing *pentiti* knew enough to earn big dividends. As was pointed out on pp. 44–5, the result was that some smaller fry are still serving long sentences, while many of the hard core, who did most of the killing, were freed long before them: this could be storing up resentment and criminalization for the future.[4] Overall, however, the price was justified by the benefits, not only the hundreds of lives saved, but also the removal from Italian politics and society of the poison of left- and right-wing political violence.

Capital punishment

Capital punishment would be counter-productive with the current level of violence and terrorism in Europe, even in Northern Ireland, not only because it is morally repugnant and demoralizing in a democratic society, but also because it would result in fewer convictions of terrorists and other murderers. People would be less ready to give tip-offs to the police if they knew that this might bring the death penalty on a young man or woman who moved in their community, (it is only from within the community that the most valuable information comes). People would be even more reluctant to give evidence, for reasons of both conscience and fear. Where juries were involved (as in England) they would for similar reasons be more reluctant to convict. Moreover the reaction of terrorist or criminal gangs would be to use more 16- and 17-year-olds to do the killing, knowing that they would not be sentenced to death. There are already too many teenagers indirectly involved in terrorist activites, and only too ready to take up the offer of a grown-up gun. If a teenager does commit himself by a murder with his own hand, he will probably remain a criminal beyond hope of redemption all his life.

On the other hand, the overwhelming majority of the public (normally around 80 per cent) do favour the return of capital punishment. If the rate of killing in Northern Ireland rose again to, say, ten times its present level, the clamour for capital punishment might persuade politicians that they had little hope of election without supporting it. It can also be argued that, with that kind of murder rate (which would be higher per head of population even than in El Salvador) drastic measures including capital punishment, might be necessary to contain it; also to avert the threat of the public's taking the law into their own hands in private 'death squads'.

With killing at that level, the counter-productive aspects of capital punishment might be overridden. Given secure means to do so, the public might become more rather than less ready to give information. And captured terrorists, faced with death rather than imprisonment, might be more ready to bargain for their lives with information. This was undoubtedly a major factor in Malaya, where unauthorized possession of a gun or even of a round of ammunition carried the death penalty, which could be avoided only by giving information. It was also a decisive factor about one of the most bizarre situations in the Second World War. By 1942, unknown to their spy-masters who had set them to work, *all* the remaining 'German' spies in Britain were in fact controlled by British intelligence to mislead the Germans, and *all* the remaining 'British' spies in Germany were controlled by German intelligence. In fact, for obvious reasons, very few of these were born either German or British, but were immigrants, usually from Central Europe, so they had no burning patriotism for which they were willing to die. But the more practical reason was that, once captured, those who refused to accept this arrangement were shot. So only those who were willing to co-operate survived at all. A stark choice.

Life-meaning-life sentences

There is an alternative to the death penalty which, for certain intolerable crimes, would have many advantages: imprisonment of offenders for the rest of their natural lives. For some criminals and terrorists the prospect of that would be a greater deterrent than that of a death sentence.

Life-meaning-life sentences should be given very rarely and only to criminals or terrorists to whom it is unacceptable that the public should ever be exposed again: first, those who have knowingly and maliciously done such appalling damage to a number of other people's lives that they have forfeited any right to live themselves; second, those who have repeated an intolerable crime which they have done before; and third, those who have committed one of the second category of crimes as a first offence, but who the courts, taking expert advice, are convinced are likely to do it again if released. Convicted prisoners of this third category should have their sentences reviewed at intervals, but the sentences for the first and second categories should not be eligible for remission; their deterrent value would come from the general knowledge, before the crime is committed, that the sentence will be perpetual.

The first category would include placing a bomb in a public place with the intention of causing a large number of indiscriminate casualties, or in such a manner that a large number of indiscriminate casualties was the likely consequence of the act; or the distribution or sale of a quantity of specified hard drugs, including cocaine, crack and heroin, likely to cause or maintain the addiction of ten or more people (see p. 113) whose lives would thereby be ruined.

Examples of the second category (repetition of intolerable crimes) would include second offences of premeditated murder; of murder committed in the course of a criminal attack (e.g. robbery); of criminal rape; of crimes committed for sexual or sadistic satisfaction, child murder or serious child abuse.

The third category (first offences of intolerable crimes which the court judged that the accused person was likely to repeat) would involve imprisonment to protect the public until such time as the competent reviewing authority decided that the risk of repetition had become so small as to be acceptable. If that judgement proved wrong, then the sentence for the repetition of the crime would be final and perpetual, as for the second category.

There is no valid moral objection to whole life sentences. No person who has committed these offences has any right to be free again to commit such a crime. The death penalty is deserved, but withheld only because it is counter-productive and irreversible (in the event of new evidence coming to light). Valid objections would, however, come from the prison service, who could fairly argue that, for a life-meaning-life prisoner, they would have no leverage by which to control him, and that he could, without further punishment, kill or maim prison officers or fellow prisoners.

This is the only serious problem, but certain experimental prison procedures have proved that it can be solved. Prisons holding life-meaning-life prisoners should have three types of regime within the prison: severe, normal and privileged. The 'severe' regime, which every such prison has to have available for prisoners who are violent or totally uncooperative, would comprise solitary confinement and minimum standards of comfort and subsistence. The 'normal' regime would be that practised in most long sentence prisons: a cell regime providing normal standards of comfort and food, with periods set aside for recreation, and association with other prisoners. The third 'privileged' regime would be based on the experiments carried out with considerable success at Barlinnie Prison in Scotland and Bullwood Hall in Essex.

This privileged regime would be in a separate building within the prison from which no escape was possible but within which prisoners would have a relaxed life, with continuous association with others and good facilities for recreation, writing, study and exercise. They would live in unlocked rooms opening on to their own recreation area (with television, library and exercise facilities), all within an impregnable perimeter.

The stability of the system would be in the contrast between the three regimes. The severe regime would need to be a real deterrent and the privileged regime a real incentive. Prisoners would be encouraged to earn transfer upwards and warned that recalcitrance or bad behaviour would mean transfer downwards. The purpose would be to place sufficient power in the hands of the prison staff to maintain order.

But the drug problem, which could become the most serious of all threats to stability in European countries, cannot be solved only by consigning drug traffickers to prison for life-meaning-life. The addicts must be got off the streets to prevent their financing their addiction by selling more drugs to new addicts. This was discussed in Chapter 9 (p. 113.)

Rehabilitation

The great majority of terrorists will not fall into any of the three categories requiring life-meaning-life sentences. The time will come when they are due for remission. It is therefore important to develop means, inside prison and after release, of preventing the prisoner from reverting to terrorism. This is difficult but there have been a great many successes. It is more likely to succeed with left-wing ideologically motivated terrorists, such as AD, BR and RAF, than with those with nationalist or religious or right-wing motivation. This is probably because most terrorists motivated by left-wing ideology are of above-average intelligence and with more than the average level of education. Yet there have also been successes with nationalist terrorists, albeit mainly small fry, in Spain.

The Spanish policy of social reinsertion, though generally applied only to auxiliaries rather than hard-core terrorists with blood on their hands, has been remarkably successful (see pp. 101–3). By contrast, rehabilitation has a poor record of success in Northern Ireland. There are probably a number of explanations for this. First, ETA members generally come from a better environment than IRA terrorists, who are mainly recruited from slum areas in Belfast and Derry, or the poorest rural areas near the border with the Republic of Ireland. Second, the Basques are in a majority in the autonomous community and there is a high degree of devolution to the regional government, whereas the Catholics are in a minority in Northern Ireland and have no prospect of devolved government, or of being other than a minority in one if it did occur (as in 1974). Third, the Basques know that their provinces will never recede from Spain, whereas British governments have always left open the possibility of secession 'if the majority in Northern Ireland so wish'; indeed, it has been clear that almost every British government would gladly be rid of Northern Ireland if only this could be achieved with a chance of peace and stability thereafter. Thus the hard-core IRA, and the inhabitants of the small deprived areas from which they are recruited, still hope that they may succeed.

Rehabilitation of *brigatisti* in Italy has generally been very successful. Many *pentiti* and *dissociati* are now free and show no sign of returning to terrorism. A factor here is that most of them are intelligent people who know that BR has no future. As mentioned in Chapter 3 and earlier in this chapter, however, there may be future problems with embittered rank-and-file, who did not have enough information to offer as a bargain for their freedom, and may have fallen prey to the influences of the *mafiosi* and other criminals in their prisons. They are, however, more likely to drift into crime than to return to political terrorism.

Rehabilitation is most likely to succeed when the approach is practical rather than ideological. The accent should *not* be on political re-education; it should offer opportunities and incentives for re-absorption into the increasingly prosperous European societies, so governments will need to take positive action to train people in the skills needed in these societies, and to assist them in getting jobs. The increased flexibility in a European internal market should facilitate this.

Part V

What is to be done?

Chapter sixteen

Future development of the threat

The rise and decline of terrorist movements

This chapter gathers together and summarizes the development of the various threats considered in previous chapters.

Crime will never go away; there will always be people prepared to use any means to get rich. Nor will terrorism; there will always be minorities unable to get their way by lawful means who will try to get it by violence and intimidation.

Fashions change in crime and terrorism as one technique is found to achieve more than another. Crime does pay. Terrorism pays in the short term, but seldom in the long term. The PLO, for example, have gained more publicity and made more money than any other comparable movement in history; but they have not recovered one square metre of Palestine for the Arabs; in fact, their terrorist activities provoked the Israeli occupation 1967, and have been the primary reason why the Israelis have refused to recognize or negotiate with the PLO or to allow them to be represented in the occupied territories; and why the rest of the world has tolerated their continued occupation (see Chapter 2).

The IRA have since 1969 killed more people than any other terrorist movement in Europe, and vastly more in terms of death per million of the population (see pp. 70 and 73). So far from bringing the reunification of Ireland any closer, they have thereby made sure that no Irish government of any political party would wish to take over the government of Northern Ireland, with its aroused and hostile majority Protestant community, in the foreseeable future (see Chapters 6 and 7).

Ever since the 1960s, new terrorist movements have emerged and declined. They have not so far achieved their long-term aims before they have spent their force. But they too have been attracted by dramatic short-term dividends: massive world publicity for their cause; huge ransoms to fund their campaigns; and repeated concessions to political blackmail, notably the release of convicted perpetrators of previous terrorist attacks. Although the great majority of the world's hijackers have been

177

Palestinians, and many have been caught, virtually none of them remains in prison.

Many European terrorist movements arose in the late 1960s and early 1970s as part of the world-wide student protest against US participation in the Vietnam War. They were anti-American and anti-capitalist. They started with non-lethal activities – demonstrations, occasional arson or sabotage, and abducting managers in support of striking factory workers. The British Angry Brigade (eleven-strong) set off twenty-five small bombs but never revived when its four leading activists were imprisoned in 1972. The German RAF survived the arrest of three generations of leaders before going to ground in 1977, reviving briefly in 1985–8. Their past resilience suggests that a further revival is possible. The Italian BR were the most enduring, reaching a peak in 1978–80, only to be decimated by defections in 1982–3. The French AD, though of similar motivation, did not emerge until 1979 and collapsed after the arrest of its leaders in 1987. The Belgian CCC had an ever shorter life (see Chapters 3, 4 and 5).

For the time being, Marxist-oriented movements of this kind appear to have passed their peak, but the techniques and organizations they used to found and develop their movements will remain available to any small group of determined people, whether they have an element of idealism or are amoral, ruthless and brutal (like most of those in the RAF and AD). These techniques and organizations were created by the classic Marxist revolutionaries – Lenin, Trotsky, Mao, Ho Chi Minh, Vo Nguyen Giap, Che Guevara and Marighela – but they are and can be used also by religious fundamentalists, neo-fascists and nationalists. The Basques' 'Action–Repression–Consciousnss' spiral adopted in the early days of ETA (p. 97) had an unmistakably Marxist ring. Moreover, all of these movements seemed to settle into the traditional Marxist concept of a regular and clandestine elite vanguard (usually between 50 and 100) plus an irregular and semi-clandestine fringe, not privy to sensitive secrets, and responsible mainly for auxiliary tasks, propaganda and the recruiting of supporters. This irregular fringe has usually numbered between 200 and 500 but their mass organizations never got off the ground. Only the nationalists (the IRA and ETA) have attracted any substantial popular support which, measured in terms of votes for their affiliated political parties (Sinn Fein and HB), amounts to around 10 per cent of the voters in their communities, though the IRA could attract only 1.5 per cent amongst the people they claimed to represent, in the Republic of Ireland.

In the Europe of the 1990s, Marxism now seems firmly discredited as a *political* philosophy. All the Socialist and most of the Western Communist parties have disavowed it as a vote loser. Nationalism, or separatism, however, seems likely to remain a strong and possibly widening influence in three forms: as a neo-fascist reaction to immigration, already attracting a disturbing percentage of voters in France and Germany; as a demand for separatism by minorities, already violent in the UK and Spain and potentially so in France and Italy; and amongst the substantial and possibly expanding immigrant communities, especially in Britain (Caribbean and Asian), Germany (Turkish) and France (Arab). It is conceivable, though at present it seems unlikely, that the South Moluccans might be led again into terrorist activity in the Netherlands. Religious fundamentalist groups may also emerge in some of these countries; and, because their leaders feel that they have a god-given right to break secular laws, including the right to kill, they can grow quickly and become the most violent of all.

If able and charismatic leaders emerge in any of these types of movements, they will all be aware of the potential of the classic Marxist _techniques_ to expand a cell of half a dozen dedicated activists into a national organization with hundreds and sometimes tens of thousands of active supporters. They can sustain themselves with the reflection that many great religious or great political movements were begun by a leader or visionary with a handful of supporters: Christ with twelve; Muhammad with thirty-nine; Castro with twelve. But those are amongst the few groups which survived. For each one of those, a hundred others will have vanished from history without trace. Success has depended on an amalgam of the quality of the leaders and of their groups; the social climate of the day; the effectiveness of the establishment they hope to overturn; their sense of timing (Lenin was a master of this); and a huge dose of luck.

Of the recent movements which have arisen and been defeated in Western Europe, the BR in Italy provided the best model for study (see Chapter 3). Most of Renato Curcio's 'historic nucleus' of about ten had some degree of idealism, and so did some of the hard core who joined later,[1] but others were militarist, opportunist and sadistic. Their strength lay in their organization. It was this, in the end, which also proved to be their Achilles' heel, because members who became _pentiti_ were able to give so much information (see Chapter 3).

Similar movements, whatever brand of politics or religion may motivate them, are likely to arise in response to the stresses in Europe in the 1990s. It will be important to understand their organization and techniques, and how best to counter them.

Less dangerous to life, but perhaps more likely to spread, are the movements which specifically reject the hierarchical organization used by BR and RAF as being too vulnerable. The German Revolutionary Cells (RZ) are one such movement. Others may well develop amongst educated young people frustrated with their inability to counter the advance of materialism, pollution of the environment (including 'social pollution' by computerized recording of personal data), the growing power of the EC bureaucracy and its concerted police and intelligence services (see Chapter 4.)

The threat of foreign terrorists fighting their battles in the EC may also grow, because it will be easier for them to find safe houses amongst sympathetic immigrant communities, and easier to evade capture by crossing one of the open frontiers when they are under pressure from the police. The countries with the weakest security (police and intelligence) will be the most likely to be chosen for spectacular terrorist media events to gain publicity for a foreign cause. The Palestinians, North Africans and Iranian-backed Hezbollah remain the likeliest perpetrators. New and violent factions (like Black September, the Abdallahs and Abu Nidal in the past) will come and go. Bitter minorities like the Armenians, Croats and Slovenes will remain and new ones, possibly including the Soviet nationalities frustrated in the USSR, may turn to West European streets to seek sympathy and publicity. Their prospects were discussed more fully in Chapter 2 (p. 25).

Is the amount of political terrorism in the EC likely to increase or decline? The SEA may increase it or could, if handled well, lead to better co-operation to defeat it. But for this, it would probably remain roughly at the same level. Terrorist movements are like wasps' nests; one is discovered and destroyed, but new ones appear. There will be peaks and troughs and some of the peaks may be higher, since indiscriminate massacres by bombs in aircraft and public places have become more common. But the average level of international and domestic terrorist incidents (like mean sea level, however big the waves) seems over the years to remain much the same. A lot will depend, however, on ensuring that terrorists cannot hide and move more freely in a Europe without frontiers and the prevention of this will be summarized in the next chapter.

Terrorist weapons

There is no foreseeable development in weapons which seems likely to make a significant difference to terrorist tactics and capabilities. It has been feasible for at least ten years to acquire or assemble a nuclear weapon or even to manufacture a simple one, and to secrete it in the cargo of a ship by substituting one crate of machinery for another in the cargo awaiting shipment. It has not been done, nor has there even been a credible hoax claim to have done it. The reasons, presumably, are complexity and lack of credibility. Though feasible, the operation would be far more complex than slipping a small bomb into aircraft baggage, driving a car bomb up to a target and firing it by delay fuse or remote control, or mounting a kidnap. There would be a much greater chance of its going wrong and a much greater chance of the terrorists' being caught. Even if the nuclear bomb were positioned and the threat made (e.g. 'Release our prisoners by noon or . . . ') the bluff would amost certainly be called, and the terrorists would almost certainly not fire the bomb, for fear of the disastrously adverse effect on world opinion. When they think about it, both sides realize this, and each knows that the other side realizes it, so terrorists are more likely to continue to rely on simpler weapons, such as hand-held guns, portable missile projectors and bombs.

Poison gas has been available for seventy-five years, and its manufacture needs no high technology. It would be easy for Gadafi to fill an adapted tanker truck with liquefied poison gas, and feasible to dispatch it, with impeccable papers as a 'dangerous liquid', into, say, Greece; thence (after 1992) to move freely across open EC borders; in due course to be concealed up wind of an undefined European city with a threat to explode it. Biological warfare has been used for centuries, famous examples being the catapulting of diseased corpses into a besieged city and the contamination of water supplies. The reasons why modern terrorists have not used these methods are similar to those applied to nuclear weapons. Since all are feasible, however, the possibility of their use cannot be ruled out.

Sophistication of bomb fuses has increased markedly in the past ten years, for example with the use of the video-recorder timing mechanism for precise delay bombs (as at Brighton in 1984) and the tilt fuse for bombs under cars (used frequently by the IRA and the INLA since 1979). Low vapour explosives have presented detection problems since 1987. Bombs to destroy passenger aircraft in the air have been fired by fuses concealed in electronic calculators and cassette-recorders. Development of bombs will undoubtedly continue, aimed to defeat detection, to booby trap neutralization and to increase their killing power. Since these developments come mainly by improvisation from other materials and manufactured products as they become available, they are the most difficult to predict. The use of multiple methods of detection (see Chapter 13) offers the best hope of countering this threat.

No revolutionary developments seem likely in small arms, but those which are occurring generally favour the terrorist, because it is almost always he or she who shoots first. Wholly plastic weapons could help the hijacker to smuggle them aboard an aircraft, but those developed so far are effective only at point-blank ranges. The three-round burst increases the accuracy of automatic weapons and conserves ammunition. Such a weapon can now be concealed in a brief-case coupled with a laser sight which projects a pinpoint of light on to the target, enabling the weapon to be aimed and fired accurately by someone holding the brief-case hanging from his hand.

Hand-held surface-to-surface missile projectors fire missiles which can be accurately guided on to a moving target (e.g. an armoured limousine) at a range of 2 km. Simple 'fire-and-forget' surface-to-air missiles have been effective in shooting down helicopters in Afghanistan and elsewhere. Developments continue all the time but there is no reason to anticipate an unexpected breakthrough, because sophisticated weapons usually take some years to develop. Developments in improvised weapons are the most likely and the least predictable.[2]

Computer games and white-collar crime

The microelectronics revolution will make it easier for criminals and terrorists to obtain money by fraud and extortion and to launder it when they do. The European internal market will make it easier still unless the free movement of persons, goods, capital and services (including electronic bank transfers) is accompanied by better means of keeping track of them anywhere inside the community.

The rapid growth of plastic money will include 'general credit cards', on the British Telecom Phonecard principle, which could be used to pay for almost any out-of-pocket expenses (such as rail and taxi fares, telephone calls and casual meals) just by putting the card in a slot under a display screen showing the amount debited and the balance. For larger amounts, charge cards with some protection against fraudulent use (such as a PIN) will be used more and more. There will therefore be less cash in the pocket, the pocket book, the till, the safe and the bank vault. Assuming that all wages will soon be paid, like salaries, by bank draft, there will be no need for the vulnerable security vans which today carry bags of cash around the streets.

Thus there will be fewer opportunities for thefts and robberies, and a corresponding increase in racketeering, fraud and extortion. We can expect more kidnaps for ransom; also more extortionary threats to contaminate food and pharmaceutical products and to disrupt computer systems by inserting a virus, or whatever new techniques become available. Money will be extorted by selecting victims who have the power to release or transfer it electronically and to coerce them into accepting that it would be the lesser of two evils to do this rather than to pay the heavier price of resisting the demand.

When the speed and ease of electronic transfer of money within the European internal market increases after 1992, it will be still easier for criminals and terrorists to launder their dirty money by splitting it up and transferring it into confidential bank accounts in tax havens and other countries which ask and answer no questions and give the courts, police and revenue authorities no access. Alternatively the money will become the assets of bogus companies (or of operating companies able to conceal illegal activities within their accounts) which can then release it as needed as supposed payment for fictitious and unverifiable goods and services.

To combat this, changes will be needed in both financial and commercial laws, and international co-operation needed both inside and outside the EC. These were discussed in Chapter 14 (pp. 156–7) and will be summarized in the next chapter.

Computer crime will certainly continue to grow unless the attitude towards it changes. Some examples of its growth and of what it is costing were given in Chapter 9 (pp. 114–15). Business corporations, manufacturers and services are becoming increasingly dependent on their computer systems each year, and their operations become more interdependent. This interdependence is also spreading nationally and internationally. To make these systems and their communications robust increases costs and decreases speed and efficiency. Duplication of all software is expensive so is building in safeguards against maliciously inserted viruses, and against fraudsters and hackers. Staff using computers all day and every day become casual about security of codes.

Another problem is that a sum of money which promises years of affluence to an individual fraudster is peanuts to a large corporation with a multi-billion turnover of goods or cash. Moreover, the most vulnerable corporations (banks, insurance companies, etc.) fear that they will forfeit public confidence if frauds are reported, so for 'relatively small' frauds they think it more profitable to turn a blind eye. This is one reason for the low rate of conviction of computer fraudsters (see pp. 114–15).

During this period of rapid microelectronic development, each generation is more advanced in its understanding than its elders. People now in top management positions have far less understanding of the capabilities and potential of computers than their employees twenty years younger. People under 30 have been brought up on computer games since early childhood; so were people under 20; but all of their computer games are old hat compared with those of children today. By the time these children enter the growing service industries, they, too, will be able to run circles round their managers.

Governments in the USA and Europe seem at last to be realizing that new legislation is urgently needed to check computer crime, whether by fraudsters or teenage hackers in search of fun. Some of the legislation in hand is discussed in the next chapter (pp. 193–5).

Racketeering (see pp. 156–7) is currently one of the biggest sources of terrorist finance but, if the measures recently introduced against it (police access to bank and company accounts and seizure of assets) are persevered with and strictly enforced, this may be checked.

Prevention of all of these crimes will be made better rather than worse if the European single market makes provision for better cross-border police co-operation and the power to impose spot checks anywhere at any time.

Drugs and international crime

The almost unbelievable profits made from trafficking in hard drugs (one kilogram of cocaine escalating to a street value of 500 times its production cost) will ensure that it will grow unless drastic action is taken (see pp. 114–15).

In Britain alone, the amount of illegal money fed into the economy by drug trafficking, fraud and counterfeiting is already around £1 billion per year and is growing. This is enough to have a significant effect on undermining the currency and fuelling inflation; addiction is even worse in some other EC countries and is rising particularly fast in Italy, where it is helping to finance the revival of the Mafia after the blows they received in the early 1980s.[3]

Throughout Western Europe, addiction is fast creating a new underclass, drawing social security and financing their addiction by crime or, more often, by recruiting new addicts. This underclass contains a disproportionate number of immigrants, whose unrewarding lives often make them prey to the drug pushers. The 'yuppie' addicts are more dangerous, because they are more likely to finance themselves by fraud or by involvement at the higher levels of drug trafficking.

Every penny of the £70,000 paid for the doses from one kilogram of cocaine comes in small denomination currency handed over by addicts (just as every penny of the turnover of a billion-dollar retail chain comes across the counters). Great as the damage is to the consumer societies it is greater still to the producing countries, notably Colombia, where the drug barons use this money to finance death squads and to corrupt the political, administrative and judicial systems. It is by no means fanciful to imagine the Medellin drug cartel taking over a major political party and using their enormous wealth and power to get themselves elected to power. Once in power, they would have the resources to offer the voters enough incentives to keep them there. There would be government of the people by the barons for the barons, financed by the addicts on the streets of Europe and the USA.

Narcotics multinationals are diversifying. Most of their subsidiaries already carry out other activities as a cover. Some of these activities are legal and some illegal. Throughout their history, the Mafia-style international criminal organizations and the Hong Kong Triads have been primarily financed by drug trafficking. So are most of the warring militias in Lebanon and Burma.[4]

The evils flowing from international drug trafficking know no bounds.

In the long term, they may be the greatest of all threats to the prospects of an orderly and civilized world. Their defeat will be amongst the most important challenges facing Europe after 1992.

Chapter seventeen

Fighting the war in a united Europe

What has worked best so far

Part II of this book covered what had been tried in tackling terrorism, drugs and organized crime in Europe from 1969 to 1989. Part III looked at technological developments. Part IV struck a balance between public safety and civil rights. This final chapter looks at what best can be done in a united Europe after 1992, first summarizing what has worked best so far.

Detection and arrest depends upon a good intelligence organization, best working with a specialized anti-terrorist force. The appointment of General Dalla Chiesa in Italy in 1974, with wide powers and a free hand, using 200 men specially trained in surveillance duties, resulted in the capture of most of the original BR hard core. The following year, his force was disbanded and the government intelligence service emasculated. The BR revived and reorganized, subjecting the Italian political and judicial system to five years of selective terror. Dalla Chiesa and his team were reactivated in 1978 and by 1983 both left- and right-wing terrorist gangs were reduced to a few small splinter groups, largely as a result of his exploitation of defecting terrorists (*pentiti*), offering leniency or release in exchange for decisive information against their former comrades (see pp. 39–45).

Most European countries do offer some form of leniency for 'state's evidence'. The equivalent of the *pentiti* in Northern Ireland (the 'supergrasses') secured numerous convictions but these were largely quashed by the Appeal Courts. One reason for this was the unsatisfactory system of single-judge courts. Both systems were widely criticized on ethical grounds, but in Italy terrorist killings fell to trickle while in Northern Ireland 400 more people have been killed since the convictions were quashed (see p. 42, pp. 44–5 and 79–81).

Also in Italy, the police were given powers for immediate tapping of telephones, subject to retrospective judicial approval, and the power to search complete blocks of apartments if it was suspected that wanted persons were in them. Similar powers were granted in Germany. In both cases these were parts of packages of emergency laws (see pp. 37–9 and 57–60). In France, police were authorized to prevent people from leaving the scene of a crime, to ask them for proof of identity, and to arrest them if they failed to provide it (see pp. 65–6).

In Northern Ireland, if weapons, ammunition or explosives were found in a person's house or car, the occupant had the onus of proving that he or she did not know they were there (see p. 159).

The Germans in 1977 installed a computerized national intelligence data bank, and this proved highly effective in finding wanted persons amongst the millions living in a city (see pp. 58–9). Most other EC countries now have a similar system and they are linked with each other.

Powers of **detention and interrogation** have been extended under emergency laws in most EC countries. Spain in 1985 authorized detention of suspects *incommunicado* for ten days, later reduced (see pp. 102 and 157). Since 1974 Britain has allowed detention of people suspected of involvement with planning or committing terrorist acts for two days, extendible to seven with ministerial permission; and knowingly withholding information on such matters itself became an offence (pp. 92 and 159). Also in Northern Ireland, though the right to silence under interrogation remains, it is now permissible for courts to be asked by the prosecution to take account of such silence in assessing guilt (see pp. 81–2). In Italy, where it became common practice for accused persons, their friends outside and sometimes also their lawyers, to disrupt and delay court preceedings and to intimidate witnesses and jurors, judges were given the power to hold accused persons in custody indefinitely if they believed that any of these things were being done deliberately (see p. 37).

Trials have been disrupted by lawyers intent on perverting the course of justice in Germany and a number of other countries. In Germany, it became necessary to ban certain lawyers from the courts for this; also if they were themselves suspected of having supported terrorist activities (see pp. 000–000). In Germany and Italy, the accused person can also be excluded from the court for disrupting proceedings.

Juries and witnesses are particularly vulnerable to intimidation, and in the Republic of Ireland (since 1962), Northern Ireland (since 1973) and France (since 1987), trials for terrorist offences have been conducted without juries (see pp. 78–81 and 65–6). For terrorist trials in France and the Republic of Ireland, the judge presides over a number of junior judges as assessors, though a single judge sits alone in Northern Ireland. No juries at all are used in the Netherlands, for any kind of trial, though assessors (found again from junior judges) are used in serious cases. Other possible ways of dealing with this problem were discussed in Chapter 15 and are summarized later in this chapter.

Rehabilitation of former terrorists has been done successfully in Italy and Spain. Despite every effort, the Dutch have been unable to reconcile the more alienated South Moluccans. Rehabilitation has generally failed with the RAF in Germany and the IRA in Northern Ireland. The most encouraging example has been the 'social reinsertion' programme in Spain, though this has been of terrorist auxiliaries rather than of hard-core killers (see pp. 101–3). In Italy, terrorists who have admitted to several murders (eight in one case) are now free. But others, who have admitted guilt but have not been willing to give information about their comrades, are still in prison, even though their offences have not included murder (see pp. 44–5).

Free movement of goods, capital and services

In their deliberations, the Schengen powers have expressed the view that ceasing to rely on internal borders should result in improved police co-operation, which could more than outweigh the value of the present border controls.[1]

The main pressure for removal of border controls has come from European business people, who are understandably more concerned with day-to-day trading profit than with hypothetical escapes of wanted persons. Border checks are estimated to add twenty-two hours to what would otherwise be a thirty-six hour journey for a truck travelling 1,200 km in Europe. The overall cost imposed by barriers is estimated at £130 billion, or 5 per cent of the EC's Gross Domestic Product.[2] If these checks are replaced by spot checks, however, the spot checks must be made equally effective, since most large consignments of drugs and explosives are concealed in cargo trucks or containers.

Britain and Ireland will also be concerned if removal of border checks allows animals and plants to be smuggled in, since they greatly prize their freedom from rabies and other diseases.

Other areas which would present problems were also listed in Chapter 10, such as weapons (more freely available in France and Belgium than elsewhere) and soft drugs (easily available in the Netherlands). All EC countries agree that there must be control of import and export of both legal and illicit drugs, and of antiques and works of art, but the means of achieving this have not yet been worked out.

Free movement of capital and services is also an aim of the SEA. This is again good for business, but there must be safeguards against facilitating crime and especially the laundering of money through shell companies and electronic money transfers. This may be easier to overcome than other problems, provided that police and Inland Revenue access to bank and company accounts is freely given; also if full use is made of the capacity of the new generations of computers to record full details of every transaction and of who carried it out, and to display it on demand without complicated procedures. This would assist police in subsequent investigation of the course taken by transfers of dirty money which came to light retrospectively. Most of the data would never be used but would be there if needed – just like the mass of fingerprints that are left all over the house or an office, which never need to be checked unless a crime has to be investigated there.

Free movement of persons

In combating both terrorism and crime, however, especially drug trafficking, ability to check the movement of people and their hand baggage is by far the most important. At peak holiday weekends, 10 million people move in to or out of the UK.[3] From 1993 the Channel Tunnel is expected to disgorge 3,000 people per hour. The tunnel will, of course, be Britain's only wholly internal frontier and, if there are to be any checks at all, it has been agreed that they will be at entry rather than exit, or on the train itself. Given the necessary personnel and equipment, this would be perfectly feasible.

British police, customs and immigration officials are convinced that the border is by far the most effective place at which to catch smugglers, drug traffickers, wanted persons and illegal immigrants. This seems to be borne out by the German experience of arresting 100,000 people every year (half of them on wanted lists) at their border check-points (see p. 125). And the problems of Denmark's no-passport agreement with Nordic countries, Switzerland's special relationship with France, Germany and Italy, and the ease with which migrants from (or via) North Africa can cross the porous Mediterranean coastlines of southern Europe were mentioned on pp. 106–7. This is particularly serious in view of Libya's continual sponsorship of terrorism, and the fact that most of the foreign terrorists who kill in Europe come from Arab or other Middle Eastern countries.

The Single European Act does specify that regulations for the movement of persons across internal borders (as distinct from goods, capital and services) will need unanimous agreement in the Council of Ministers; the Act also leaves member states free to take necessary measures to check illegal immigrants, criminals and terrorists, and to re-establish whatever controls they need in an emergency.

These provisos will certainly need to be exercised regularly for some years to come until the effectiveness of the spot checks has been developed and proved that it is as good or better than the border controls.

Spot checks will replace internal border checks effectively only if every EC country does issue machine-readable identity cards, passports and visas; if the police and excise officers are equipped and free to do spot checks whenever they think necessary; and if the necessary personal data are recorded on linked national computers. With the technology now becoming available for identification and anti-impersonation, and for handling, storing and instant access to data, this would need very little extra staff. The problems will be for all to agree to face the initial outlay and to have the political will to use the capabilities to the full, and to find effective means of preventing or detecting abuse in order to conserve civil liberties.

Identification and anti-impersonation

The potential of machine-readable identity cards, passports and visas, and of recording personal data on national computers, were discussed in Chapters 11 and 12 and some of the implications for civil liberties in Chapter 14. So were the capabilities and implications of the various means of detecting impersonation – matching digital fingerprint data, vein patterns, retina patterns, voice characteristics and (for subsequent investigation) DNA in body fluids.

Innocent people have nothing to fear from such data being recorded, provided that there are effective curbs on any abuse. Large numbers of people already have identity cards; many more have bankers cards, credit cards, and so on. All of these involve recording of data both electronically on the card and in a central computer. Virtually none feels deprived of liberties and the Data Protection Act is at people's disposal if they do. The addition of anti-impersonation data would prevent them from using someone else's card, which is itself a gross abuse of civil liberties. Machine-readable anti-impersonation identity cards, passports and visas would help to deter and catch not only terrorists and drug traffickers, but also fraudsters, other criminals and football hooligans, all of whom abuse their civil liberties at the expense of the rest of the community.

The power to make spot checks could be abused just like any other police powers (eg. the 'sus-laws' and random breathalyser tests). The huge memory capacity of the computer systems now coming on stream (see Chapter 11) offers a better guard against this than ever before. It is perfectly feasible for such a system to be programmed to record not only the identity of the person been checked, but also the identity of the police officer or official making the check. If the person later complained of harassment, all the data could be brought forward by pressing a few keys, and it would immediately be apparent if the patterns revealed officiousness, harassment or victimization.

Air travel security

Air piracy (bombing and hijacking) has international political repercussions out of proportion to the number and scale of incidents, and the casualties from bombing passenger aircraft can be very heavy. Air travel security is largely a matter of access control, and of checking of passengers, baggage and cargo before embarkation and loading. Given the electronic means now available for processing and linking check-in data about passengers, there should be a better chance of detecting hijack teams before they board, not least because it will be possible to concentrate the investigation and interrogation effort on passengers who might conceivably be suspects and not waste it on those who clearly are not. This is discussed in Chapter 12 (pp. 139–41) and would require harmonization of national procedures and data links between the countries of a united Europe.

Emerging technology for bomb and gun search, coupled with checking passengers' personal data, would now permit a radical improvement to check-in and boarding procedure. A comprehensive proposal for this is set out in Chapter 13 (pp. 146–50).

A world war on drug trafficking

The alarming spread of drug addiction and the enormous profits it places at the disposal of international criminal organizations were described in Chapters 9 and 16. Huge sums of money will continue to flow into the already enormous reserves held by the drug barons and their multinational trafficking empires. Much of this is held in property and commodities and in banks in countries where, under present world banking practices, it cannot be seized. These range from tax havens where no questions are asked or answered, to nations which are themselves governed by illegal regimes.

The only long-term solution will be to cut the demand in the consumer countries. Possible methods were discussed in Chapter 9. Legalization of drugs, with heavy taxation (as for alcohol) would slash the drug baron's profit and provide instead revenue for public education and the cure of addicts, but at the price of condemning many more of the weaker people to ruination of their lives by addiction.

The answer proposed is compulsory clinical treatment of addicts (where necessary in custody) and life-meaning-life sentences for anyone proven to have been involved in substantial distribution and sale of narcotics (see p. 113). For this to work after 1992, it would be necessary for all the EC countries to harmonize their policies.

In parallel with this, it will be necessary to smash the infrastructures of the narcotics multinationals, in Latin America, the Caribbean and Asia, and in the distribution networks in the USA and West Europe, especially in Colombia, which is in real danger of a political take-over by the drug cartels, much as General Noriega took over Panama.

The problem is so urgent that it should be regarded as a world war. All but a small minority of countries would in principle support such a war, though not all could afford to contribute materially to it. The first step would be to get the UN Security Council and General Assembly to give this legal backing. This is how the UN Charter was designed to operate, and as it did operate over the Korean war in 1950, when the USSR had walked out of the Security Council, and was not there to veto it. Neither the USSR nor any of the other permanent members, however, would veto a war on drugs.[4]

Despite the ending of the Cold War, the USA, USSR and East and West Europe are still likely to need to keep substantial armies, navies and air forces, certainly until there is no further risk of a hardline reaction in the USSR, and thereafter so long as there are still a number of governments in the world which have shown their readiness to use armed force internationally. (At the time of writing there are at least twelve in this category and, when their leaders die or are replaced, other leaders of the same kind will undoubtedly appear in these or other countries.)

The NATO and Warsaw Pact countries will be able to reduce the armed forces facing each other drastically and would be able to divert many army, naval and air patrol units to the drugs war. This would, in fact, keep them much more battle-worthy than training in barracks at home.

This war would not be a conventional war. It would be much more akin to policing – on land, sea and air. For example to break up the transit of drugs across the Caribbean needs large numbers of ships, aircraft and personnel, carrying out surveillance to detect the traffic and then checks and searches to intercept it and arrest the traffickers. Armed forces in this role, like police, would fire only if fired upon.

Certain countries would probably welcome the assistance of troops and aircraft in this role to police their frontiers, harbours and small airstrips. Such requests could be met. Given assistance, the Colombian army (which, contrary to some press comment, is highly efficient and experienced), would be able to concentrate more effort on intercepting and arresting members of the drug barons' killer squads in Bogota, Medellin, Cali and the countryside, and wearing down the guerrilla organizations whom the barons sponsor. Peru would probably welcome similar assistance, enabling the army and police to concentrate on eliminating the Sendero Luminoso terrorists who currently protect the coca growers and traffickers. Both countries would also probably welcome training teams from professional units like air forces, VIP protection units and anti-terrorist commandos.

Co-ordination would be needed rather than a central command structure, to allocate forces to assist sovereign governments to fight the battles they are already trying to fight. This co-ordination would best be done by a headquarters jointly run on behalf of the United Nations by the USA and the USSR, with staff and liaison officers from both the assisting and assisted countries.

This can be regarded as a substantial enlargement of the kinds of assistance dispatched by the USA and Britain to Colombia and the Caribbean in September 1989 – British SAS and US army training teams, naval patrol craft, and so on. The significance would be the practical co-operation of the previously rival power blocks to help police the world. This, again, was precisely the original concept of the UN.

Similar assistance would be needed in Asia to support the governments fighting the heroin traffic. Thailand, Laos and Pakistan would almost certainly welcome such assistance. Britain could deploy whatever extra effort was needed in Hong Kong; in future years – who knows? – the other countries (the Golden Crescent and the Golden Triangle, including newly stabilized regimes in Afghanistan, Burma and Iran), might join the common effort for this particular war. Once again, the very existence and process of such co-operation could have far-reaching results. And it cannot be many years before the horror of the 1989 Tiananmen Square massacre fades and China resumes her proper place in the international community.

A parallel campaign in this war on drugs would be to tackle the money-laundering process by mobilizing the international banking community. This will be discussed next, after consideration of the other forms of international crime which generate illegal money to be laundered.

International crime and money laundering

The malign domestic and international influences of the international Mafia, the Triads and other criminal secret societies were discussed in Chapter 9. Many of them are closely associated with the cocaine and heroin industries, so they would be proper targets for the proposed war on drugs.

The rate of growth of international fraud, counterfeiting and other white-collar crime is almost as alarming as the growth in drug trafficking. The courts do not seem to regard it as a serious crime; only a tiny percentage of fraudsters and hackers are prosecuted, and very few of these sent to prison. This was discussed in Chapters 9 and 16, which also drew attention to the reluctance of computer manufacturers and major users to build in or to operate effective computer security measures, and their reluctance to prosecute computer criminals.

Europe should break away from these attitudes. Computer crime develops skills and techniques which are used by more dangerous criminals, notably *mafiosi* and drug traffickers, to launder the proceeds of their crimes. No sympathy should be shown to the computer criminals themselves. They are mainly in-house employees betraying their trust, relying on the lack of will to prosecute them, or young computer buffs (often in early teenage), initially hacking into computer systems for kicks, but who are thereafter tempted to use their skills for personal gain. All are relatively affluent and in good jobs. Their opportunities for defrauding the remainder of the community will be increased as international computer links develop, so the Council of Ministers should enact and harmonize laws to enable the courts to prosecute and to give deterrent penalties.

Late in 1989, it looked as though Britain might be considering effective legislation against computer crime. The Law Commission reported on the scale of disruption and expense which hackers, fraudsters and extortioners were causing to both government and commercial computer operators (see pp. 114–16), and the inadequacy both of the legislation under which they could be charged and the penalties awarded by the courts. They proposed that there should be a basic offence of knowingly entering a computer system without authority, which should carry a summary punishment of a maximum of three months' imprisonment. If this unauthorized entry were made with the intent of committing a serious crime (eg. fraud or embezzlement) the maximum penalty would be five years; and the person should be liable for such a charge immediately his or her entry was detected without waiting for the more serious crime to be committed, it being necessary only to prove the intent beyond reasonable doubt to make the person liable for the five-year sentence.

Similarly if the intent of the unauthorized entry were to alter computer data or programs, or to insert viruses or 'time bombs' or to put infected discs into operation, this intent would again make the offender liable for five years' imprisonment.[5]

The USA has had a law of this kind for six years. The Computer Fraud and Abuse Act 1984, strengthened in 1986, made intentional and unauthorized access to a computer used by government agencies a criminal offence; also, entry to two or more computers in different states; also altering or destroying information which caused losses of more than $1,000. The first successful prosecution under this Act was completed in January 1989 when a 17-year-old hacker was sentenced to nine months in prison. Another 'mischievous' hacker was sentenced to six months in prison to be followed by a year in a rehabilitation centre to be treated for 'addiction to computers'.[6]

The California State Assembly has recently passed a law banning academic institutions from awarding degrees related to computer science to anyone convicted of computer crimes.[7] If extended world-wide, this could be a powerful disincentive to the teenage hacker. The EC would do well to emulate and improve upon this US legislation without further delay.

The various means available for laundering money were described in Chapter 9; through drug trafficking, fictitious dealings in shell companies and exploitation of the ease of electronic transfer of money from bank to bank all over the world. Since laundering plays a big part in facilitating and concealing the most serious crimes and terrorist activities, it is urgent for the EC to stifle it before the SEA makes it easier still. The essential antidote is ease of police access to accounts in banks and commercial companies, subject to judicial control to prevent abuse of privacy if nothing untoward is found; but a claim of the right to privacy in order to conceal crime at the expense of the community must not be accepted, and the only way to discover if this is being done is to have a look at the accounts.

Several EC countries have made provision for such access, notably Italy in dealing with criminal 'organizations of a mafia kind' (see pp. 156-7), and the UK to counter racketeering and extortion by terrorist organizations in Northern Ireland (see pp. 81-2). In both cases, if evidence of crime is revealed by the examination, the police can freeze the assets pending prosecution and confiscate them after conviction. In the UK senior police officers have power of access on their own initiative in emergency, subject to retrospective endorsement by the courts.

Some progress has been made in extending this power internationally. In December 1988 the Central Banks of twelve countries (including the Summit Seven, Benelux, Sweden and Switzerland) signed the Declaration of Basel, committing themselves to identifying sources of funds and co-operating with international judicial enquiries. The UN Vienna Convention in the same month aimed to extend this more widely and at government level, but this has still to be ratified (see pp. 116-19). The EC must see to it that full access is open to police and other authorities from any one of its countries to another, subject to judicial safeguards to prevent abuse, and this will not work if there is a requirement to *prove* the crime before gaining access. The police, in co-operation with local authorities, must be able to pick up the apple to see if it is rotten, with no danger to the innocent if it is not.

The Achilles' heel lies at present in the number of banks in tax havens and other (mainly small) countries which themselves make fat profits from the trade and will not allow access.[8] The only way to overcome this is for the responsible countries (starting with the signatories of the Declaration of Basel) to introduce currency regulation requiring a collective ban on the transfer of any money in and out of banks which will not co-operate in giving this access (see p. 117).

The rule of law

Most EC countries have found it necessary to adapt their judicial processes to counter the intimidation of witnesses and jurors by terrorist or criminal gangs and, in some cases, to counter abuse of their privileges by lawyers actively supporting (as distinct from legally defending) terrorist groups. These measures are described in the chapters on individual countries (3–8) and in Chapters 14 and 15.

As an alternative to trial of terrorist offences by wholly professional courts (judges sitting with qualified assessors and no juries), a proposal is made in Chapter 15 for protecting the anonymity of witnesses and juries, and if necessary also of members of professional courts, by greater use of video-cameras and CCTV (pp. 166–8).

Action is also needed to revise detention and interrogation procedures, both to safeguard fairness to the accused person, and also to ensure that these safeguards are not abused by guilty people and their lawyers to pervert the course of justice. While highest priority must be given to ensuring that no innocent person is convicted, some of the safeguards designed for nineteenth-century conditions are now used by professional criminals and terrorists and dishonest lawyers to get much too high a percentage of patently guilty people acquitted, and this not only releases them to commit further crimes but also encourages others to do so in the confidence that, even if caught, they will be able to get away with it by using their 'rights'. In Northern Ireland, while the 'right to silence' remains, there is now the parallel right for the prosecution to ask the court to take note of such silence in arriving at their verdict. This is discussed in a wider context in Chapters 14 (pp. 158–9) and 15 (p. 168).

In the interests of both the public and the accused, the processes of appeal and confirmation of sentences must not be unnecessarily prolonged. Unless prevented, some lawyers will do this as a means of making more money. This has been particularly rife in Italy, where in 1989 the procedures were revised to curtail such opportunities. This kind of abuse must not be allowed to hamper European judicial co-operation.

It will be important in the European single market to harmonize judicial processes, though the very different legal traditions between member countries will prevent a completely integrated system for many years, if not always. It should, however, be possible to agree on expenditious trial in any one member country with witnesses available from any other. An important factor will be to obviate obstacles and delays in extradition procedures.

Political and professional co-operation

Interpol provides useful channels for promoting bilateral co-operation, but its wide membership (136) and its bar on investigating matters classed as political will *always* limit its effectiveness in dealing with terrorism.

For similar reasons the United Nations has been virtually useless in this field (see p. 120).

The Tokyo, Hague and Montreal Conventions against hijacking, though all were ratified by more than 100 countries, are hamstrung by the ease with which any member country can evade its obligation to extradite hijackers by going through the process of prosecution with no intention of conviction (pp. 120–1). The European Convention for the Suppression of Terrorism, despite a determined attempt to exclude terrorist offences from being regarded as political, left several loopholes for any signatory to evade its obligations by doing just that, so it has proved virtually useless in practice (pp. 122–3).

The meetings of the Summit Seven have ensured that the seven most powerful non-Communist countries have committed themselves publicly and morally to not giving way to terrorism, and to co-operating over extradition and other matters, but sadly experience has shown that even some of these countries will find loopholes to evade actions which they judge to be counter to their national interests (pp. 123–4).

By far the most effective international anti-terrorist organization is TREVI, under which EC ministers, officials and professionals meet regularly to discuss and co-ordinate their actions. It has two major strengths: it succeeds in carrying out its work without media attention (which so often poisons international co-operation when ministers have to take up postures to impress their electorates); and it provides the machinery and the authority for the operations, especially police and intelligence services, to co-operate discreetly in their common professional aim of combating terrorism and crime (p. 121.)

This is the most valuable co-operation of all – *bilateral* co-operation between the professionals. Once police and intelligence officers get to know their opposite numbers personally at TREVI meetings, they will develop trust and confidence in knowing how far they can go in exchanging information: this is in full accord with the 'need to know' principle. Even amongst a group of trusted colleagues, individuals will go furthest with sensitive information if they are speaking only to the one who needs to know it. There is on this basis outstanding co-operation between British, Dutch, French and German police and intelligence officers (pp. 121–2).

This co-operation will need to be facilitated by laws and agreed procedures enacted in the final provisions of the SEA, covering such things as links between their national computer data banks and ready access for using them; interchange of wanted lists; readiness, either at external borders or spot checks, to search positively for people on those lists and extradite them; and the right of hot pursuit by police across borders, subject to keeping all concerned informed. In all of these areas, especially intelligence and aggressive search for terrorists from neighbouring countries, Belgium has always lagged behind the others, probably with the aim of letting sleeping dogs lie; it will, however, be important for Belgium to live down the reputation it has earned amongst terrorists (eg. the IRA, RAF and AD) as a useful rest-and-recreation area and as a good place for a secure base, untroubled by the police. There must be no such secure bases in a united Europe.

Co-operation between Europe's anti-terrorist commandos, notably the British SAS, the Dutch BBE and the German GSG9, has been extremely successful. Proposals for an international anti-terrorist force, however, must be resisted. The necessary skill, precision, teamwork and morale of these national elite forces could never be matched by an international force, in the same way that a 'European' or 'Latin American' football team would not beat the Dutch, German, Italian or Argentine national teams. Moreover, the success of such commandos depends on their having unequivocal political direction, and the ability to get instant political decisions for action at the critical moments of an operation. No group of governments, however closely allied, could achieve this as quickly as a national government. The best arrangement is, as now, for one government with its own commando to take the decisions and actions and for the others to be available to participate (as was done successfully at Glimmen and Mogadishu) without affecting the chain of responsibility (see p. 122).

The united Europe must also be bold about making full use of the enormous potential offered by the technological developments now so rapidly advancing. These should give greatly increased capability in fighting terrorism, drug trafficking and international crime, in fields such as intelligence; detection of terrorists, and their devices and of drugs and explosives; identification; security of premises; and the provision of evidence for conviction. As with all other powers mentioned in this book, there must be safeguards to prevent abuse. The single market should give greater opportunities to apply these technologies to good effect in defeating terrorism and reversing the growth of computer crime and drug trafficking. The professionals will always be keen to use all the weapons available, and to co-operate in using them. It would be a tragedy if the Community failed to use these opportunities due to misplaced caution, petty rivalries or lack of political will.

Widening co-operation to the East

The co-operation developed under the Single European Act will undoubtedly spill over to Switzerland, Norway, Sweden and Austria, but it need not stop there. Many East European countries, with Poland and Hungary in the van, are already expanding their economic and cultural links with Western Europe. This trend is being positively encouraged by President Gorbachov, who clearly sees advantages of both sides in these links. Unless the spectre of a hardline Communist Party backlash materializes in the USSR, there is every reason to hope that this trend will spread to the rest of Eastern Europe and to the USSR itself.

This could in turn be the beginning of a development as far-reaching for world security as the parallel reduction of nuclear and conventional armed forces. Eastern and Western Europe and the rest of NATO all have a common interest in eliminating the poisonous effects of drug trafficking, international fraud and terrorism on international relations. Few people now believe in the theory of a world terrorist network based in Moscow. The USSR no longer benefits from a continuation of the Arab–Israeli or Lebanese conflicts. It is in the interest of neither side to see Islamic fundamentalists reaching out from Iran or Afghanistan.

Co-operation between the Warsaw Pact and NATO countries, and especially between the USSR, the USA and the now potentially equal political and economic power of a united Western Europe, has breathtaking potential in the fields of both economics and security. Along with co-operation in the war on drugs, proposed earlier in this chapter, one of the most promising starting-points will be this co-operation in countering terrorism, especially by denying support to internal terrorist movements (such as ETA, the IRA and ideological terrorists as out-dated now as Stalin and Brezhnev) and to foreign terrorists wishing to fight their battles on European streets. With the EC, USA and USSR united in this aim, one or other or all of them will be able to apply overwhelmingly powerful restraints on any country sponsoring, harbouring or supporting terrorists.

Sadly, part of the price of freedom is its abuse by terrorists. Stalinist stifling of freedom (especially freedom of speech and of the media) brought the paradoxical benefit of stifling terrorism. *Perestroika* and *glasnost* will inevitably provide incentives for extremists to grab the headlines as they do in the West, and to use terrorism as the means. The East will increasingly share both the problem and the benefit of co-operation in handling it.

In January 1989 a meeting took place in Moscow between twenty-six US and Soviet lawyers, academics and senior journalists, to discuss Soviet-American co-operation against terrorism. This was in response to a statement by Mikhail Gorbachov in his 1987 book, *Perestroika*: 'the Soviet Union rejects terrorism in principle and is prepared to co-operate energetically with other states in eradicating this evil'. Both governments approved of the meeting, though they wisely agreed that, at this stage, exchanges would be more frank if neither government was officially taking part. After five days of discussion the group agreed on a nine-point recommendation to their respective governments.[9]

A second meeting took place at the Rand Corporation in the USA in

September 1989, this time including two former senior KGB officials, and a former Director (William Colby) and Deputy Director (Ray Cline) of the CIA. This meeting set up four working groups: on intelligence; on the Middle East; on practical measures; and on legal matters. It was also agreed to set up a fifth working group to prepare a Soviet–US Simulation Exercise for current and former policy makers, playing their own roles in a scenario involving a joint Soviet–US response to terrorist incidents.

The second meeting was fully reported in the *Los Angeles Times*.[10] A book will appear in 1990 about these meetings, to be edited by Eric Grove of the British-based Foundation for International Security, who attended both the meetings as a member of the US team. Other meetings are planned, including one between Soviet and West European representatives.

The results of these meetings were highly encouraging, though their reports give full weight to differences in perception as well as to areas of agreement. There is no doubt about the sincerity of the desire to co-operate. It would be folly, however, to imagine that either side will do other than act in its own national interests. This applies to every international venture and is also very apparent at meetings of the EC Council of Ministers. The art of international co-operation is to agree on objectives which will advance the national interests of all concerned. In developing co-operation against terrorism, drug-related and other crime, all participants will be aware that their own national interests will be served best by concerted action against common enemies. This will apply equally to the European single market as to joint Soviet/US/European action. Their united effort would offer the most exciting prospect for overcoming these evils, and perhaps as 1992 approaches, we are on the brink of it.

The world, however, remains unstable and dangerous. Nationalist and religious fervour will continue. The dramatic changes in Eastern Europe in 1989 created new problems as well as new opportunities. The Baltic States, Ukraine, Moldavia and some of the southern Soviet republics have been further encouraged to reject their Communist Parties and try to break away from the USSR. Hardliners in Moscow, blaming Gorbachov, may try to oust him and repress them. Alternatively, Gorbachov may be impelled to take a harder line to hold the Union together and prevent the loss of some of its most economically successful areas. Either of these could lead to political demonstrations becoming more violent and, if these are violently repressed, to terrorism. If it comes to that, what should be the attitude of the West?

We must stick to three principles: first, we should encourage peaceful change through enabling people to express a majority desire for this by democratic means, but keeping to a pace which will not lead to instability or anarchy; second, we should not tolerate the use of terrorism to further these or any other ambitions; third, within these parameters, we should encourage and support President Gorbachov and other leaders willing to initiate or accommodate such peaceful change under reasonable control.

Gorbachov must be given credit for the most dramatic year of change ever achieved in Europe without war or violence (with Romania an exception, thanks to President Ceausescu). We should not demand that such changes continue at too fast a pace in the USSR if that is going to result in Gorbachov's being ousted by a reactionary regime. We must not forget that attempts by demostrators to force the pace too fast in China resulted in the dismissal of two reformist Party General Secretaries in turn – Hu Yaobang and Zhao Ziyang – and then to the tragedy of Tiananmen Square on 4 June 1989, tragic not only for China, but also for international relations and thus for the whole world. And we should not connive at terrorism, that is coercion by killing one to frighten ten thousand, regardless of its aim or by whom it is done.

Provided that, with help from the West, a progressive regime remains in power in Moscow, we should not take too much counsel of our fear that it might not last. We should base our policies on the realization that such a regime will not survive unless it acts in what it perceives to be its own national interests – political and economic. We should do our best to help it to do so, and should take full advantage of any opportunities it offers in co-operating to curb terrorism and to avoid the continual wastage of the world's resources on armaments and conflicts; but because no regime is immortal (as we were reminded in 1989) we should maintain a balance of power and keep our powder dry. An unstable Soviet Union with a collapsing economy, and a disbanded NATO, would not be a recipe for peace.

The 1990s could be the most dangerous or the most progressive decade of the century. Which it is to be will depend mainly on far-sighted, realistic and sympathetic co-operation between the USA, the USSR and the united European Community.

Notes and bibliography

1 The challenge of 1992

Adams, J. *The Financing of Terror*, London, New English Library, 1986. Concentrates particularly on the finances of the PLO and the IRA.

Butt Philip, A. *European Border Controls: Who Needs Them?*, London, Royal Institute of International Affairs, 1989. A concise analysis based on a seminar of officials from the five Schengen countries, held in London in 1989.

Clutterbuck, R. *Industrial Conflict and Democracy*, London, Macmillan, 1984. Chapter 19 forecasts the pattern of life and work in the 1990s.

Clutterbuck, R. *Terrorism and Guerrilla Warfare*, London, Routledge, 1990. Political and technological developments affecting terrorism in the 1990s.

Korthals Altes, F., Address by the Dutch Minister of Justice at a conference on the theme 'Towards a European Response to Terrorism' held at Leiden University in March 1989.

Wistrich, E., *After 1992: The United States of Europe*, London, Routledge, 1989. A comprehensive account of the arguments in favour of the European internal market.

Notes

1 *Annual killing rates*

Place	Period	Deaths over period		Per year	Population (millions)	Per million per year
Northern Ireland	1969–88	Traffic	5,240	262	1.5	175
Northern Ireland	1969–88	Terrorism	2,712	135	1.5	90
Basque country	1969–88	Terrorism	800	40	2.1	19
Italy	1969–88	Terrorism	421	21	58.0	0.4

2 Simpson, J., *TVI Journal* 1985, 6, 1, p. 12
3 Wistrich, p. 99
4 Butt Philip, pp. 2, 21 and 28.
5 Clutterbuck, *Industrial*, pp. 1, 93–203.
6 Adams, p. 109.
7 Clutterbuck, *Terrorism*, p. 108.

2 Foreign terrorists in Europe

Adams, J., *The Financing of Terror*, London, New English Library, 1986.
Gives a good account of the financing of the PLO.

Clutterbuck, R., *Kidnap, Hijack and Extortion*, London, Macmillan, 1987.
Analyses terrorist actions world-wide, with sixty-one case studies.

CRIS, *Briefing Book*, London, Control Risks Group, 1982–9. A monthly
record and analysis of terrorist incidents world-wide.

Dobson, C. and Payne, R., *War Without End*, London, Harrap, 1986. A
digest of Palestinian terrorist groups in action since 1968, with some
useful case studies.

Mickolus, E.J., *Transnational Terrorism*, London, Aldwych Press, 1980.
Accounts of terrorist incidents world-wide, 1968–79.

Smith, C., *Carlos*, London, André Deutsch, 1976. Covers the activities of
the PFLP in Europe, 1971–5.

Notes

1 Mickolus, pp. 952–3, lists fifty-five Black September incidents, with
   dates, and gives an account of each in the body of the book; these
   accounts (world-wide) are in chronological order.
2 Dobson and Payne, pp. 145–56.
3 Adams, p. 109.
4 Mickolus, pp. 208–15, describes the multiple hijack in detail.
5 Smith, pp. 99–217, gives a full account of the European Commando's
   operations.
6 Mickolus, pp. 321–4.
7 Dobson and Payne, pp. 164–8.
8 CRIS, October 1989.
9 Dobson and Payne, pp. 54–66.

3 Italy

The author was in Rome a few days after the kidnap of Aldo Moro in March
1978, spending a day on the streets with the Carabinieri and interviewing its
Commander, General Corsini. He revisited Rome in July 1978, when he
interviewed General Corsini again, and also the Minister of the Interior, Virginio
Rognone, and Judge Galucci, who was at that time responsible for allocating
examining magistrates to investigate all terrorist incidents and to supervise their
investigation. In 1980 he attended the Council of Europe Conference described
below and took part in the discussion of the paper by Senator Bonifacio, the
former Italian Minister of Justice.

His main source for these chapters, however, has been Alison Jamieson, long
resident in Italy, with whom he exchanged visits in Italy and the UK and
corresponded over the period 1987–9 during the writing of her book, for which
he wrote the foreword. Her research and especially her interviews are without
parallel in this field. This book, and the writings of Vittorfranco Pisano (whom
he has also interviewed) have been the main documentary sources.

Notes and bibliography

Bonifacio, F.P., *Limitation of Individual Rights in the Fight against Terrorism*, a paper presented to the Council of Europe Conference on the Defence of Democracy against Terrorism in Europe held on 12–14 November 1980 and published in Strasbourg by the Council of Europe, 1981. Senator Bonifacio is a former Minister of Justice in Italy, and this is a comprehensive analysis of Italian anti-terrorist legislation up to 1979.

Jamieson, A., *The Heart Attacked: Terrorism and Conflict in the Italian State*, London, Marion Boyars, 1989. A definitive account of the rise and decline of the Red Brigades, and especially of the kidnap and murder of Aldo Moro, based mainly on interviews in depth with convicted BR terrorists, the families of victims, politicians, judges, police and prison officers.

Pisano, V., *The Red Brigades: A Challenge to Italian Democracy*, London Institute for the Study of Conflict, 1980. The author is a lawyer who practises in both Italy and the USA.

Pisano, V., *Terrorism – The Italian Case*, New York, International Association of Chiefs of Police, 1984. A concise account of the rise and decline of right- and left-wing terrorism in Italy.

Pisano, V., 'Terrorism of the Right in Italy', *TVI Journal* 1985, 6, 1, pp. 20–33. This goes more deeply into right-wing terrorism.

Seton-Watson, C., 'Terrorism in Italy', in J. Lodge (ed.) *The Threat of Terrorism*, London, Wheatsheaf, 1988. Includes a useful analysis of Italian anti-terrorist laws from 1975 to 1985.

Notes

1 Jamieson, pp. 19–25 and 296–9.
2 Pisano, 'Terrorism of the Right in Italy', pp. 20–3.
3 Jamieson, pp. 30–1.
4 Seton-Watson, pp. 105–6.
5 Jamieson, pp. 82–6.
6 Seton-Watson, pp. 103–4, and Bonifacio, pp. 8–9.
7 Pisano, *Terrorism – The Italian Case*, p. 2.
8 Jamieson, pp. 19–25 and p. 294.
9 ibid., p. 108.
10 ibid., pp. 112–70, gives a full account of the Moro kidnap and response.
11 Bonifacio, pp. 10–12, gives a detailed analysis of the Cossiga Laws. This section is also based on the author's interviews in Rome in July 1978 with the Minister of the Interior, Virginio Rognone, and Judge Gallucci; and with Alison Jamieson in Italy in 1988 and the UK in 1989.
12 Seton-Watson, pp. 104–6, and Jamieson, p. 174.
13 Pisano, *Terrorism – The Italian Case*, p. 3.
14 Jamieson, pp. 174–92.
15 ibid., pp. 193–208.
16 Pisano, *Terrorism – The Italian Case*, p. 3.
17 Jamieson, pp. 201–8.

4 West Germany

Becker, J., *Hitler's Children*, London, Granada, 1977. The best book on the early days of the Baader-Meinhof Group and Red Army Faction from their foundation to the hijack to Mogadishu, 1977.

Becker, K.-H., 'Competence and strategy concerning suppression of terrorism in the Federal Republic of Germany', a paper presented to the Council of Europe Conference on the Defence of Democracy against Terrorism in Europe held on 12–14 November 1980 and published in Strasbourg by the Council of Europe, 1981. Dr Becker was at that time head of the anti-terrorism section of *Bundeskriminalamt*.

Clutterbuck, R., *Kidnap and Ransom*, London, Faber & Faber, 1978. Contains an analysis of the kidnap and murder of Hanns-Martin Schleyer and the hijack rescue at Mogadishu prepared durng a visit to Germany shortly after the event.

Cobler, S., *Law, Order and Politics in West Germany* (translated by F. McDonagh) Harmondsworth, Penguin, 1978. A highly critical analysis of the German response to terrorism by a lawyer at that time writing his doctoral thesis.

CRIS, *Briefing Book*, London, Control Risks Group, 1982–89. A monthly record and analysis of terrorist incidents world-wide.

Dobson, C. and Payne, R., *Terror! The West Fights Back*, London, Macmillan, 1982. Describes the German computerized intelligence system and anti-terrorist force (GSG9).

Dobson, C. and Payne, R., *War Without End*, London, Harrap, 1986. A dossier of terrorist movements and a chronology of terrorist incidents from 1969 to 1985, some with detailed accounts.

Fanning, M., 'Recent developments in French and German anti-terrorist law', 1987, unpublished research paper prepared for the Airey Neave Trust.

Horchem, H.-J., 'Terrorism in Western Europe', in R. Clutterbuck (ed.) *The Future of Political Violence*, London, Macmillan, 1986. Dr Horchem was formerly Director of the Hamburg Office of the *Bundesamt fur Verfassungsschutz*.

Koch, P. and Hermann, K., *Assault at Mogadishu*, London, Corgi, 1977.

Kolinsky, E., 'Terrorism in West Germany', in J. Lodge (ed.) *The Threat of Terrorism*, London, Wheatsheaf, 1988. Concentrates particulaily on anti-terrorist laws.

Mickolus, E.J., *Transnational Terrorism*, London, Aldwych Press, 1980. Concise accounts of terrorist incidents world-wide, 1968–79.

Smith, C., *Carlos*, London, André Deutsch, 1977. Contains a useful account of the PFLP/RAF seizure of OPEC hostages in Vienna in 1975, Chapter 10.

Notes

1 Mickolus. Dates and other details of incidents taken from Mickolus, where they are described in chronological order.

2   Koch and Hermann, pp. 26–42. See also Clutterbuck, pp. 150–4.
3   Koch and Hermann, pp. 125–50. See also Clutterbuck, pp. 155–7.
4   CRIS, *Briefing Book*, provided dates and other details.
5   Horchem, pp. 147–52.
6   Kolinsky, pp. 71–80. See also Horchem, pp. 152–6.
7   Dobson and Payne, *War*, p. 246.
8   Fanning, pp. 21–2.
9   Cobler, pp. 33–6 and 162.
10 Dobson and Payne, *Terror*, p. 123.
11 Fanning, p. 24.
12 Kolinsky, pp. 83–5.

5 France, Benelux, Denmark and Ireland

Clutterbuck, R., *Kidnap and Ransom*, London, Faber & Faber, 1978.
   Contains case studies of selected incidents, 1969–77.
Clutterbuck, R., *Kidnap, Hijack and Extortion*, London, Macmillan, 1987.
   Contains case studies of selected incidents, 1975–86.
CRIS, *Briefing Book*. London, Control Risks Group, 1982–89. A monthly
   record and analysis of terrorist incidents world-wide.
Dobson, C. and Payne, R., *Terror! The West Fights Back*, London,
   Macmillan, 1982. Describes the training, organization and operations of
   European anti-terrorist squads, including British, Dutch, French,
   German, Italian and Spanish.
Dobson, C. and Payne, R., *War Without End*, London, Harrap, 1986.
   Contains useful case studies of both foreign and domestic terrorist
   attacks in Europe, mainly from 1977 to 1985.
Fanning, M., 'Recent developments in French and German anti-terrorist
   law', 1987, unpublished research paper prepared for the Airey Neave
   Trust.
Moxon-Browne, E., 'Terrorism in France', in J. Lodge (ed.) *The Threat of
   Terrorism*, London, Wheatsheaf, 1988. Concentrates particularly on
   anti-terrorist laws.
Mickolus, E.J., *Transnational Terrorism*, London, Aldwych Press, 1980.
   Accounts of terrorist incidents world-wide, 1968–79.
Smith, C., *Carlos*, London, André Deutsch, 1976. Contains an excellent
   account of the activities of the PFLP European Commando in Paris and
   London, 1971–5, in Chapters 4 to 9.

Notes

1   *The Times*, 27 May 1986.
2   Dobson and Payne, *War*, pp. 95–107.
3   Fanning, pp. 10–12.
4   CRIS, (incidents in chronological order).
5   Moxon-Browne, pp. 221–4.
6   ibid., pp. 224–5.

7   CRIS.
8   Fanning, pp. 12–15.
9   Moxon-Browne, pp. 226–7.
10 CRIS.
11 Dobson and Payne, *War*, pp. 103–7.
12 Clutterbuck, *Kidnap and Ransom*, pp. 150–4.
13 Dobson and Payne, *Terror*, pp. 127–37.
14 Dr R. Mulder, psychiatric adviser to Dutch government in all the incidents described. Interviews with the author, 1989.
15 Clutterbuck, *Kidnap, Hijack*, pp. 164–5.
16 Mulder, interview, 1989.
17 See, for example, Clutterbuck, *Kidnap, Hijack*, pp. 161–4.

6 Northern Ireland

Adams, J., *The Financing of Terror*, London, New English Library, 1986. Includes two chapters on IRA finance.
Arthur, P. and Jeffery, K., *Northern Ireland since 1968*, Oxford, Basil Blackwell, 1988. By two young Northern Irish academic colleagues (one Politics, the other History, one Catholic, the other Protestant, one from Derry, the other from Belfast) giving a balanced perspective of the twenty years of conflict up to 1988.
Bishop, P. and Mallie, E., *The Provisional IRA*, London, Corgi, 1988. A detailed account of the origins, organization and performance of the IRA, based mainly on interviews with IRA and Sinn Fein members, politicians, officials, soldiers, police and journalists of all shades of opinion. It gives a vivid and convincing picture of life inside the IRA.
Clutterbuck, R., *Protest and the Urban Guerrilla*, London, Cassell, 1973. Gives an account of the early years of the troubles.
CRIS, *Briefing Book*, London, Control Risks Group, 1982–9.
Devlin, B., *The Price of My Soul*, London, Pan, 1969. A vivid account of the run-up to the troubles written by one of the leading republican student activists in 1969 just before the first person was killed. Her passion and sincerity shine through, and the book gives an insight into how such passions build up into violence.
Kenny, A., *The Road to Hillsborough*, Oxford, Pergamon, 1986. A good account of the shaping of the Anglo-Irish Agreement of 1985, and analysis of its provisions.
Magee, J., *Northern Ireland: Crisis and Conflict*, London, Routledge & Kegan Paul, 1974. A very valuable reference book containing extracts from the most important documents concerning the partition of Ireland and the subsequent troubles, up to and including the Diplock report in 1972 and the 'Sunningdale' proposals for power sharing in 1973.

Notes

1   Bishop and Mallie, pp. 61–81.
2   ibid., pp. 82–118.

3 Compiled from RUC statistics.
4 Clutterbuck, pp. 96–100.
5 Kenny, pp. 29–36.
6 ibid., pp. 28–31.
7 Bishop and Mallie, pp. 391–3.
8 *Guardian*, 20 January 1972, and Clutterbuck, pp. 97–8.
9 Adams, pp. 166–75, and Bishop and Mallie, pp. 393–400.
10 Bishop and Mallie, p. 408.
11 Kenny, pp. 95–104.
12 CRIS, October 1989.

7 Great Britain

Bishop, P. and Mallie, E., *The Provisional IRA*, London, Corgi, 1987. A
picture of life inside the IRA by two journalists with good access and
contacts.

Clutterbuck, R., *Britain in Agony*, Harmondsworth, Penguin, 1980. An
analysis of political violence in Britain in the 1970s.

Clutterbuck, R., *Kidnap and Ransom*, London, Faber & Faber, 1978.
Includes case studies in the 1970s.

Dobson, C. and Payne, R., *Terror! The West Fights Back*, London,
Macmillan, 1982. Gives a good account of the British SAS and other
European anti-terrorist units.

Gibson, B., *The Birmingham Bombs*, London, Barry Rose, 1976. A
detailed account of the IRA bombings in the Midlands in 1974 and of
the arrest, interrogation and conviction of the bombers, by an
experienced BBC journalist who was there.

Jellicoe, The Rt Hon. Earl, *Review of the Prevention of Terrorism Act*,
Cmnd 8803, London, HMSO, 1983. The fullest of the periodic reviews
presented to Parliament by the Home Office. Contains the text of the
Act current at the time, statistical data on its implementation up to 1982,
detailed analysis of its clauses and recommendation for their amendment.

Observer, Siege, London, Macmillan, 1980. A contemporary account of the
siege of the Iranian Embassy in London and of the rescue of the
hostages by the SAS, published within a week of the rescue. What it
loses in hindsight it gains over subsequent accounts from the absence of
special pleading. It is still probably the most reliable published account
of the incident.

Smith, C., *Carlos*, London, André Deutsch, 1976. Contains an excellent
account of the PFLP European Commando which Carlos commanded
from 1973–75, it includes details of the operation of his (sometimes
unwitting) safe houses in London.

Walker, C., *The Prevention of Terrorism in British Law*, Manchester
University Press, 1986. A critical analysis of the Prevention of
Terrorism Act based on a doctoral thesis. Its conclusion is that the Act
was unnecessary and that civil liberties would have been better served
by using powers within existing laws.

Notes

1 Bishop and Mallie, pp. 253–4.
2 Gibson, *passim*, and Bishop and Mallie, pp. 257–9.
3 Bishop and Mallie, pp. 255–61, and Clutterbuck, *Britain*, pp. 151–7.
4 Clutterbuck, *Kidnap and Ransom*, pp. 135–6, and Bishop and Mallie, p. 257.
5 Bishop and Mallie, pp. 423–7.
6 ibid., pp. 427–30.
7 Smith, pp. 145–65.
8 ibid., pp. 206–9.
9 Dobson and Payne, pp. 37–45. See also *Observer, Siege, passim*.
10 Jellicoe, pp. 97–114 (the full text of the Prevention of Terrorism Act).
11 Walker, pp. 133–7 and 175–83.
12 Jellicoe, pp. 127–44, gives statistics of arrests, charges and convictions under the Act.

8 Spain, Portugal and Greece

CRIS, *Briefing Book*, London, Control Risks Group, 1982–9. A monthly record and analysis of terrorist incidents world-wide.

Dobson, C. and Payne, R., *Terror! The West Fights Back*, London, Macmillan, 1982. Describes the Spanish anti-terrorist force, with examples of its use.

Janke, P., *Spanish Separatism: ETA's Threat to Basque Democracy*, Conflict Studies no 23, London, Institute for the Study of Conflict, 1980. Describes the moves towards Basque autonomy and the ETA split.

Fanjul, J.M., 'Nature of terrorism', a paper presented to the Council of Europe Conference on the Defence of Democracy against Terrorism in Europe held on 12–14 November 1980 and published in Strasbourg by the Council of Europe, 1981. The author was Spanish Attorney-General at the time and he explains the philosophy behind Spanish anti-terrorist laws.

Laina Garcia, F., 'The security forces of the state and the population in the struggle against terrorism', a paper presented to the Council of Europe Conference (see Fanjul above) and published in Strasbourg 1981. The author was Spanish Secretary of State for National Security at the time.

O'Ballance, E., *Terrorism in the 1980s*, London, Arms & Armour, 1989. A narrative of the activities of selected terrorist movements from 1980 to 1989, including those in Spain, Portugal and Greece.

Pollack, B. and Hunter, G., 'Dictatorship, democracy and terrorism in Spain', in J. Lodge (ed.) *The Threat of Terrorism*, London, Wheatsheaf, 1988. Analyses the Spanish government's conflict with ETA since the Franco era, including discussion of anti-terrorist laws.

Notes

1 CRIS, October 1989.
2 Pollack and Hunter, p. 126 (up to 1984; thereafter from CRIS).
3 O'Ballance, pp. 89–90.

4   Pollack and Hunter, pp. 123–4.
5   Janke, *passim*.
6   Pollack and Hunter, p. 125 (up to 1985; thereafter from CRIS).
7   O'Ballance, pp. 90–1.
8   ibid., pp. 82–3.
9   Dobson and Payne, pp. 171–3.
10 O'Ballance, pp. 86–7.
11 CRIS, October 1989.
12 Janke, intrview, 1988.
13 Dobson and Payne, pp. 176–8.
14 Fanjul, pp. 14–15.
15 Laina Garcia, pp. 9–11.
16 Pollack and Hunter, p. 133.
17 O'Ballance, pp. 91–2.
18 Pollack and Hunter, pp. 135–7.
19 CRIS, August 1989.
20 ibid.
21 O'Ballance, p. 25.
22 CRIS, October 1989.
23 ibid.

9 International crime and drug trafficking

Clutterbuck, R., *Terrorism and Guerrilla Warfare*, London, Routledge, 1990. Includes three chapters on drug trafficking.

Jamieson, A., *The Modern Mafia: Its Role and Record*, Conflict Study no 224, London, Research Institute for the Study of Conflict ad Terrorism (RISCT), 1989. A concise but comprehensive account and analysis of the Sicilian Mafia and its international operations up to mid-1989.

The Economist, 'Drugs: It doesn't have to be like this', 2 September 1989, pp. 21–4. The case for legalizing drugs, eloquently put.

Naylor, R.T., *Hot Money*, London, Unwin, 1987. An alarming account of the scale of the flow of illegal money around the world.

Naylor, R.T., *Money Laundering*, transcript of lecture given at a conference in Florence on 19 May 1989.

Parker, D.B., *Crime by Computer*, New York, Scribner, 1976. The essentials of computer crime, written in readily understandable terms by one who continues to be one of the world's leading experts.

Richardson, L.D., 'The urgency of detergency', *TVI Report* 1986, 6, 3, pp. 12–21 (Part I), and 4, pp. 43–50 (Part II). A comprehensive account of money laundering through domestic and international banks, tax havens, bogus deals with shell companies and a hundred and one different ways. Written in a style understandable to the non-expert.

TVI, 'Interpol's response to terrorism', *TVI Journal* 1985, 6, 1, pp. 3–13. Text and analysis of Interpol General Assembly Resolutions on Terrorism, 1984, with interviews with the Secretary-General (Ray Kendall) and the President of the General Assembly (John Simpson).

Notes

1 TVI, p. 12.
2 Jamieson, p. 1.
3 ibid., p. 4, and an article in the *Birmingham Post*, 19 September 1989.
4 ibid., p. 17.
5 ibid., p. 29.
6 *The Times*, 14 October 1989.
7 Clutterbuck, pp. 91–5.
8 *The Economist*, 2 September 1989, pp. 21–4.
9 George Potter, computer crime consultant, interview with the author, April 1989.
10 *The Times*, 17 October 1989.
11 Parker, pp. 71–9, gives a detailed account of a similar embezzlement. There are others in *The Times* of 16 and 17 October 1989.
12 *The Times*, 16 October 1989.
13 *The Times*, 17 October 1989.
14 Naylor, *Money Laundering*, p. 2.
15 ibid., p. 5.
16 ibid., p. 11.
17 Richardson, pp. 12–21, gives some good examples, e.g. the tiny independent Pacific island of Nauru, packed with banks and shell companies, whose inhabitants enjoy a standard of living 50 per cent higher than the average in the USA.

10 European co-operation against terrorism

Butt Philip, A., *European Border Controls: Who Needs Them?*, London, Royal Institute of International Affairs, 1989. Paper based on a seminar of officials from the five Schengen countries, held in London in 1989.
Council of Europe, *Defence of Democracy against Terrorism in Europe*, Strasbourg, Council of Europe, 1981. A report of a conference in Strasbourg in November 1980 to review the performance of the European Convention of the Suppression of Terrorism, 1977. It contains the text of the Convention, a number of papers presented at the Conference, and a record of the discussion. The author presented one of the papers and was rapporteur for one of the discussions.
Korthals Altes, F., Address by the Dutch Minister of Justice at a Conference on the theme 'Towards a European Response to Terrorism' held at Leiden University in March 1989. A masterly analysis of the implementation of the Schengen Agreement and a discussion of the problems which will arise over the implementation of the European internal market in 1992. It will be published by Leiden University in a collection edited by Alex P. Schmid in 1990.
Lodge, J. (ed) *The Threat of Terrorism*, London, Wheatsheaf, 1988. Chapters 1, 'Terrorism and Europe', and 9, 'The European Community and terrorism', both by the editor herself, give a useful analysis of some of the problems and solutions attempted up to 1987.

TVI, 'Interpol's response to terrorism' and 'Interpol's resolutions on terrorism', *TVI Journal* 1985, 6, 1, pp. 3–12. Text and analysis of Interpol's resolutions to overcome its constitutional shortcomings in furthering international police co-operation against terrorism, with a record of their discussion at the 1984 General Assembly and interviews with senior officials.

Wilkinson, P., *Terrorism and the Liberal State*, London, Macmillan, 1986. A revised second edition of a classic work (1977) on the response of democratic states to terrorism, and of their co-operation in this response.

Wistrich, E., *After 1992: The United States of Europe*, London, Routledge, 1989. A comprehensive account of the arguments in favour of the European internal market by one who has been closely involved with the negotiations leading up to the Single European Act.

Notes

1 TVI, pp. 3–7.
2 Wilkinson, pp. 284–6.
3 ibid., pp. 254–5.
4 Lodge, pp. 234–59 and Korthals Altes, pp. 4–5.
5 Wilkinson, pp. 290–4.
6 Sobel, L.A., *Political Terrorism, Vol. 2*, Oxford, Clio, 1978, pp. 37–40.
7 Wilkinson, p. 256.
8 Butt Philip, pp. 16–17.
9 ibid., p. 2.
10 Korthals Altes, pp. 8–9.
11 Butt Philip, pp. 7 and 22.

11 Computerized intelligence systems

Clutterbuck, R., *Terrorism and Guerrilla Warfare: Forecasts and Remedies*, London, Routledge, 1990. Chapter 7 goes more deeply into the computer techology behind the development of intelligence systems, and was based largely on a series of interviews with:

> Professor Richard Gregory, of Bristol University, who has combined medical and computer science to become Britain's leading thinker on artificial intelligence.

> Dr John Hulbert, whose qualifications in computer science and psychology made him Britain's most highly qualified police officer in these fields (as a Chief Superintendent) before starting his own computer research and development company, Cogitaire, in Lustleigh, Devon.

> Chief Superintendent David Webb, now with the Police Requirements Support Unit at the Home Office in London.

> Mr Masoud Yazdani, Lecturer in Computer Science at the University of Exeter.

Hulbert, J., 'The use and potential use of artificial intelligence for police, security and intelligence activities', paper presented to the Institute of Police and Technology Management Symposium in Florida, 23 February 1988.

Webb, D., 'Artificial intelligence: its potential to create an impact in the fight against terrorism', paper presented to a Symposium at the Office of International Criminal Justice, University of Illinois at Chicago, August 1987.

Yazdani, M. and Narayanan, A. (eds) *Artificial Intelligence: Human Effects*, Chichester, Ellis Horwood, 1984.

Notes

1 An example of this technique was described in Clutterbuck, R., *Conflict and Violence in Singapore and Malaysia*, Boulder, Col., Westview Press, 1985, pp. 251–2.
2 Hulbert, p. 3.
3 *Independent*, 7 September 1987, reporting on Police Conference IPEC 87.
4 *The Times*, 15 September 1987, reporting on Police Conference IPEC 87, p. 15.
5 Hulbert, p. 15.
6 ibid., p. 3
7 Webb, pp. 5–8.
8 Yazdani, pp. 26–35.
9 Webb, pp. 11–12.
10 Hulbert, in a letter to the author (February 1987) printed in full in Clutterbuck, *Terrorism*, pp. 72–3.

12 Identification and detection of impersonation

Clutterbuck, R., *Terrorism and Guerrilla Warfare: Forecasts and Remedies*, London, Routledge, 1990. Contains a more detailed investigation of access control and other security equipment in a wider context.
Federal Bureau of Investigation, *Crisis Reaction Seminar*, held at the International University for Presidents, Maui, Hawaii, 1982, Washington, DC, FBI, 1982.

Moore, K.C., *Airport, Aircraft and Airline Security*, Los Angeles, California, Security World, 1976.

Sitrep International, a periodical published every two months since September 1987, with articles and manufacturers' details on new developments in security equipment.

Webb, D., 'Artificial intelligence: its potential to create an impact in the fight against terrorism', paper presented to a Symposium at the Office of International Criminal Justice, University of Illinois at Chicago, August 1987.

Two manufacturers of identification and anti-impersonation systems,

Ferranti and Logica UK Ltd, provided much detail, including demonstrations of their equipment.

Notes

1 Stephen Thompson, Ferranti, interview, May 1987.
2 J. Hulbert, letter to the author, February 1987.
3 Ferranti Security Systems Ltd, demonstration to the author, May 1987.
4 Logica UK Ltd, letter to the author, April 1989.
5 Mickolus, E.J., *Transnational Terrorism*, London, Wheatsheaf, 1987. Case studies, best found from dates, in chronological order.
6 Clutterbuck, R., *Kidnap, Hijack and Extortion*, London, Macmillan, 1987, pp.19–21.
7 D. Webb, interview, 1987. See also Clutterbuck, *Terrorism*, p. 78.
8 Clutterbuck, *Terrorism*, p. 77.

13 Searching for guns, explosives and drugs

Bozorgmanesk, H., 'Bomb and weapon detection', *Terrorism: An International Journal* 1987, 10, 3, 285–7. Examines Thermal Neutron Activation and other developments in the pipeline.

Clutterbuck, R., *Terrorism and Guerrilla Warfare: Forecasts and Remedies*, London, Routledge, 1990, Chapter 6 gives a more detailed analysis of bomb search technology in a wider context of terrorism and rural guerrilla warfare world-wide.

Kindel, S., 'Off the shelf technology', *Terrorism: An International Journal*, 1978, 10, 3, 281–4. Describes the technology of tagging explosives, and of measuring dielectric properties as a means of detection.

Knowles, G., *Bomb Security Guide*, Los Angeles, Calif., Security World, 1976. A useful general guide to the subject, based on technology available or coming into use.

Wyatt, J.R., 'Defensive search', *Royal Engineers Journal*, April 1989, 103, 1, pp. 47–52. British army techniques for bomb search. Major Wyatt also demonstrated some of the detection equipment under test to the author at the Royal School of Military Engineering in November 1987. He is now working in the same field with International Military Services, and gave further information and demonstrations to the author in November 1989.

Notes

1 Clutterbuck, pp. 53–5.
2 Wyatt, interview, November 1987.
3 Kindel, pp. 282–3.
4 From material supplied by Ferranti Security Systems Ltd.
5 Wyatt, demonstrations to the author, November 1987 and November 1989. See also *Terror Update*, July 1989, pp. 6–7.
6 Demonstrated to the author by Graseby Security Ltd, November 1988.

7 Demonstrated to the author by Singapore Airport police, August 1986.
8 Bozorgmanesk, pp. 285–7.
9 Wyatt, demonstrations to the author, November 1987 and November 1989.
10 Kindel, p. 283.
11 Bozorgmanesk, pp. 286–7.

14 Detection, arrest and civil liberties

Cobler, S., *Law, Order and Politics in West Germany*, Harmondsworth, Penguin, 1978.

Fanning, M., 'Recent developments in French and German anti-terrorist law', 1987, unpublished research paper prepared for the Airey Neave Trust.

Hewitt, P., *The Abuse of Power*, Oxford, Martin Robertson, 1982. A critical analysis of civil liberties in the UK by the former General Secretary of the National Council for Civil Liberties.

Jamieson, A., *The Modern Mafia: Its Role and Record*, Conflict Study no 224, London, Research Institute for the Study of Conflict and Terrorism (RISCT), 1989.

Jellicoe, The Rt Hon. Earl, *Review of the Prevention of Terrorism Act*, Cmnd 8803, London, HMSO, 1983.

Lodge, J. (ed.) *The Threat of Terrorism*, London, Wheatsheaf, 1988.

O'Brien, C.C., 'Freedom to peddle murder', London, *The Times*, 16 September 1989. The case against broadcast interviews with spokesmen for terrorist organizations.

Richardson, L. D., 'The urgency of detergency', *TVI Report* 1986, 6, 3, pp. 12–21 (Part I), and 4, pp. 43–50 (Part II).

Walker, C., *The Prevention of Terrorism in British Law*, Manchester University Press, 1986.

Notes

1 Hewitt, pp. 35–55.
2 Richardson, pp. 12–14.
3 This view was regularly confirmed by police officers in discussion after lectures by the author at the Police Staff College and other police colleges.
4 Jellicoe, pp. 83–9.
5 ibid., pp. 41–4.
6 Lodge, pp. 255–9.
7 O'Brien, *The Times*, 16 September 1989.

15 Trial and sentence in face of intimidation

Clutterbuck, R., *Conflict and Violence in Singapore and Malaysia*, London, Books of Asia, 1985 and Boulder, Col. Westview Press, 1985. Gives a detailed account of the techniques used to recruit informers in Malaya, both amongst terrorist supporters and surrendered terrorists (the forerunners of the *pentiti* and the 'supergrasses').

Clutterbuck, R., *Terrorism and Guerrilla Warfare: Forecasts and Remedies*, London, Routledge, 1990. Contains a fuller account of the narcotics chain from producer to consumer; also a discussion of the balance between anti-terrorist action and civil liberties.

The Economist, 'Drugs: It doesn't have to be like this', 2 September 1989, pp. 21–4. The case for legalizing drugs.

Fanning, M., 'Recent developments in French and German anti-terrorist law', 1987, unpublished research paper prepared for the Airey Neave Trust.

Jamieson, A., *The Heart Attacked*, London, Marion Boyars, 1989.

Lodge, J. (ed.) *The Threat of Terrorism*, London, Wheatsheaf, 1988, with chapters on all main EC countries.

Mark, Sir Robert, *In the Office of Constable*, London, Collins, 1978. Autobiography of a distinguished Commissioner of the Metropolitan Police. Includes extracts from his 1973 Dimbleby Lecture in which he criticizes some criminal lawyers.

Walker, C., *The Prevention of Terrorism in British Law*, Manchester University Press, 1986.

Notes

1 Mark, pp. 68–9.
2 ibid., pp. 154–6.
3 Clutterbuck, *Conflict*, pp. 253–6, provides a full account of the handling of the equivalent of *pentiti* or supergrasses in Malaysia. This, including the handling of the media by the Malaysian Prime Minister, was a model for subsequent operations of this type. It completely broke the jungle-based terrorist organization within two years.
4 Jamieson, pp. 199–201.

16 Future development of the threat

For bibliography, see notes for relevant previous chapters.

Notes

1 Jamieson, A., *The Heart Attacked*, London, Marion Boyars, 1989, includes on pp. 266–84 a remarkable prison interview with Adriana Faranda, serving thirty years for complicity in the kidnap and murder of Aldo Moro. It gives an insight into the motivation of some of the more idealistic members of the Red Brigades.
2 Clutterbuck, R., *Terrorism and Guerrilla Warfare*, London, Routledge, 1989, includes two chapters on weapon development, pp. 22–52.
3 Jamieson, A., *The Modern Mafia: Its Role and Record*, Conflict Study

no 224, London, Research Institute for the Study of Conflict and Terrorism (RISCT), 1989, p. 27.
4 Clutterbuck, op. cit., pp. 98–9 and 103–4.

17 Fighting the war in a united Europe

For bibliography, see notes for relevant previous chapters. Also:
Jenkins, B., *The Possibility of Soviet-American Cooperation Against Terrorism*, Santa Monica, Calif., Rand Corporation, March 1989.
Jenkins, B., *Terrorism: Policy Issues for the Bush Administration*, Santa Monica, Calif., Rand Corporation, May 1989.

Notes

1 Butt Philip, A., *European Border Controls: Who Needs Them?*, London, Royal Institute of International Affairs, 1989, p. 27.
2 Wistrich, E., *After 1992: The United States of Europe*, London, Routledge, 1989, p. 5.
3 Butt Philip, p. 2.
4 Jenkins, *Terrorism: Policy Issues*, pp. 38–9.
5 *The Times*, 11 October 1989.
6 *The Times*, 16 October 1989.
7 ibid.
8 Richardson, L.D., 'The urgency of detergency', *TVI Report* 1986, 6, 3, p. 14.
9 Jenkins, *Possibility*, pp. 16–18. This paper also gives an account of the meeting and a list of participants.
10 *Los Angeles Times*, 25 and 29 September and 1 and 2 October 1989.

Index

Abdallah, Georges, 23–5, 61, 66, 180
abduction, *see* Kidnap
Abu Daoud, 123
Abu Nidal, 19, 21–2, 24–5, 90, 106, 180
access control, 136–8, 147–8, 191, 198
Achille Lauro hijack, 18
AD (France), 7, 30, 50, 62–7, 105, 121, 172–3, 178, 198
Adams, Gerry, 75–6
addiction (drugs), 8, 9, 68, 110, 112, 172, 184–5
  average cost of, 113
  cure of, 113, 191
  financing of, 113, 172, 184
Afghanistan, 25, 110, 182, 193, 199
AG (Germany), 52–3
air travel security, 5, 190–1
  air travel permits, 141
  airport layout, 147–50, 191
  baggage checks, xii, xviii, 140, 142–8, 150, 191
  check-in time, 140
  cost of, xix, 145, 147
  enforcement of, 124, 147, 150
  Frankfurt, 21, 54, 148
  Greece, 106–7, 121
  'naive carrier', 147–8
  passenger checks, xii, xviii, 140–1, 147–8, 150, 191
  ramp security, 147–8
  Singapore, 145, 148

suicide bombers, 147
vetting, 141, 147
aircraft, attacks on,
  Air India (1985), 146–7
  on the ground, 20, 124, 190–1
  over Greece (1986), 149–50
  over Lockerbie (1988) 12, 20–1, 53, 146–8
  see also Bombs, Hijack
airports, attacks on,
  Lod (1972) 20
  Rome (1985) 21–2
  Vienna (1985) 21–2
Al Fatah, 17–19
Algiers, 123, 124
Andreotti, Giulio, 28, 34–6, 39
Anglo-Irish Agreement, 67, 82–4
Angry Brigade (UK), 85, 178
anti-terrorist units, 186, 192–3
  British (SAS), 11, 49, 75, 91, 122, 193, 198
  co-operation between, 49, 122, 198
  Dutch (BBE), 68–9, 122, 198
  Egyptian, 21
  German (GSG9), 49, 55, 122, 198
  Israeli, 47–8, 90
  Italian, 10, 31, 39, 42, 154
  Spanish (GEO), 101
ARB (France), 64
Armenians, 8, 25, 53, 61, 180
Athens, 20, 21, 106–7
Audran, René, 63

Baader, Andreas, 46, 49, 58, 85

Baader-Meinhof group, *see* RAF
Bakhtiar, 61
Balcombe Street, 87, 90
Bani Sadr, 61
banks
  boycott, threat of, 117, 156–7, 195
  computer crimes against, 114–15
  confidentiality, 116–18, 182, 191
  corruption of, 109, 111, 157
  deposits and transfers, control
    of, 38, 156–7, 188–91
  electronic transfer between, 7,
    116–18, 156–7, 182, 188–9
  international, 7, 116–18, 156,
    188–9, 193
  police access to, 10, 81, 93,
    117–18, 156–7, 182–3,
    188–9, 191, 195
  robberies, 76, 98
  see also laundering
Barlinnie Prison, 172
Basel, Declaration of, 117, 195
Basques, *see* ETA, Spain
BBC, 161
BBE (Netherlands) 68–9, 122, 198
Beckurts, Karlheinz, 51
Belgium, 10, 20, 49
  bank control in, 117, 156, 195
  CCC, 50, 62, 64, 67, 178
  extradition from, 160
  IRA in, 25, 67–8, 160
  security weaknesses, 62, 68,
    126, 188, 198
  terrorist havens in, 25, 50, 67–8
Berufsverbot, 56–7, 155
Besse, Georges, 63, 64
BfV (Germany), 55–6, 121
Birmingham bombs (**1974**), 86–7,
  97, 163
BKA (Germany), 55, 59, 121
Black, Christopher, 79–80
body fluids, for identification, 59,
  138, 190
Boeynants, Paul Vanden, 67
Bolivia, 9, 111
bombs, bombing
  detection of, xviii, 12, 91,
    142–50, 191, 198; *see also*
    explosives

firing circuits, concealment of,
  12, 20, 91, 142, 181
fuses, barometric, 20–1, 54,
  149; delay, 87–8, 142,
  180–1; remote control, 180;
  tilt, 88, 142, 181
  in aircraft, 12, 20–1, 53, 91,
    142, 146–7, 149–50, 180,
    190–1
  in Belgium, 67
  in England, 85–9, 171
  in France, 61–5, 121
  in Germany, 51–3
  in Italy, 26–7, 30–1, 34, 40, 97
  in Northern Ireland, 72, 75, 161
  in Portugal, 105
  in Spain, 96–8, 100, 102–3
  in trains, 27, 34
  nuclear, 180–1
  suicide bombers, 3, 23, 147
  see also Birmingham, Bologna,
    Brescia, Brighton, Enniskillen,
    Lockerbie, Milan, Munich
    (Oktoberfest)
Bonn declaration (**1978**), 124
BR (Italy)
  hardcore and irregulars, 7, 32–4,
    40, 130, 178, 186
  in Genoa, 32, 40
  in Milan, 30, 32, 35, 39–41
  in Rome, 32, 35–42
  in Turin, 32, 35, 40
  in Veneto, 41–2
  operations and tactics, 5 28–37,
    40–2, 178
  organization, 7–8, 32–5, 39–42,
    52, 130, 178–9
  recruiting and propaganda, 33,
    40–1, 178
  rise and decline, 10, 31–4, 40–5,
    154, 178–9
  see also, Bologna, Bombs,
    Brescia, Cirillo, Costa,
    Curcio, *dissociati*, Dozier,
    D'Urso, Franceschini,
    Gallinari, Kidnap, Milan,
    Moretti, Moro, *pentiti*,
    Senzani, Sossi
Brescia bomb (**1974**), 27, 30, 31, 34

Brighton bomb (**1984**), 87–8, 163,
181
Britain, British, *see* UK
Buback, Siegfried, 48
Bulgaria, 25, 90
Bulwood Hall, 172
Burma, 110, 184, 193

Callaghan, James, 122
Canada, *see* Summit Seven
capital punishment, 169–70
Carette, Pierre, 62
Caribbean, 9, 179, 191, 193
Carlos, 20, 47, 90
Carrero Blanco, Admiral, 97
Carvalho, Colonel, 105–6
CCC (Belgium), 50, 62, 64, 67,
178
Channel Tunnel security, xvii–xviii,
189
China, 118, 193, 201
Cirillo, Ciro, 41
Civil liberties
and acquittal of the guilty, 165
and banning broadcasts, 161
and computers, 12, 155–6, 190,
198
and concealment of identity, 12,
139, 155, 190
and impersonation, 12, 139, 190
and intelligence, 56, 135, 154–5,
198
and law enforcement and public
security xii, 12–13, 37, 39,
102, 153, 155, 157, 159,
186–8, 190, 195
right to kill, claim of, 13, 179
right to live, 13, 146
Cocaine and crack, 9, 112–13, 142,
171, 193
Coco, Francisco, 32–3, 44
Collins, Michael, 71, 76
Colombia, 108, 111–12, 114, 154,
168, 184, 192–3
Communist Parties, 5, 178,
199–201; *see also* Italy, political
system
computer crime
espionage, 114–15

extortion by, 115–16, 182, 194
fraud, 10, 114, 137, 156, 182–4,
190, 193–5
growth of, 9, 114–15, 183,
193–5, 198
hackers, 9, 114–15, 183, 193–4
legislation against, 183, 193–5
leniency towards, 9, 114–15,
193–5
proceeds from, 114
prosecution, low rate of, 10,
114–15, 183, 193–5
virus, 115, 182–3
computers
and civil liberties, 12, 155–6,
190, 198
expert systems, 133–4
fingerprint matching, 59, 66,
130, 137–9, 141, 148, 190
in drug war, 118
knowledge based, 132–3
linking of data, 129–30, 137,
141, 147, 155, 191
logical inferences by, 131–3
miniaturization, 131–2, 134
national police, xviii, 11, 49,
56, 129, 136, 139, 148, 187,
190–1; links between, xviii,
126, 139, 148, 187, 190–1,
194–5, 197–8
neural, 135, 137, 139
parallel, 130–1, 133
personal data, 11, 155, 157, 190
photographs, matching of, 130
see also intelligence, smart card,
surveillance
corruption, 9, 29, 41, 153
of banks, 109, 111, 157
of intelligence services, 8,
109–10
of judges, 8, 111
of juries, 166
of police, 8, 9, 155
of politicians and officials, 8,
29, 155
Corsica, *see* France
Cossiga, Francesco, 38–9, 42–5,
204
Costa, Pietro, 32–3, 38

Council of Europe, 11, 122–4
Crack, *see* Cocaine
CSPPA (France), 61, 67
Cuba, 144
Curcio, Renato, 30–2, 44, 85, 179
Czechoslovakia, 56, 142, 155

Dalla Chiesa, General, 10, 31–2,
    35, 39–43, 129, 154, 169, 186
data protection, 59, 190
Denmark, 126, 154, 189
dielectric properties, 12, 142, 146
Diplock Courts, 78–81, 165–6, 168,
    186; *see also* juries, trial without
dissociati, 44–5, 173
DNA, 59, 138, 190
dogs, 12, 142, 148
Dozier, James, 41–2
drug traffickers, xii, 29
    action against dealers, 113–14,
        141, 191
    corruption by, 9, 111, 184–5
    generation of crime, 4, 8, 24,
        45, 114, 121, 191; of
        terrorism xii, 8, 24, 108,
        111, 114, 121, 192
    growth of, 8, 191, 193, 198
    international organization, 9,
        111–12, 155, 184–5, 191
    Mafia links, 110, 121, 184
    money laundering by, 116–18
    murders by, 9, 111, 114
    political power of, 111, 184, 191
    turnover and profit, 8–10,
        111–12, 184
    world war against, 9, 112, 118,
        155, 191–3, 199–201
drugs
    control of, 126, 184–5, 188
    curtailing demand for, 24, 113,
        184–5, 191
    detection of, 144–5, 192–3, 198
    legalization of, 9, 112, 191
    price of, 9, 112–13, 184
    see also addiction, cocaine,
        heroin
D'Urso, Judge, 33, 40–1

Eastern Europe

developments in, 125, 200–1
co-operation against terrorism,
    11, 139, 150, 192–3, 198–201
EC (European Community)
    bureaucracy and Parliament, 5,
        180
    co-operation with USSR and
        Eastern Europe, 11, 139,
        144, 150, 192–3, 198–201
    Council of Ministers, 4–5, 189
    drug addiction in, 9, 24, 45,
        112–14, 184–5, 191
    external frontiers, 5, 107, 125–6,
        197–8
    foreign terrorists, access to, 4,
        17, 153, 180, 189; fighting
        their battles in, 7–8, 17, 19,
        23–5, 63, 180, 199
    immigrants in, 6, 17, 22, 61,
        125–6, 153, 179–80, 184
    internal frontiers, opening of,
        xii, 5, 10, 17, 106–7, 125–6,
        161, 180, 182, 188–90;
        economic gain from, xi, 188
    uniting of, 4–6
    see also Extradition, Immigration,
        International cooperation,
        Judicial processes,
        Jurisdiction, Laws, Police,
        SEA, Shengen, TREVI
economic immigrants, 6, 107, 126
ECST (Council of Europe), 11,
    122–4, 197
Egypt, 18, 19, 21
El Al (Israeli Airlines), 19–21, 91,
    139–40
El Salvador, 108, 154, 170
Enniskillen bomb (**1987**), 75–6, 89
Ennslin, Gudrun, 46, 49, 58, 85
ETA (Spain), 7, 199
    assistance from IRA, 99
    extradition from France, 99–100
    finance, 98, 101
    French businesses, attacks on, 104
    hard core, 98, 173
    in France, 25, 63, 95, 98
    intimidation by, 98
    murders by, 96–9 *passim* 102,
        104

negotiations with, 104–5
origins of, 95–6
philosophy of, 97, 173, 178
rehabilitation of, 173
security forces, attacks on, 98,
    103, 104
split of, 97
support for, 96, 103–5, 178
see also HB
Ethiopia, 25
explosives and bombs, detection of,
    191, 198
dielectric properties, 12, 142,
    146
dogs, 12, 142, 144
magnetometer, 142
multiple checks, xx, 12, 146,
    148, 181
neutron, xviii, 12, 142–3, 145–6,
    148
tagging, 143–4
vapour, xviii, 12, 91, 142, 144–5
    148, 191
X-rays, xviii, 91, 142, 145, 148
extortion, 69, 76, 115–16, 182, 194
see also computer crime, kidnap,
    product contamination,
    ransom
extradition, 66–7, 81–3, 95, 98,
    111, 125–6, 160, 196
or prosecution, 121, 123–5, 160
political offences, 121, 123, 197

False alarm rate (FAR), 138,
    142–3, 145
Faranda, Adriana, 216
fibre optics, 143
financing terrorism
    BR, 32–3
    ETA, 98, 101
    IRA, 7, 76–7
    PLO, 7, 18–19, 177
fingerprints, 59, 66, 130, 137–9,
    141, 148, 190
Fletcher, WPC Yvonne, 70, 91
FLNC (Corsicans), 63–4
FP25 (Portugal), 105–6
France, French, 20, 22, 49, 50,
    Chapter 5, 121, 123–6, 150,

    160, 188–9
Action Directe, *see* AD
asylum in, 61
bomb attacks in, 23
concessions to terrorism, 3, 23–4
Corsicans (FNLC), 63–4
emergency legislation, 10–11,
    62, 64–7, 69, 166, 187
foreign terrorists in, 23–5, 61–3,
    90
intelligence services, 10–11,
    65–7, 123, 197
murders in, 61–7 *passim*
separatism in, 8, 63–4, 179
surveillance service (DST), 66,
    121
see also bombs, GAL, judges,
    judicial processes, juries,
    laws, murder victims, police,
    Schengen, Summit Seven
Franceschini, ALberto, 30–1, 44
fraud
    computer, 10, 114, 137, 156,
        182–4, 190, 193, 199
    tax, 77, 156

Gacha, Jose Gonzales Rodriguez,
    111, 155
Gadafi, 23, 70, 90, 91, 142, 181
GAL (France and Spain), 63, 100
    suspected police involvement in
        100
Galan, Luis Carlos, 111, 155
Gallinari, Prospero, 35–6
Germany, 5, 20–2, Chapter 4,
    66–7, 121, 150, 155, 179, 189
concessions to terrorists, 23, 47
emergency legislation, 10–11,
    46, 57–60, 62, 93, 159,
    186–7
foreign terrorists in 23–5, 53–5
frontiers, arrests at, 125, 189
GSG9, 49, 55, 122, 198
intelligence organization, 10–11, 46,
    55–60, 136, 187, 197
kidnapping in, 35–6, 38, 48–50
police powers in, 58–60, 93, 136
political system, 46, 55–6, 60,
    85–6

Red Army Faction, *see* RAF
revolutionary cells, *see* RZ
see also Berufsverbot, BfV
  BKA, Intelligence, laws,
  lawyers, murder victims,
  Schleyer, Schmidt, Shengen,
  Summit Seven
GEO (Spain), 101
Greece, 20, 21, 106–7, 181
  EC's weakest frontier, 107, 121,
    189
  political instability, 107
  sympathy for Palestinians,
    106–7, 121
Grove, Eric, 200–1
GSG9 (Germany), 49, 55, 122, 198

Habash, Dr George, 19–20
Hamadei brothers, 23, 121
HB (Spain) 101, 103–5, 178
heroin, 110, 144, 171, 193
Herrhausen, Alfred, 51
Hezbollah, 23–5, 124, 180
hijack, 120, 123, 124, 140
  Bonn declaration (**1978**), 124–5
  from Athens, 21, 23, 106–7
  from Munich (attempts **1970**),
    139
  from Rome (**1968**), 19
  of ships, 18
  of trains, 68, 122
  political effect of, 140, 146,
    190–1
  to Algiers (**1988**), 124
  to Beirut (**1985**), 3, 23, 66, 124
  to Entebbe (**1976**), 47–8
  to Jordan (**1970**), 20
  to Malta (**1985**), 21
  to Mogadishu (**1977**), 49, 54,
    122, 198
  to Zagreb (**1972**), 54–5
  see also air travel, international
    co-operation
hijackers
  detection of, 139–41, 147, 191,
    198
  extradition of, 120, 123, 124–5
  weapons for, 142, 147–8, 181–2
Hindawi brothers, 24, 91

Hong Kong, 9, 24, 110, 184, 193
hunger strikes, 46–7, 50, 87

IATA, 147, 150
identification, 58, 66, 125, 147–8,
  155 198
identity (ID) cards, 125, 136–7
  machine-readable, xvii, 12, 60,
    136–7, 139, 147–8, 189–90
  murder to obtain, 137–8
immigration and customs, xviii, 12,
  17, 22, 61, 125, 141, 148,
  189–90
impersonation, detection of, 125,
  137–9, 147–8, 190
  see also DNA, fingerprints,
    retina, vein-check, voice
    prints
India, Indians, 25, 146–7, 150
infra-red detection, 12, 146
INLA (Northern Ireland), 76, 80,
  86, 161, 181
insurance, 52, 115
intelligence, 186–7, 197–9
  accountability, 154
  artificial (AI), 131
  computerized, 39, 49, 50, 56,
    58, 129–35, 137, 141
  corruption of, 8, 109–10
  effect of capital punishment on,
    170
  human and technical, 129–31
  organizations, 10, 29, 34–6,
    55–60, 72–4, 123, 136
  scanning search, 58–60, 129,
    135
  spies, turning of, 170
  trawlnet search, 58–60, 93, 129,
    135
  see also computers, France,
    Germany, international
    co-operation, Interpol, Italy,
    Netherlands, Northern
    Ireland, surveillance, UK
international co-operation against
  terrorism, drugs and crime
  Basel, declaration of (**1988**),
    117, 195
  bilateral, 11, 62, 66–7, 119,

121–2, 124–5, 196–8
Bonn declaration (**1978**), 124
ECST (Council of Europe,
    1977), 11, 122–4, 197
Hague (**1970**), 11, 120, 123, 197
Montreal (**1971**), 11, 120, 123,
    197
self-interest and, 11 123–4, 197,
    201
Tokyo (**1963**), 11, 120, 123, 197
see also East Europe, Interpol,
    NATO, Summit Seven,
    TREVI, United Nations,
    USSR, Warsaw Pact
Interpol, 4, 11, 108, 119, 196
interrogation, 79, 92–4, 153, 196
lawyers presence at, 37, 159
validity as evidence, 37, 158–9,
    168–9
video-taping, 13, 158–9, 168–9
see also silence
intimidation, 12, 98, 108, 153,
    156–7
see also judges, juries, lawyers,
    Mafia, police, prison officers,
    witnesses
IRA (Northern Ireland), 199, 207
assistance to ETA, 99
broadcasts on behalf of, 161–2
financing, 7, 76–7
hard core, 75–6, 130, 162, 173,
    178
in Britain, 70, 86–9, 163
in Continental Europe, 25, 67–9,
    76, 89, 162, 198
in Irish Republic, 69, 163
kidnapping by, 80
Libya, support from, 76, 142
murders by, 70–80 *passim*, 89,
    162, 177, 181
organization and tactics, 74–8,
    161
origins, 70–2
popular support, *see* Sinn Fein
proscription of, 92
splits within, 74–6
see also Adams, Black, bombs,
    Collins, Diplock, extradition,
    judges, juries, jurisdiction,

laws, Magee, Northern
    Ireland, O'Brien, police,
    Prevention of Terrorism Act,
    racketeering, Ryan, Semtex.
    silence, 'supergrasses',
    witnesses
Iran, 8, 21, 23–5, 47, 54, 110,
    144, 180, 193, 199
Iranian Embassy siege (London,
    1980), 23, 90–1, 208
Iraq, 20–5
Ireland
history, 70–4
Northern, *see* Northern Ireland
population structure, 70–1, 95
Republic of, 67–8, 70–1, 81,
    160, 161, 163, 187–8
unification of, 71, 77, 82–3,
    173, 177
Islamic fundamentalism, 24–5, 54,
    124, 179, 199
Israel, Israelis, 7, 18–25, 52, 177,
    199
as terrorist targets, 7, 18–22,
    120
intifida, 18–19
invasion of Lebanon (**1982**), 21
see also anti-terrorist units,
    El Al, hijack
Italy, 8–9, 18, Chapter 3, 66, 126,
    150, 179, 184, 195–6
concessions to terrorism, 3, 41
corruption, 8, 29, 35, 41,
    109–10
emergency legislation, 10, 31–2,
    37–9, 42–5, 110, 154,
    157, 159, 187
foreign terrorists in, 22–5
intelligence organization, 10, 29,
    34–6
left wing terrorism, 26–8, 31,
    154, 169; *see also* BR, PL
level of violence, 26–30, 32, 34
police organization, 29–32, 39
political system, 28–30, 34–7,
    85–6
Red Brigades, *see* BR
right wing terrorism, 26 –8, 31,
    34, 154, 169

see also Achille Lauro,
anti-terrorist units, bombs,
Dalla Chiesa, *dissociati*,
judges, judicial processes,
juries, laws, lawyers, Mafia,
murder victims, Peci, *pentiti*,
police, Summit Seven

Japan, 11, 19–20, 112
see also Summit Seven
Jibril, Ahmed, 20
Jordan, 19–20
JRA (Japan) 19–20
judges
as assessors, 65, 69, 81, 166,
168, 187
corruption of, 8, 111
government influence on, 123
intimidation of, 10–11, 29, 37,
153, 159
murder of, 28, 40–1, 47, 111,
114, 168
judicial processes
arrest and detention, 37, 78–9,
93
bail, 32, 37
conviction, deterrent effect of,
165
custody, duration of, 32,
37–8, 45, 78–9, 92–3, 102,
157, 187, 196
detention without trial, 72, 162
disruption and delay of, 13, 29,
32, 36–7, 58, 157, 159, 187
failure of, in Northern Ireland,
169
leniency for co-operation, 37, 39,
42–5, 60, 65, 80, 102, 186;
see also Malaysia, pentiti,
'Supergrasses'
'life-meaning-life' sentences,
113, 171–2, 191
trial, duration of, 29, 38, 196
verbal statements as evidence,
78–80, 158
see also judges, juries,
jurisdiction, laws, lawyers
juries
acquittal rate (UK), 165

anonymity, using video, xix, 13,
166–70, 196
corruption of, 166
intimidation of, xix, 12–13, 24,
32, 36–7, 63, 78, 153, 159,
165, 187, 196
trial without, 63–6, 69, 71,
78–82, 160, 165–6, 168,
186–7
jurisdiction
co-operation, 117, 123, 160, 196
cross border, 81, 160, 196
harmonization, 4, 13, 126, 160,
191, 194–6

kidnap, 39, 65, 80, 182
in Belgium, 67
in Columbia, 154
in Germany, 17, 46, 35–8,
47–50, 54
in Irish Republic, 69
in Italy, 10, 30–1, 34–7, 39, 41,
154, 178
in Netherlands, 68–9
in Northern Ireland, 80
in Spain, 101
see also kidnap victims, ransom
kidnap victims, see, Boeynants,
Cirillo, Costa, Dozier, D'Urso,
Moro, Palmers, Peci, Revilla,
Schleyer, Sossi
Kuwait, 124

laundering illegal money, xii, 4, 7,
12, 38, 111, 114–15, 118, 153,
157, 182–5, 188–9, 193–5
shell companies, 10, 116, 156,
182, 188, 195
tax havens, 117–18, 182–3, 191,
195
see also banks, fraud, police,
racketeering
laws
access to bank and business
accounts, 10, 38, 81, 93,
117–18, 156–7, 182–3, 188,
195
aggravating factors, 37, 60, 65,
101

assets, freezing and seizure of, 81, 108, 110, 113, 117–18, 183, 195
association,c rimes of, 38, 45
concealment of identity, 32, 60, 66, 154
emergency legislation held in draft, 92, 162–4
lodging registration, 32, 163
malicious damage, 5, 64–5, 102
onus of proof, possession of arms and explosives, 78, 159, 187
onus of proof, source of assets, 12, 93, 110, 156
powers of search: of buildings, 38, 48, 78, 186–7; of persons, 37, 78
see also France, Germany, interrogation, Italy, judges, judicial processes, juries, jurisdiction, Northern Ireland, *pentiti*, police, Prevention of Terrorism Act, silence, 'supergrasses'
lawyers
    abuse of privilege, 13, 29, 32, 36–7, 45, 58, 157, 167, 187, 196
    barring from court, 58, 157, 187
    intimidation and murder of, 32, 36, 37, 168
    perverting course of justice, 13, 167
    prison visits by, 32, 49, 58, 158
    supporting terrorism, 49, 58, 157, 196
Lebanon, 19–24, 100, 124, 184, 199
Libya
    Abu Nidal group in, 20, 106
    hit squads in Europe, 24–5, 90
    murder of London policewoman, 70, 91
    support for international terrorists, 124, 139, 142, 144, 189
    support for IRA, 76, 142
    US bombing of, 23, 53

Lockerbie bomb (**1988**), 12, 21, 53, 146–8
Lod Airport massacre (**1972**), 20
Luxembourg, 4, 117, 125–6, 156, 195

Mafia, 108, 116, 162, 193–5
    drug trafficking, 110, 121, 184
    enforcement of silence, 108, 111
    in UK, 110
    in USA, 108, 110
    intimidation by, 108–9, 156
    Italian 8, 10, 26, 34, 40–2, 45, 109
    murders by, 10, 40, 45, 154
    organization, 109
    pentiti in, 45, 109
Magee, Patrick, 87–9
magnetometer, 142
Malaysia, 44, 163, 168, 170
maritime security, 5, 18, 107, 121
Mark, Sir Robert, 154, 167
media, 3, 5, 24–5, 47, 90–1, 155, 177, 197
Meinhof, Ulrike, 46, 50, 58
Menigon, Nathalie, 62–4, 67
MIK (Germany), 51–2, 60
Milan bomb (**1969**), 27, 30, 34
MNF (Lebanon), 3, 23
Moretti, Mario, 30–6 *passim*, 39, 44
Moro, Aldo, 28–37 *passim*, 38, 40, 203, 204
Munich
    bomb (*Oktoberfest* **1980**), 53, 97
    Olympics (**1972**), 17, 46, 54, 120, 123
murder victims, individual
    in Colombia, *see* Galan
    in France, *see* Audran, Besse
    in Germany, *see* Beckurts, Buback, Herrhausen, Ponto, Schleyer, von Braunmühl
    in Italy, *see* Coco, Dalla Chiesa, Moro, Peci Roberto
    in Spain, *see* Carrero Blanco
    in UK, *see* Neave

NATO

as terrorist target, 49–52, 62–4
co-operation with Warsaw Pact, xix–xx, 192, 199–201
new roles for, 192–3, 199–201
terrorist alliance against, 50, 62, 64, 105
Neave, Airey, 86, 161
negotiation, 4–5, 36, 41, 49, 135
neo-fascists, Nazis, 5, 28, 42, 53, 56–7, 75, 97, 101, 155, 178–9
Netherlands
bank controls in, 117, 156, 195
BBE, 68–9, 122, 198
crisis management organization, 69
IRA in, 25, 67–8
police and intelligence services, 69 co-operation within EC, 121–2, 197
product contamination, 68–9
terrorist attacks in, 20, 68–9, 179, 188
Triads in, 24
trial without jury in, 69, 187
see also Shengen, South Moluccans
neutron detection, xviii, 12, 142–3, 145–6, 148
cost of, 145
Nigeria, 90
Noriega, General, 118, 191
North Africa
immigrants from, 22, 107, 126, 189
terrorists from, 23, 61, 67, 107, 180, 189
Northern Ireland, 7–8, 25, Chapter 6, 145, 157, 160, 196
British army in, 72–4, 78–9
capital punishment, 169
direct rule from London, 73, 78
Emergency Provisions Act (1973), 78–9, 166, 187
intelligence in, 72, 74
level of violence, 3, 11, 26, 70, 72–4, 80, 96, 153
politics in, 73–4, 95–6
power-sharing in, 73–4
Protestant militants, 74, 78, 83,

163; murders by, 73–4, 83
racketeering, 76–7, 81, 93, 156–7, 195
'revolutionary taxes', 76
RUC, 72–4
UVF, 79
see also bombs, Diplock, extradition, INLA, IRA, judges, judicial processes, juries, jurisdiction, laws, 'supergrasses'

O'Brien, Conor Cruise, 161–2

Pakistan, 108, 110, 114, 124, 193
Palestinians, 7–8, 19, 24–5, 46, 49, 53, 62, 100, 123, 142, 177–80
intifada, 18–19
see also Abu Daoud, Abu Nidal, *Achille Lauro*, aircraft, airports, Al Fatah, El Al, Greece, Hamadei, hijack, hijackers, Hindawi, Lockerbie, PFLP, PFLP-GC, PLO
Palmers, Walter, 50
Panama, 117–18, 191
passports, xvii, xviii, 136, 140–1
machine-readable, 12, 60, 136, 137, 139, 148, 189–90
Peci
Patrizio, 40
Roberto, 41
pentiti (Italy)
arrests and convictions due to 11, 43–5, 154–5, 179, 186
ethics of, 11, 27–8, 45, 155, 169, 186
in Mafia, 45, 109
laws governing, 37, 39–45
lives saved by, 45, 168–9, 186
rehabilitation of, 172–3
see also Dalla Chiesa, *Dissociati*, Peci
Peru, 22, 111, 192
PFLP, 19–20, 47–8, 90, 200
PFLP-GC, 19, 21, 54
PL (Italy), 28, 40
PLO, 7, 18–19, 21, 62, 90, 123, 177

police and army
  access to accounts, 10, 81, 93,
    117–18, 156–7, 182–3, 188,
    195
  corruption of, 8–9, 109, 115
  detection and arrest, 37, 153,
    155
  hot pursuit by, 126, 197
  informers, 31, 51, 65, 157; *see
    also* Malaysia, *pentiti*,
    'supergrasses'
  international co-operation, 11,
    62, 66–7, 108, 119, 121–6,
    180, 183–4, 188, 192–3, 195–8
  intimidation of, 12, 24, 37
  murder of, 25, 46
  search of buildings, 36–8, 48,
    78, 186–7
  spot checks by, 6, 12, 31, 36,
    59, 93, 125, 184, 188–90,
    197–8
  tapping telephones, 31, 154, 186
  see also anti-terrorist units,
    computers, Germany,
    identification, impersonation,
    intelligence, interrogation,
    Italy, Netherlands, Northern
    Ireland, Prevention of
    Terrorism Act, Spain
Ponto, Jurgen, 48
Portugal, 105–6
Prevention of Terrorism Act, 81,
    92–4, 102, 157, 159, 162–4,
    208
  exclusion orders, 92, 160
  lives saved by, 94
  offence to withhold information,
    92, 159
  ready in draft (**1974**), 162–4
  terrorists caught through, 92–4
  see also judicial processes, laws
prison officers, intimidation of, 28,
    37, 153
prison service
  in Italy, 10, 31–2, 37–45
  'life-meaning-life' sentences,
    113, 171–2, 191
production contamination, 69,
    114–15, 182

protection money, 76, 156–7
  see also racketeering
publicity for terrorism, 20, 24, 47,
    90–1, 177, 180
  see also media

racketeering, 12, 76–7, 81, 93,
    117, 153, 156–7, 182
RAF (Germany) 7, 22, 30, 46–51,
    198
  anti-NATO alliance, 50, 62, 64,
    105
  hard core, 51, 56, 130, 178
  lawyers in, 58–9, 157, 167
  militant activists, 51
  murders by, 46–51 *passim*, 56,
    62–3, 137–8
  organization of, 51, 179
  rehabilitation of, 172–3, 188
  resilience of, 51, 178
ransoms, 32, 41, 47, 49–50, 67,
    98, 101, 103, 116, 154, 177,
    182
rehabilitation of terrorists, 44,
    101–3, 105, 172–3, 188
retina reading, 138, 190
Revilla, Emiliano, 103
'revolutionary taxes', 76, 98
right to silence, *see* silence
Rognone, Virginio, 39, 110, 203,
    204
Rouillan, Jean-Marcc, 62–4, 66
Ryan, Patrick, 67–8, 83, 89, 160
RZ (Germany), 8, 51–3, 179–80

SAS (UK), 11, 49, 75, 91, 122,
    193, 198
Schleicher, Regis, 63, 65–6, 78
Schleyer, Dr Hanns-Martin, 35–8,
    48, 50, 56, 58–9, 122, 129
Schmidt, Helmut, 36, 47, 49, 122,
    124
SEA (Single European Act), 4,
    125–6, 180, 188–9, 198
Semtex explosive, 76, 142
Senzani, Giovanni, 40–2
Shengen Agreement, 125–6, 188
Shia Muslims, 23, 124, 179, 199
Sicily, 8, 10, 40, 42, 154

Sikhs, 25
silence
    right to, 3, 82, 158, 168–9,
        187, 196
    right to take account of, 82,
        158–9, 168–9, 187, 196
Singapore, 145, 148
Sinn Fein, 71, 79, 207
    banning of broadcasts by, 161–2
    electoral support for, 71, 76–7,
        161
    legality of, 75
    support for IRA, 161, 178
smart card, 137–8, 141
Somalia, 25, 49, 54, 122, 198
Sossi, Mario, 30
South Moluccans, 68–9, 179, 188
Spain, Chapter 8
    appointment of judges, 102
    Basque autonomy, 8, 95–6,
        101–2, 173; referendum on,
        101
    co-operation with France, 95,
        100
    emergency legislation, 99,
        101–2, 157, 187
    King Juan Carlos, 99–100
    level of violence, 26, 96, 102,
        104, 179
    police and army, 98–103
    politics in, 99, 103–4
    population structure, 8, 95,
        105
    propaganda, 102
    'revolutionary taxes', 98
    right-wing terrorists, 63,
        99–101
    social reinsertion, 101, 103,
        105, 173, 188
    see also ETA, GAL, GEO,
        HB, kidnap, murder victims,
        PNV
Sri Lanka, 25, 163
'Summit Seven', 11, 117, 124–5,
    144, 150, 156, 195
Sun Tzu, 3
'supergrasses' (Northern Ireland)
    convictions due to, 11, 45, 80;
        quashing of, 11, 45, 80, 166,

    168–9, 186
    ethics of, 11, 80–1, 169, 186
surveillance, 5, 31, 35, 68, 121,
    126, 129, 186, 192–3
Sweden, 47, 117, 126, 150, 156,
    195, 198
Switzerland, 20, 50, 117, 126, 150,
    157, 189, 195, 198
Syria, 19–25, 24, 91, 139, 144

technological developments, 6–7,
    24, 198
    see also access control, bombs,
        explosives, identity cards,
        impersonation, intelligence,
        passports, surveillance, visas,
        weapons
Tejero, Colonel, 99–101
television see media
terrorism, tactics and techniques,
    see Achille Lauro, aircraft,
    airports, bombs, BR, ETA,
    extortion, hijack, Hezbollah,
    INLA, intimidation, IRA,
    Iranian Embassy, kidnap, kidnap
    victims, Libya, MIK, MNF,
    murder victims, Northern
    Ireland, product contamination,
    racketeering, RAF, RZ, weapons
terrorists, terrorist organizations
    age and education of, 53, 173
    aims, short and long term,
        177–8
    concessions to, 3, 23–4, 41, 47
    hard core, 7, 32–4, 51, 56.
        74–6, 130, 173, 178
    irregulars and auxiliaries,
        32–4, 51–2, 74–6, 173, 178
    Marxist, decline of, 178, 199
    recruiting and propaganda, 33,
        51–3, 71, 76–7, 95–6, 102,
        178
    rise and decline of, 10, 31–4,
        40–5, 51, 154, 177–80
    see also Abdallah, Abu Daoud,
        Abu Nidal, AD, BR, CCC,
        CSPPA, ETA, Hamadei,
        Hezbollah, Hindawi, INLA,
        IRA, Islamic fundamentalists,

JRA, North Africa, PFLP,
PFLP-GC, RAF, RZ, South
Muluccans, UVF
Thailand, 110, 193
Thatcher, Margaret, 82, 87–8
TREVI, (EC), 11, 22, 67, 121–2,
124–5, 197
Triad Secret Societies, 9, 24, 108,
110–11, 184, 193
Turkey, Turks, 8, 25, 53, 61, 112,
179

UK, British, 4, 20–1, Chapter 7,
121, 126, 150, 160, 179, 193,
195
acquittal rate by juries, 165
concessions to terrorism, 3, 24
drug abuse in, 9, 111–14, 172,
184–5, 191
foreign terrorists in, 24, 70,
89–91
indigenous terrorists in, 85
intelligence organization, 55, 92,
121–2, 197
international co-operation, 11,
139, 144, 150, 192–3,
199–201
Mafia in, 110
murders in, 70, 80–91 *passim*,
94
numbers crossing frontiers,
189–90
SAS, 11, 49, 75, 91, 122, 193,
198
see also Angry Brigade, bombs,
extradition, IRA, judicial
processes, juries, laws,
Northern Ireland, police,
Prevention of Terrorism Act,
'Summit Seven'
United Nations, 120, 192–3, 197
USA, Americans, 18, 22, 150, 157,
193
as a common market, xi
as targets for terrorism, 20,
50–1, 53–4, 120, 137,
139–40
aviation security, 142, 145
bombing of Libya, 23, 53

concessions to terrorism, 3, 23–4
co-operation with USSR, 111,
118, 139, 144, 150, 192–3
drug abuse in, 9, 114, 184–5,
191
extradition of drug runners to,
111
homicide rates in, 3
homogeneity of, 4, 125
in Panama, 117–18
international co-operation, 11,
118, 139, 144, 150, 192–3,
199–201
Mafia in, 108, 110
see also NATO, Summit Seven
USSR, Soviet, xi
co-operation against terrorism
and drugs, 11, 118, 139,
144, 150, 192–3, 199–201
national minorities in, 8, 180,
200–1
prospect of domestic terrorism
in, 199–201
see also Eastern Europe,
Warsaw Pact

vapour detectors, xviii, 12, 91, 142,
144–6. 148, 181
cost of, 145
vein-check, xviii, 138–9, 148, 190
Vienna, 21–2, 50
Convention (drug traffickers),
117, 195
OPEC kidnapping, 47, 50, 90
VIP protection, 35, 37, 48, 192
visas, xvii–xix, 66, 140
machine-readable, xvii–xix, 12,
139, 148, 189–90
voiceprint, 59, 138, 190
von Braunmuhl, Gerold, 51
von Drenkmann, Gunter, 47

Warsaw Pact, co-operation with
NATO, xix–xx, 192–3, 199–201
weapons, 181
biological, 181
control of, 68, 126, 188
detection of, xviii, 142, 147–8,
191

improvised, 182
missiles, 181–2
nuclear, 180–1, 199
poison gas, 181
small arms, 181
witnesses
intimidation of, 24, 29, 32,
36–7, 78, 105, 153, 187,
196
video protection for, 166–8, 196

X-rays, xvii, 91, 142, 145, 148

Yassir Arafat, 17–21 *passim*
Yugoslavia, Yugoslavs, 8, 25, 53,
67, 180

Zimmermann, Dr Ernest, 50